Performing Popular Mus

This book explores the fundamentals of popular music performance for students in contemporary music institutions. Drawing on the insights of performance practice research, it discusses the unwritten rules of performances in popular music, what it takes to create a memorable performance, and live popular music as a creative industry. The authors offer a practical overview of topics ranging from rehearsals to stagecraft, and what to do when things go wrong. Chapters on promotion, recordings, and the music industry place performance in the context of building a career. *Performing Popular Music* introduces aspiring musicians to the elements of crafting compelling performances and succeeding in the world of today's popular music.

David Cashman is an Adjunct Associate Professor of Popular Music at Southern Cross University, and a working pianist. David's research area is live music, with a particular emphasis on regional music and live music and tourism. As a pianist, David has performed all over the world, worked on cruise ships, and remains an active performer in Sydney and on regional and international tours.

Waldo Garrido is a Lecturer in Contemporary Music at Western Sydney University. He is a well-known bassist, composer, and producer. Waldo has produced two solo albums and has had two radio hits in his native Chile. As a songwriter, he is currently signed to BMG. Waldo researches and writes on the music of Chile and on the migrant experience of Syrian musicians in Berlin.

Performing Popular Music
The Art of Creating Memorable and Successful Performances

David Cashman and Waldo Garrido

Routledge
Taylor & Francis Group

NEW YORK AND LONDON

First published 2020
by Routledge
52 Vanderbilt Avenue, New York, NY 10017

and by Routledge
2 Park Square, Milton Park, Abingdon, Oxon, OX14 4RN

Routledge is an imprint of the Taylor & Francis Group, an informa business

© 2020 Taylor & Francis

The right of David Cashman and Waldo Garrido to be identified as authors of this work has been asserted by them in accordance with sections 77 and 78 of the Copyright, Designs and Patents Act 1988.

Library of Congress Cataloging-in-Publication Data
Names: Cashman, David, author. | Garrido, Waldo, 1962- author.
Title: Performing popular music: the art of creating memorable and successful performances/David Cashman and Waldo Garrido.
Description: [1.] | New York: Routledge, 2020. | Includes bibliographical references and index.
Identifiers: LCCN 2019037493 (print) | LCCN 2019037494 (ebook) |
ISBN 9781138585058 (hardback) | ISBN 9781138585065 (paperback) |
ISBN 9780429505560 (ebook)
Subjects: LCSH: Popular music–Vocational guidance. |
Popular music–Instruction and study. | Music–Performance.
Classification: LCC ML3795 .C345 2020 (print) | LCC ML3795 (ebook) |
DDC 781.64/143–dc23
LC record available at https://lccn.loc.gov/2019037493
LC ebook record available at https://lccn.loc.gov/2019037494

ISBN: 978-1-138-58505-8 (hbk)
ISBN: 978-1-138-58506-5 (pbk)
ISBN: 978-0-429-50556-0 (ebk)

Typeset in Goudy
by Deanta Global Publishing Services, Chennai, India

https://www.routledge.com/9781138585065

For Phil Hayward. In appreciation.
The authors would like to acknowledge the hundreds of musicians whose
views contributed to this book. We're very grateful.

Contents

Introduction

The music industry began with performance. In the middle of the 19th century, composers, mirroring the industrial revolution, began writing and selling music to a mass amateur audience. This was in stark odds with composers of the past such as Haydn, Mozart, and Tchaikovsky who had composed their complex and virtuosic music under the patronage system. This new 'popular' music was written specifically for performance. At the time, there were few ways of recording music. Then came the first abortive attempts at recording music—the first music boxes and player pianos, Edison's wax cylinder, Berliner's flat record. Eventually, recording became the main way of making money in the music industry. Live performance was regarded as a necessary evil, a way of promoting new recordings and albums. Record companies held enormous power and generated huge profits. It got so that they actually believed they were selling these small round pieces of plastic called records, when they were actually in the intellectual property business. They believed this so much that they utilised new technologies to digitise their music and put it on small pieces of plastic called compact disks. These were supposed to reproduce sound perfectly (they did pretty well, but weren't perfect), they were supposed to last forever (not even close), and they were readable by CD players and computers. It was computers that brought them unstuck. When the public found they could use their PCs to 'rip' CDs and make perfect copies, they replicated the same behaviour from the 1960s with cassettes. If a friend had the latest Billy Joel recording (for instance), you could burn it and have it for the cost of the blank CD. Things got worse, much worse, when four things happened in the 1990s. First, Karlheinz Brandenburg and the German Fraunhofer Institute developed a popular compression format called an mp3. The mp3 took the huge music files stored on a CD and compressed them down to a much smaller size, with a comparatively small loss in quality. Second, internet speeds developed to the point of being able to transmit these mp3s between computers in relatively short times. Third, two computing students, Shawn Fanning and Sean Parker, developed a peer-to-peer file sharing service called Napster, which became extremely popular for sharing computer files, including mp3s. Fourth, insiders in CD pressing plants began ripping and releasing CDs even before they were officially released. The huge profits of record companies plummeted and the industry impotently cried foul. Tabloids announced the death of the music industry.

However, music is a profoundly human phenomenon. Ethnomusicologists call music a key marker of humanity. People are always, *always* going to want to listen to music. There is an enormous amount of historical rock to listen to, but people also want to have music that speaks to them right now. So the industry has had to adapt. For a while, the role of the recording industry became one of talent development. Slowly, however, live music moved to the centre of the industry. The production of live music experiences became the principle manner of commodifying music and generating revenue. The development of streaming services such as Spotify has enabled recorded music to start a comeback, but live music performance is still front and centre of the industry. It's an interesting time to be learning about being a musician.

Now, as you and I start this book, we're going to assume that you're a performing musician. You are at least competent and likely brilliant on your instrument. You probably play in a popular music genre such as jazz, rock, country, Latin, or whatever. And you have, for whatever reason, picked up this book. Perhaps you're undertaking a performance course at music college and it's a set text. Perhaps you want to learn how to be a better performer. Perhaps you're trawling through the library bookshelves. Whatever. As the title says, we're going to discuss the art of creating memorable and effective musical performances. Now some might think that's easy. Get a venue, plug in your amp, flail away, and start raking in the cash, right? Sadly, it's not quite that simple. You might be the best saxophonist in your school or your city. But—and this is decades of industry and teaching experience here—most emerging students and beginning musicians have no idea—none—of how to create an effective and memorable musical performance. Newly minted music grads might have done some gigs. They might have a few years of performance classes under their belt. But the art and craft of making memorable musical performances is a big fat unknown to them. They may not even know that they don't know. This gap in their knowledge results in staid and boring musical performances. Music institutions, with their background in art music traditions, are adept at producing technically brilliant musicians. But they are, perhaps, not quite so good at producing performers. There are plenty of musicians who have been comparatively very average musicians from a technical point of view: Bob Dylan, Leonard Cohen, Ed Sheeran, and Kylie Minogue to name a few. However, these musicians still create amazing, memorable, and successful performances. Musicians, even classical musicians, can no longer rely on their considerable musical ability. We all need to learn to *perform*!

There's a music industry term: 'musical wallpaper'; music that is in the background and exists but doesn't particularly excite or inspire an audience.[1] Now, if you spend time working on your performance, you'll get better. That's natural. But this book presents industry knowledge and experience drawn from experts in the field from all over the world, as well as our own not inconsiderable practice. It is, if you like, a shortcut to what you would learn on your own. Over the next 12 chapters, we're going to discuss the process of making your performances memorable and effective. We're going to see what you can do to engage your fans and make them want to come and see you again.

Our good friend Tim, an experienced record industry executive, observes that there are three aspects to the music industry: composing, recording, and performing. Books exist for some of these aspects. There are courses and books that discuss the technical aspects of songwriting. They talk about how to rhyme, how to use scansion, how to use metre and simile and so forth. Some books talk about music publishing, which commodifies those songs. There are some books that discuss the recording industry. However, there are very few books that discuss the nature of performance except in passing. It is this lacuna that this book seeks to address.

Your authors come from different backgrounds. I originally come from a classical music background. When I finished my bachelor's degree, I fully expected to be a rich and famous classical pianist. Rare as they are. I expected to write symphonies and live in a rarefied and artistic environment. That didn't happen. Instead I got a gig in a rockabilly band. Now, playing piano licks on old Elvis and Louis Prima and Johnny Cash hits was about as far from Mozart and Beethoven as I could expect to be. Gradually, I got a reputation as a decent pianist who wasn't a jerk and could play. I played in a lot of different bands over the years. Jazz quartets; 1970s and 1980s rock. A Sting show. A Prince show. A Michael Bublé cover band. I worked on cruise ships, in theatre pits, wrote for corporate videos; I did anything I could to earn a living from music. And I loved it, and I'd be miserable doing anything else. Waldo grew up playing Latin and Andean music, first in Chile and then in Australia. In his late teens, he started playing in pop, rock, and funk bands in Sydney and was venturing into recording studios as a session musician and then as a producer. In 1991, he was signed to Warner Chappell Music as a songwriter. He spent a few years signed to the iconic Albert music (home of AC/DC) as a producer and composer. Now he's signed to BMG Publishing. His music is a mix of funk, Latin, and electronic music. He also works with migrant musicians in Berlin creating some new sounds in high-resolution platforms.

When I moved into teaching popular musicians at music colleges, I began to notice the different approaches and processes that rock and classical musicians took to both performance and rehearsal. Classical musicians are taught from their youth how to practice. They learn to rehearse. They learn how to behave on stage (very formally). They learn how to interact with an audience (as little as possible). Yes, it might seem like an alien world to many rock audiences; dull, not as immersive, not as exciting. Not as much fun. But classical performers *know* their performance world. They know it well. When a classical ensemble rehearses, not a second is wasted. Everyone prepares beforehand, and they come to the rehearsal knowing their stuff.

In the classical world, there's a branch of study called performance practice. This looks at the musical techniques applied to musical genres in certain periods.

If you're a baroque specialist, a recorder player say, you need to know how the doctrine of affects works to play the music. If you're a classical musician, you need to know how classical fingering worked on the fortepiano, how to ornament, and how to improvise in the classical tradition. Many of these practices are not notated. You're just expected to know them. There's even a word for it: HIP, or Historically Informed Performance. Rock too has a performance practice. You'll approach the guitar very differently if you're a folk musician compared to if you're a metal head (unless you play folk-metal). You might even play differently whether you're playing in the world of classic metal (classic metal or the NWOBHM) or one of the multitudes of modern genres.

This book discusses popular music performance practice. There are parts that are reflective and philosophical. We'll consider the process of creating a musical experience, of what goes into creating a memorable performance, of the place of recordings in the industry. Then there are parts that are practical. We'll consider the process of live sound, of practice, of group rehearsal. We'll talk about planning your musical product and manifesting that in performance. These are all unwritten laws of live music performance, and you need to know them.

As performers of music, we all need to be informed and self-aware. We need to be purposeful and considered, both as artists and as entrepreneurs. Our art, our performances and songs, need to be the best they can be. We need to be all over both our art and our industry, because the competition is white-hot. If we're going to perform, we all need to take our performances seriously!

Live Music as a Creative Industry

Make no mistake: music is a business. I'll regularly hammer this concept home. Unless you grasp it, your music career will be short. The music industry is part of what are called the **creative industries**. This term is used to describe the group of industries that generate revenue by the commodification of intellectual property. It includes different sectors depending on who you ask, but typically includes the fashion industry, television, radio, film, music and the performing arts, museums, games, animation, and the like. They produce vastly different products, and often rely on other creative sectors.

There are a few terms here that perhaps need unpacking. First, **commodification**. This is the process of taking something that has no intrinsic value in itself and assigning a dollar value to it. Goods … a cup of coffee, a sack of potatoes, a new TV, have intrinsic value because they are things. Services, someone making the coffee, delivering the sack of potatoes, servicing the TV, have intrinsic value because they are created by direct human labour working on tangible things (things you can touch). By contrast, a song, a computer game, or a television program are intangible, meaning you can't touch them. Because of this, the human labour is much harder to quantify. Such products gain value as they are processed by their respective creative industry. In music's case, a song gains value as it is promoted, recorded, and played, either in live performance or in recorded form. This process is called commodification.

Intellectual property is the intangible (untouchable) product of the creative industries. This is the computer program, the TV show, and (in our case) the song. How do you touch and hold a song? You can hold the representation of a song (the sheet music) or a reproduction of a song (a recording), but the song itself? More than that, what goes into creating a song? Obviously, the lyrics. Probably the melody. Probably not the groove. Certainly not the chords. The trouble is that there are so many jurisdictions and (in common law countries) so many legal cases and precedents that what a song is has become a keenly debated topic.

Intellectual property in general is protected by a series of laws called **copyright**. While the details of copyright vary from jurisdiction to jurisdiction, they share a few common features, derived largely from the operation of the UN Berne Convention, originally signed in 1886. By 2019, this treaty includes 176 member countries (and, in effect, through the operation of the World Trade Organization, is in place for all UN signatories). It established a few principles necessary for the successful operation of the creative industries.

- It established the principle of copyright.
- It established a copyright term, a duration when copyright can exist. This is usually the life of the author plus a certain number of years.
- It established a set of protections that must be met (for music). These include:
  - The right to perform in public (performing rights).
  - The right to communicate to the public the performance of such works.
  - The right to broadcast (broadcast rights).
  - The right to make sonic reproductions (mechanical rights).
  - The right to use the work as a basis for an audiovisual work (synch rights).

Copyright creates a method of treating (intangible) intellectual property like (tangible) physical property. If someone stole your laptop, you would expect to have a method of punishment and recompense. You could get the police involved and have them track down the thief. Copyright takes these property laws and applies them to the intangible property of intellectual property. If someone uses your song without asking permission (such as sampling a recording in which your song appears) then you can take legal action and expect to be recompensed for that.

The process of commodification of intellectual property in the music industry occurs in two main manners. The first is through recording and release through industry channels. This is traditionally through record shops via CDs and records. It can also be through release on film, TV, video, or games. The other way is through the live performance of songs at gigs. It is this second way of writing that concerns us here. How do you create value from the process of commodifying the intellectual property of the music industry within the experiential space of live music? Or, if you like, how do you make people come to your gigs, remember your gigs, and want to come again?

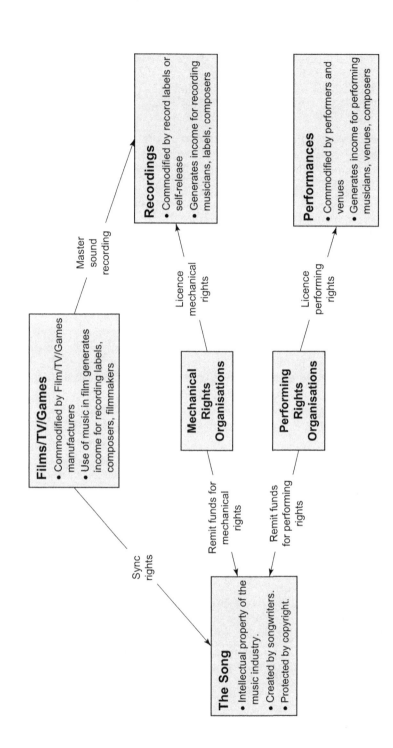

Figure 0.1 Commodification in the music industry.

Your Value

Let me tell you something about you. You possess something that is impossible to download digitally or copy, something that is eminently marketable, and completely unique to you. Something people will pay money to access. You have musical talent. Probably considerable musical talent. You've spent many hours learning your instrument, working on technique, and developing your own musical identity. Talent is, however, not the only aspect of creating a career. You need to work hard and sustainably over a long period. You also need to treat your career as part of an industry. To do that, you need to regard and reflect on your performances unflinchingly.

The music industry of the new millennium has performance at its core. If you're going to create a career in a popular music genre, be that rock, hip hop, country, Latin, jazz, or even classical music or any other genre, your performances need to be superb. They need to be memorable. They need to be informed by insider knowledge of performance practice. They need to be integrated into the industry. If they are not, your industry career will be short-lived.

KNOW YOUR WORTH

I heard about this one singer because he did a wedding at our club. And everyone said, "We thought that they had a recording on", except it was this guy singing. Every song he sang sounded like the original artist. All the young staff, the older staff, everyone, were raving about him. So, I thought I'd better find out who this guy was. I contacted him, and found out his father was managing him at the time. So, his father said to me, "Yes, you know, he's very good". And I said, "So how much does he charge?" Now, solo acts charge $350 around here. That's top dollar. He said, "He's $750". And I said, "$750 for three hours and he sings to backing tracks?" He said, "Yes, but he's very good". And I was like, "You've got to be kidding ... " He interrupted and said, "Anthea, trust me, he will fill your venues". And there was just something about his dad that made me stop. I would never have paid that much for a solo act. I could get a little band for that. But I got him in. Sure enough, he got a standing ovation in the bloody restaurant. He was unbelievable. And you know what it was, apart from the fact that, yes, he had an amazing voice? In every break, he would sit down and go talk to people. He would find out what songs they liked, and he would then go and do them in the next set, even if it meant he had to go on Spotify and find the songs, or he would say, "Next week I'll do it for you". And he would, he would find that song and he would learn it, and he would go and do it the following week.

Anthea, Promoter and singer

Making Your Performances Memorable

It's easy to talk of music being an experience, but just what does that mean? Think of the best concert you've ever been to. What made it stand out from all the others? Sure, the band may have been amazing musicians, but a performance is more than just the music. It is an *experience*. It is the hyper-energetic singer bouncing off the walls, the light show, the proximity of talented musicians producing music out of nothing, the rumble of the sub, the seemingly easy banter on stage, the smells of the venue, the taste of cheap beer in plastic cups. A musical experience doesn't just stimulate the aural sense; it stimulates many senses. (It is telling that we say we're going to see a band rather than hear a band.) It is planned and thoughtful, designed to give the audience the best possible experience of the band's musical performance. It makes people want to go to the merchandise stand and pay still more money for CDs, t-shirts, and recordings.

It is this multi-layered and multi-dimensional experience that creates memorable performances. Fans are giving you their money to spend time within the musical experience you create at a certain time and place. Done well, a purposely and thoughtfully designed musical experience will create memorable performances. Often, however, they are done badly, thoughtlessly, and without consideration of the experience. Too many musicians think that all they need to do is turn up, play, and fans will swoon. Sometimes they don't even acknowledge the audience. This leads to forgettable performances. As a musician interested in a long and successful career, you need to avoid forgettable shows and create memorable ones.

Finding Your Place in the World

If I can get philosophical for a moment, there's a concept from Okinawa Prefecture in the south of Japan called Ikigai (生き甲斐). You might have come across it in your social media travels. The philosophy of Ikigai states that finding your place in the world means doing something that fulfils four characteristics:

- Doing what you love.
- Doing what you are good at.
- Doing what you can be paid for.
- Doing what the world needs.

All of these are important. If you don't do what you love, you will feel empty. If you don't do what you're good at, you will feel uncertain. If you don't do what the world needs, you will feel useless. If you don't do what you can be paid for, you will be poor and probably too busy doing other stuff. However, once you incorporate these into your life, you have achieved Ikigai. You have achieved your reason for being.

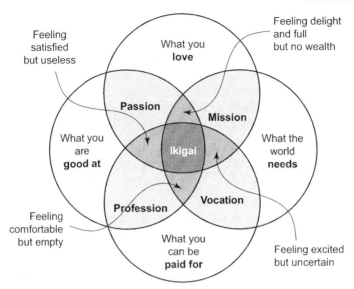

Figure 0.2 A visual representation of Ikigai.

As musicians, what can we take away from this? Well, let's look at them in turn. Do you do what you love? Do you love being a musician? Really love it? Can you see yourself being in the music industry for your whole life? Fine, good. Next. Are you good at being a musician? There are plenty of mediocre musicians out there. If you feel you're really good at being a musician, what about the next criterion? This is where a lot of people fall down. Music is, as I say, a business. You need to be paid for what you do. You can't be paid in exposure. Nor can you be paid by doing lots of charity gigs. You need to ensure that you have a wide range of income streams. Play live music. Record. Teach. Compose. Arrange. Do anything you can to generate opportunities to be paid for. What about the last one? Does the world need music? Specifically, does the world need your music? What is it about your music that makes the world better?

If two of these are missing, you have a mission, a passion, a vocation, or a profession, but you don't have Ikigai. If one of them is missing, you can nearly get there, but there will be something missing still. If you can truly state that you have all four, then you're lucky. You'll probably be successful in the music industry.

If you are going to be a performer of music, you are going to need to cast that musical performance as effectively as possible within the music industry. Over the course of this book, that's just what we are going to do. We're not going to discuss publishing deals or record contracts, except as to how they impact upon performance. We're going to focus on how your performances can be integrated into the industry. This means talking about festivals, touring, organising gigs, working with venues, and creating merchandise.

The Voices in this Book

The preparation of this book involved interviewing more than 200 musicians, venues, agents, and music business people from Australia, the United States, the UK, Canada, New Zealand, Germany, India, and Syria. Their views and thoughts permeate this book and have shaped our thinking on live popular music. What you're reading is the distillation of Waldo's and my ideas based on a lifetime of performing combined with lived experience. You'll hear all sorts of voices in these pages.

So, let's start.

Note

1 All through this book, we're going to use industry jargon. If you're not sure what it means, look it up in the glossary at the back of the book.

Section 1

Creating Memorable Performances

In the first section of the book, we examine the performance itself. We will consider what makes a memorable performance and speculate how to go about making it. We'll examine the process of preparing for that performance through personal practice and ensemble rehearsal. Then we'll go on to examine who your audience are and how to play to them. Finally, we will consider the processes, pitfalls, and practice of working in a band. We might get a little philosophical, but don't worry. We'll counter it with practical advice.

1 What Makes a Performance Memorable?

When we musicians first begin to perform in public, it's common for us to focus on ourselves and our music. This is understandable. Being a musician is hard work, and a lived experience. We get caught inside our own heads. You might have focussed on your instrumental technique. Perhaps you've concentrated on developing your skills as a songwriter. Or maybe you studied how to record music on your computer or in a studio. These things are undeniably important, but they're not the whole package.

There's a fundamental difference between your experience of a performance, and the audience's. Your experience of a particular show might be great, or it might be awful. Maybe the guitarist got drunk. Maybe the sound was hideous. Maybe there was a train wreck. However, from an audience's viewpoint (and they are, after all, paying to attend), a performance is either memorable or it is not. It will make them want to tell their friends about this great gig they attended, and how they should all go to this venue, or go to all your gigs, or it will not. As a working, performing musician, you need everyone in the audience to go home thinking that your gig was the most awesome gig ever; you need them to join your Facebook group that night, and buy all your merchandise. And there's an art to that. It's the art of purposefully and cleverly crafting a memorable experience.

But what is this experience? How do you make it memorable for the audience? How do you create a group of fans who want to come to every gig you do? It's not entirely about technique. It's not entirely about recording. It's not entirely about the songs you write. Though they're all a part of it. It's mostly about how good a performer you are. It's about the way you move and perform, about the engagement you have with the audience, both on and off the stage; it's about making every audience member think you're singing to them, and about generating stage excitement. That's what will make an audience remember your performances.

There's one thing all of our informants said that we should mention at the outset: Go and see some gigs. See performers you know, and performers you don't. If you're not playing one night, see what concerts are on. While you're there, and on the way home, think about whether you'll remember the performance in a month or a year. Will it enter your mental catalogue of gigs you want to emulate? Learn from every performance you attend. And attend a lot of them.

THE BEST ROCK CONCERT

The best concert I ever attended was Queen in 1986. Just those four individuals, so strong as players and as songwriters, just coming together with this incredible unity. There's a special chemistry that happens sometimes that makes it much more than just a simple performance. And that was one of those shows. What I was saying about filling a room, I mean ... my god ... those guys ... just their presence, the presence of Freddie Mercury alone, it was just unbelievable. This guy just struts to the front of the stage and opens his voice and sings and it's just ... you just go on from that straightway. He was an incredible performer. But all the other three guys were unbelievable musicians and they could all sing incredibly as well. But just the power and simplicity of what they could do as a four-piece band, given that the compositions and the writing was not complex ... They took the pieces of music and yet they were able to just perform them with such ease. That stands out.

Cameron, Venue owner and jazz bassist

The Gig as Experience

One of the questions we asked our interviewees was about their best, their most memorable concert experience, and we'll mention those responses right through the book, like we have done with Cameron here. We also asked the opposite question: "Tell me about a bad performance you've seen". The response was almost always the same: "Oh, there's been so many!" Any musician who's gone to a lot of gigs will have seen bad performances by musicians who do not understand how to engage. Bands or singers that show up, plug in, perform in the corner of a pub meeting no one's eyes, and then wonder why no one pays attention or buys their merchandise. There could be many reasons for this, but often it's because they are playing at the audience instead of engaging with them. The one thing that everyone talked about was the importance of the audience. If you watch the superstar performers live, they engage the audience. Watch Taylor Swift stand on a stage and wordlessly look out at the audience. Watch Bruce Springsteen. Even though he is playing to a large stadium, fans often say how he seems to be playing to them alone. Watch Harry Connick Jr bounce around and talk to the audience. Watch the movement and enthusiasm of the Big Bad Voodoo Daddies. Musicians fascinate audiences. Even though their idols are sweating on stage and working their hardest, they are having fun.

Before we go any further, we should consider what fun is. Fun is the unexpected, informal, and purposeless enjoyment of pleasure. It is a psychological state and a philosophical concept. As humans we can't be serious all the time. We can't work all the time. Large-brained mammals such as humans need to experience diversion, pleasure, and fun or we go crazy. Many animals play and it is supposed that human play predates human culture.[1] The Epic of Gilgamesh, written at the dawn of human civilisation around 2100 BC, advised: "Fill your belly. Day and night make merry. Let days be full of joy. Dance and make music day and night … These things alone are the concern of men". Play and fun are so important that a philosophical school—Hedonism—grew up around the pursuit of fun and relaxation as the primary task of humans. There are concepts of hedonism and fun that are advocated by many of the modern-day world's religions. Fun makes our temporal perception (chronoception) appear to go faster.[2] It is infectious and engaging. People in groups (such as at a live music event) seem to generate more fun. Lack of fun and recreation have been linked to obesity,[3] depression,[4] mental health issues,[5] alcohol and drug addiction, and suicide.[6] It is precisely because fun is so important, so fundamental to the human experience, that creating live music experiences is so important.

You've probably heard the term 'experience' many times. You might have had your teachers tell you that you "need to make your performance an experience". But what does the concept of experience mean? What is an experience, and how does it relate to music? There's been a reasonable amount of work done on the concept of experience in the last few years, notably that of Harvard business scholars Joseph Pine and James Gilmore.[7] To paraphrase what they say:

1. An experience is an event that happens at a certain time.
2. An experience happens within the confines of a certain place.
3. An experience is designed specifically to engage consumers of the experience.
4. In fact it is so engaging that audiences will pay money for the privilege of spending time within the experience.

A vast array of experiences occur. Having a coffee in St Mark's Square in Venice is an experience. Visiting a theme park such as Disneyland is an experience. Going on a cruise is an experience. A musical performance is an experience. Consider a musical performance through the four points above.

1. A musical performance happens at a certain pre-advertised time.
2. A musical performance happens within the confines of a certain place. It might be the space of a festival, with its clearly delineated differentiation between festival space and the outside. It might be at a venue with the space inside the experience only available to those who pay the entrance price.
3. A musical performance is designed to engage the audience, to get them listening and applauding.
4. It is because of the designed engagement that audiences pay money to spend time within the physical and temporal confines of the musical performance.

There are many types of experiences. We mentioned a few above: cruise ships and St Mark's Square and so forth. All these different experiences have a few aspects in common:

- Experiences are sensory.
- Experiences occur in a defined space at a defined time.
- Experiences are planned.
- Experiences are commercial.
- Experiences are engaging.

Let's look at each of these in turn.

An Experience is Sensory

As humans, we experience the world through our senses. They are the conduit between our brains and our environment. We see things to know where and what they are. We hear things to communicate and to be aware of danger. We smell things to know if they're good to eat. We cannot exist without our senses. If you take one away, our other senses need to work more actively.

Music primarily engages the aural sense. You listen to music, on a CD, streamed, or in performance. However, if your performance is to truly be an experience, it needs to engage as many of the senses as possible, not just the aural. The visuals can be stimulated by light shows, by projected images, or by the physical appearance and stage costumes of the performers. Smell can be stimulated by the smell of food or the smell of other sweaty dancers. Consideration of, and planning for, the other senses move a performance from just another gig into the realm of a memorable performance.

But wait, there's more! When we think of our senses, we traditionally think of the five 'traditional' (or 'Aristotelian') senses of sight, smell, taste, touch, and hearing. However, humans can also sense beyond these basic but important senses. Consider the following senses:

- Chronoception (our sense of time passing).
- Mechanoreception (our sense of vibration).
- Thermoception (our sense of hot and cold).
- Nociception (our sense of pain).
- Equilibrioception (our sense of balance).
- Proprioception (our sense of the position and movement of our bodies).

If a gig is fantastic, it seems to be over all too quickly. That's our chronoceptive sense. When you feel the rumble of the subs in your chest and your gut, that's stimulating our mechanoreceptive sense. Movement on the dancefloor affects our equilibrioception and our proprioception. Planning beyond the five main senses into others increases the memorability of the experience.

These senses can be engaged positively or negatively. For example, gigs are often loud and exciting because humans are excited by loud noise (activating our aural and perhaps our mechanoreceptive senses). However, if a gig is too loud, it can also activate the nociceptive (pain) sense and create a less enjoyable experience. It will be memorable, but perhaps for the wrong reasons.

When you are planning a performance, plan for these senses. I suggest you consider them individually until you have your experiential product thoroughly planned. Revise and reconsider after every gig until you have a working product.

An Experience Occurs at a Certain Time and in a Certain Defined Space

An experience is an ephemeral event. It occurs at one place and one time only. The Bee Gees performed their final One Night Only tour across many nights and dozens of cities. Despite the name, each performance was slightly different. In the entire history of the world, of the untold number of musical performances that have ever happened, each performance occurs only once in a given place. It's worthwhile putting some effort into it. It's not just a gig. It's the only time that gig will ever happen.

Invariably, the general public exchange money for time spent within the space and the time of an experience. That might be through ticket sales or it might be through bar revenue, but make no mistake, once they enter the space/time of a performance, they are paying money and they expect to be engaged. You'd better make that space and time rewarding.

Figure 1.1 It doesn't get more engaging than this. Bruce Springsteen in Sydney with our friend, astrophysicist Dr Jessica Bloom. I'll bet that she remembers this moment. Source: Jessica Bloom.

An Experience Is Purposefully Planned

The planning of an experience is one of the most contradictory processes of a performance, and something often missed by learning musicians. In our experience, they concentrate on getting the music right, and spend a long time on this. However, they often give only cursory thought to planning the performance. An effective musical experience deals with both the music and the performance. Omit one at your peril.

When you're preparing a gig, everything has to be prepared. Everything has to run well. There can be no unpleasant unexpected problems. It has to be planned to the nth degree. Yet it also has to appear spontaneous, joyful, and easy. The banter on stage has to seem easy and unplanned, just like banter that might happen in a living room. How do you mount a performance that is at the same time thoroughly prepared and organised, yet apparently unprepared and in the moment? Consider the planning of a performance like the scaffolding around a building. It exists. It is there for safety. But it is not the building itself. The planning of a performance ensures that it goes well and that there will be no obvious mistakes. It permits the performers the ease to relax and concentrate on their performance. But to the audience it seems that it happens by magic.

SPONTANEITY IN PERFORMANCE

Despite the need for preparation, music performances also require a certain amount of spontaneity. There might be some kind of improvisation, and there are bands who will occasionally do a request that they haven't researched. I saw Patti Smith tentatively play a Prince song at the State Theatre after an audience member engaged her in conversation about Prince's previous gig there. That certainly enhanced the memorability of the gig. I also once spoke to guitarist Danny Adler when we were both in the bathroom during his band's mid-set gig at the Golden Lion in London. I asked him whether his band ever played The Clean Up Woman, because I thought it would be great for his guitar style. He said they hadn't. But when he came back on stage he played the opening riff because "some dude in the toilets told him to". Made it pretty memorable for me!

Phil, Music academic

A successful experience takes intellectual property that has no dollar value in itself (in our case, songs) and converts it into something that does. It is this value for which the general public (not-audiences) become consumers (audiences), by exchanging money for time spent within the experience. Ideally, you then want to take these audiences (people who come to see your performance) and make them into fans (audiences who come to see your performances regularly).

By creating audiences and then fans, you generate revenue for yourself and for the venue, and become financially successful musicians. Easy, right?

Our friends Pine and Gilmore state that the value of an experience is created by carefully planning four realms that go on to create an experience. These realms are entertainment, escapism, and the aesthetic and educational aspects. They exist on the two spectrums of absorbing or immersing audiences and actively or passively engage them. If you can blend all four of these realms effectively, you achieve the sweet spot and create the most successful experiences. Figure 1.2 shows this model.

Firstly, the obvious one. As musicians, we are entertainers. But what actually is entertainment? In this model, entertainment is a process of absorbing a musical experience through human senses. Now, you might react actively to that performance. You might dance to a funk band. You might tap along to a singer/songwriter. You might thrill to a star performer. But as far as the experience is concerned, being entertained is a passive aspect of the experience. It moves from the performer to the audience and, as such, it is entirely on you as a musician to consider how you are going to entertain an audience. You have to plan for the control here. You have to plan to give such a good, entertaining performance that you (figuratively) grab them by the shirtfront and occupy their attention for the duration. It may not always happen because of some external factor; maybe the sound is not great, the promotion has been underwhelming, or you're playing on the night of the football final. However, you have to plan for active entertainment. Memorable performances always involve entertaining an audience.

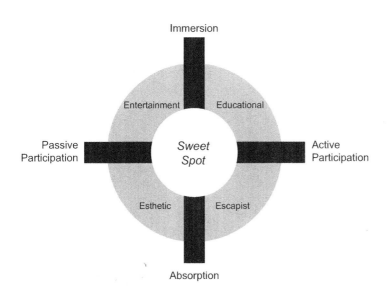

Figure 1.2 Aspects of the experience.

To make a performance memorable, you also have to consider the aesthetics. You won't always have control over your environment, but you need to consider it. Aesthetics concerns the physical and performative environments in which you find yourself. It can include concepts of beauty; however, practically, it involves considerations of the performative space. Does the venue work as a performance space? Is it too narrow for the audio, is the bar positioned badly, what are the sightlines like? Does the lighting contribute to the performance, or is the operator inexperienced? Are the ceilings too low for effective lighting? How is the sound? Is it too loud or too soft? What about your performance? Is it aesthetically pleasing within the confines of the genre? You don't (generally) go in and shred loud distorted guitar in a folk club or play heartfelt acoustic songs in a metal concert. Or if you do, you are making an aesthetic decision, and it is incumbent upon you to explain it within the context of the performance.

Memorable performances are escapist, immersive, and active. Escapism describes a journey from a place (everyday life), to a new place (the performance you are creating). It is this journey that you need to consider. Think back to the amazing performances you have previously identified. Think of the journey that the performers took you on. Did you feel like a passive observer, or did you feel like an active traveller as the performer took you on a journey? One reason performances fail is because they are not active. They do not take audiences on a journey. Memorable performances involve treating audiences as active participants in your performance.

Last, experiences are educational. Does this mean that you need to have a slide presentation and hand out qualifications at the end of a gig? Of course not. But memorable performances can make people think and reflect. Whether that's by engaging people in a jazz gig, performing songs that challenge their worldview, or by other means. Music is an art form and sometimes needs to provoke and encourage discursive thought. This is not to suggest that performances that are fun for the sake of fun (totally escapist) are not worthwhile—they are. But the thoughtful side of performance is also important.

The people we spoke to in preparing this book regarded these realms in similar fashions, but with nuances depending on if they were musicians, industry members, or audiences. Musicians and industry members regarded entertainment, escapism, and aesthetic values as all being equally important to the creation of a successful performance. Audiences rated entertainment as being the most important, aesthetic elements as secondary, and escapism as third. All rated the educational/challenging aspects as being less important, marginally in the case of industry members, somewhat less in the case of musicians, and significantly less in the case of audiences.

Different performances will emphasise different aspects of each of these axes. They are not discrete. Let's consider the 'escapist/educational' axis. Some gigs are entirely escapist. People dance and have fun rather than thinking about their issues. Others are more educational and reflective. An earnest singer/songwriter might sing songs that deal with politics, the problems of modern life, or relationship issues. People reflect on that and go away thoughtful. The sweet spot is found if you are able to balance all of these. But that doesn't mean that you can't emphasise other areas. Just do so thoughtfully.

THE WORST PERFORMANCE

One of the worst performances I ever saw was a concert of jazz/pop music students. They appeared neither authentic nor humble, they seemed to imitate singers they had heard somewhere on the radio or seen on TV, imitating the timbre of their voices, their movements on stage and also their confidence. The music seemed empty and boring. The students were behaving like 'wannabes' who neither had their own voice nor their own mind. They didn't inspire, surprise, or touch me at all.

Olivia, Jazz singer and pianist

Experiences Are Commercial

Musicians think of themselves as artists, which they clearly are. However, successful musicians also think of themselves as businesspeople. Their performances are a commercial and experiential product with a target group of consumers who pay to hear them perform. Every genre of music, even the ones that aspire to the status of high art, such as jazz or classical music, is commercial. You might aspire to be a jazz musician. Great. You might be able to solo on "Donna Lee" at crotchet 240. Awesome. You might think (as many jazz musicians do) that Michael Bublé is a lightweight performer. However, Michael Bublé is estimated to be worth $60 million. He is successful. He makes a living from what he does. Classical musicians often disparage Dutch violinist André Rieu as showy, imprecise, and catering to the lowest common denominator. Showy, supposedly imprecise André Rieu is estimated to be worth $40 million. Other musicians are worth even more. Taylor Swift is reputed to be worth around $400 million. Bruce Springsteen? $500 million. Dolly Parton? $500 million. Paul McCartney? A staggering $1.28 billion.

Believe it or not, it is not a sin to be successful in the music industry. Bublé and Rieu are doing what they love and they're being successful at it. Being a successful musician in whatever genre you perform in means adopting a commercial approach to your art. Performances are business enterprises jointly hosted by you and the venue. If you do not adopt a dollars and cents approach to the music industry and your performances, the dollars and cents will not come.

Experiences Are Engaging

One thing that you need to learn really fast and well is: If you want to be successful in the music industry, never be boring. There is already one Dr Dre in the world, so why would the world need 50? You need to plan your musical product so it is unique to you. Be a singer-songwriter, sure. Have a jazz piano trio, or a Cuban salsa band. Run a newgrass band. Be influenced by people. But your 'product', your brand, needs to be interesting and distinctive.

A FORK IN A WORLD OF SOUP

In 2008, I was at a meeting in LA with other Universal execs from different parts of the world for an Interscope conference. Every night there was a showcase of artists, mainly new, some established. Separate to this, a manager I knew offered me tickets to an exclusive Metallica show … he was incredulous when I turned him down, opting for the 'ladies night' showcase. The first band on were a facsimile of the Pussycat Dolls (huge at the time). They performed, met us, gushed about how much they were looking forward to coming to Australia, Canada, France, England, etc. Second band on … more of the same. The third performer was dressed from neck to foot in black leather. The songs were great. Similar but different, with her own take. Add a couple of mime artist dancers behind her and the concept of ArtPop shone through. It was brilliant. When she finished, she didn't come over and gush … she just left the stage and walked away. My immediate thought was, "Wow, she's a star! It's just that the world doesn't know it … yet". At the end of the conference we were all asked to name our standout artist … Australia and Canada said Lady Gaga and committed to breaking her if Interscope delivered her to market. They did; we did … and the rest of the world followed. Australia was the first market to give her a gold #1 award. If you want to stand out, know who you are … take your concept to the edge of its creativity and, to misquote Noel Gallagher, be a fork in a world of soup. Gaga did just that.

Tim, Record Executive

Historical Music Experiences

The popular music industry didn't spontaneously appear with Taylor Swift, or even Elvis Presley. Popular music has existed as long as there has been consumers of music and the means to disseminate it to a mass audience. This dates the origins of the popular music industry back to the mid-19th century. In this section, we'll consider four historical examples of popular music performances: the Ziegfeld Follies, the performances of Cab Calloway, the Beatles' performance in the Washington Coliseum, and Queen's performance at Live Aid.

The Ziegfeld Follies

The 1920s was the era of revue. The revue was a high-class theatrical entertainment involving lots of music, dancing, and revealing costumes. The headquarters of the revue was Broadway in New York, with its attendant composers nearby in Tin Pan Alley. The greatest and showiest of these revues was the Ziegfeld Follies produced by (male) impresario Florenz "Flo" Ziegfeld (1867–1932).

Revue had a surface similarity to both the minstrel show and vaudeville; however, it was actually quite different. It originated within the French tradition of cabaret, which had itself begun after the Napoleonic wars (1799–1815) when a decimated Paris desperately needed entertainment. The quintessential French cabaret was the *Folies Bergère*, which opened in 1872 in the 9th arrondissement. They produced a beautiful and thoroughly French series of cabarets featuring extravagant and outrageous costumes, startling sets and effects, and frequent nudity. In the 1920s, the famous African-American performer Josephine Baker performed here.

Ziegfeld was a manager, entrepreneur, producer, director, bully, advocate, and ringmaster all in one. He produced great art, entertaining and titillating performances, and supported important songwriters while simultaneously making squillions. From 1907 to 1927, he produced these annual lavish productions performed by beautiful and talented men and women and written by songwriters and composers, such as Irving Berlin, Jerome Kern, Franz Lehar, Buddy DeSylva, Eddie Cantor, Harry Tierney, Harry Von Tilzer, and Rudolph Friml. The postwar Follies embodied the excesses of the 1920s, prohibition, and the jazz age. Unlike later 'book' musicals, there was no plot to a Follies. They comprised a series of self-contained performances. A comedian would follow a tableau and then be followed by a musical number with a chorus line. The series of performances meant it was acceptable to arrive late and leave early without sacrificing the performance. Many of the best-known stars of the twenties and thirties performed here, accompanied by the 'Ziegfeld girls', a chorus line of beautiful women dressed in revealing costumes designed by the best designers in New York. The success of Ziegfeld's follies led to other lookalike performances.

The follies were an escapist experience. People paid to go in and be transported to a world of beauty, glamour, and decadence. Eventually, Ziegfeld built his Ziegfeld Theatre, the most beautiful theatre in New York, and a testament to the Follies. In this gorgeous space, he mounted revues and early book musicals to widespread acclaim. He was responsible for mounting the hugely influential musical Showboat.

Even after the stock market crash of 1929, Flo Ziegfeld continued to mount lavish productions in the face of declining audiences and harsher conditions. His last follies were in 1931. He died the following year from pleurisy, at the age of 65.

Takeaway: Florenz Ziegfeld was a pioneer of the performance-as-experience. He created spectacular and aesthetically beautiful performances through the 1920s. He took risks and spent significant money on his Follies, and they made him rich. His shows were engaging, enthralling, and relevant to the time.

Figure 1.3 Ziegfeld girl Rose Dolores wearing her famous Peacock costume in 1919.

Cab Calloway's Performances at the Cotton Club

At the same time that Flo Ziegfeld was developing his revues, jazz, transposed from Louisiana to New York City, was changing from a vulgar novelty, a crude depiction of the improvised African-American music of New Orleans, into a truly popular art form. When producers combined jazz and revue, it made for a particularly unique event. Most New York revues used predominantly white performers; however, a few black revues, such as Blackbirds of 1928 existed. For commercial purposes, producers of these revues exoticised African-American music as the 'primitive' 'jungle' music of Africa to appeal to the prejudices of the audience. Black dancing girls wore skimpy costumes for scenes set in the jungles of Africa, or the pre-bellum south … anything that would play to white audiences and turn a buck. Into this mix, in the early 1930s, swaggered Cab Calloway, strutting across the stage of the Cotton Club.

Cable "Cab" Calloway (1907–1994) was an early and influential jazz singer. He grew up in Baltimore with a love of performing and took over a band called The Missourians in 1930. In 1931, he took over for Duke Ellington's band at the Cotton Club. The Cotton Club was a gangster-owned white-only venue in Harlem, which used black performers to depict African-American life using the racist imagery of the time. By the 1930s, it had become the premiere jazz venue in the country. The bands of Fletcher Henderson, Count Basie, Duke Ellington, and Jimmie Lunceford graced its stage. Calloway used his performances at the Cotton Club to cement his particular brand of performance. He became known as the "Hi-Dee-Ho Man" because of the chorus of his hit Minnie the Moocher. His was a particularly physical performance. He was a superlative singer, and a

Figure 1.4 Cab Calloway.

virtuoso scatter, but his physicality was unique and forceful. Consider this review of a 1934 performance in London:[8]

> To one rather shy of the black arts it seemed that Mr. Cab Calloway began gently. The showmanship of his Cotton Club Band was skilful, his smile persuasive. This gentleness, however, masked the wrath to come. His band began to quiver. The news of the bass violist contracted tremors as if a sapling foretelling a tempest, or a sensitive blancmange or an impending earthquake. The drummer showed signs of possession by demons as his whirling sticks caressed or crashed on the tympani that surrounded him like a glory. Then the storm burst and, as I caught my breath, I wondered what Dr. Livingstone might have thought of us. Those feline plaints and bull-roaring rhythms, the scandalised scale with its distressed intervals, the tunes, too brief to exhaust but swift to execute, roused the London Palladium to cup-final frenzy.

How old fashioned seems Sousa's brassy band beside this Voodoo virtuosity! Mr Calloway dances, sings, howls, gesticulates, grimaces; but though apparently at his last gasp gives neither in nor quarter. What need to drag in Bach (as enthusiasts do for comparisons odious to Bach?) Here are older more primitive rhythms and a kind of devilish artistry. London audiences will not get nearer to the ju-ju in the jungle that Mr Calloway delivers twice nightly.[9]

This description, stuffy and offensive to modern readers, demonstrates a few points about Calloway's performance. First, it was energetic and physical. His musicality was exceptional, but that was not all of his performance. Calloway did not sit back and wait for audiences to engage with him. He was physical. He engaged with the audience. Second, he had a strong persona on stage. He was the Hi-Dee-Ho man, a name taken from his propensity to scat. Third, he planned his performance as an entirety. He did not go out on stage and trust to luck that everything would go well in the moment. There was an arc. He started this performance understated, against the expectations of the audience, then gradually built up into an extraordinary and memorable performance. And lastly, he was unique. There was no one at the time that was doing what he was doing as successfully as he was doing it.

Why did Calloway become one of the best-known swing performers? His musicality was unquestioned. He popularised an improvisatory approach to singing and rhythm whereby both could be changed at will while still remaining recognisable. But he was a memorable performer and a singer. His performances were novel and energetic. He had a strong persona on stage and performed his music with commitment and determination.

Calloway had enormous influence on the popularisation of swing and jazz. He voiced a Betty Boop cartoon, performed in a series of Paramount shorts, sang duets with Al Jolson in the 1934 feature *The Singing Kid*. He recorded prolifically from the early 1930s until the late 1940s. To modern audiences, Calloway is probably best known as Curtis from the 1984 Blues Brothers Movie. In this role, he sang Minnie the Moocher in a virtuoso musical and physical performance he undertook at the age of 77. If you can, watch some of his performances. He's worth a YouTube search.

Takeaway: Calloway was a physical and engaging performer who played to and engaged his audience. It made him successful.

The Beatles' 1964 Tour of the US

By the 1950s, swing and jazz was transitioning from contemporary music into the more esoteric art form of bebop. A new form of contemporary music emerged to fill the gap. This music was called rock and roll, and it was a hybrid of post-war R&B, country music, western swing, and gospel. Moreover, it was music to dance to. Rock concerts were usually dances. This is reflected in shows like American Bandstand in the US, which featured shiny, bright (typically white) teenagers dancing to Chuck Berry or Little Richard or Jerry Lee Lewis. With the decline of rock after the Payola Scandal, American rock at a national level became very industry controlled. Good-looking young white men sang corporately approved songs of romantic love written by professional songwriters. More full-on bands like The Kingsmen had local appeal but did not make the national charts. Two things changed these restrictions. First, The Beatles toured the US in 1964. Second, amplification technology improved to the point that high-power systems that didn't distort sound could be transported and set up temporarily.

In the dying days of 1963 America discovered The Beatles, a little later than the UK, but that was perhaps understandable. Little contemporary music of international interest had emerged from the UK before. Suddenly, in December, The Beatles were everywhere: on the radio, in record shops, in store windows. Teenagers were buying their records and playing them on high repeat. The Beatles were cheeky, good-looking, had weird-looking hair, and had exotic Liverpudlian accents. Interest was high enough for an American tour to be hastily organised. On 7 February, they arrived in the United States and, on 9 February, they appeared on the Ed Sullivan show, watched by 73 million people (about 40% of what was then the US population). Two concerts were organised. The main show was to be on 12 February at the 2,000 seat Carnegie Hall, but an out-of-town opening was to be held the previous night at the Washington Coliseum.

The Washington show turned out to be a watershed performance. The Washington Coliseum was not a performance venue. It was a sporting stadium that was occasionally adapted for other uses such as a ballroom. There was no stage. The design was 'in the round', meaning that the audience were seated 360° around the central area. These issues took some creative thinking. How could the Fab Four perform with their backs to part of the audience with the primitive amplification technology of the time. This took some working out. A boxing ring stage was placed in the middle and Ringo's drums were placed on a revolve in the middle of the ring. The other members of the band would literally have to pick up their instruments and amplifiers and move them ninety degrees, so they played to all of the audience at some stage. To make matters more complicated, on the day of the performance, a major east-coast snowstorm had dumped eight inches of snow on the city, meaning the opening act, The Chiffons, could not make it.

On the night, far from being deterred, fans showed up in droves. 8,092 of them—four times what Carnegie Hall would hold—braved the snow to see one of the first stadium pop performances. A video recording taken at the performance shows a slick and easy performance between the four. They were excited at their first American performance, performing to eight thousand screaming fans.

Takeaway 1: John, Paul, and George had been playing together for five years at this stage. They had played together every night in Hamburg on several stints. Ringo had been playing with them for 18 months. These musicians knew each other. They knew each other's performance. They liked each other (at this stage). This knowledge contributed to the easy banter and fun on stage.

Takeaway 2: This was an unusually difficult concert to organise. However, this difficulty did not deter organisers, and they worked hard and creatively to ensure a successful performance. Preparation is key to contemporary music performance.

Queen and the Live Aid Concert

In 1984, with the horrors of the Ethiopian famine being shown on British televisions nightly (via the memorable reporting of Michael Buerk), Bob Geldof and Midge Ure wrote a song, "Do They Know it's Christmas", and convinced British rock and pop royalty to record it. A grand total of 37 musicians–including Bono, Phil Collins, Chris Cross, Bananarama (Sara Dallin, Keren Woodward, and Siobhan Fahey), Boy George, George Michael, Jody Watley, and Sting–performed on the song. It became the biggest selling single in Britain's music history, sold nearly 12 million copies, and raised £8 million within the year. It inspired the American industry to record We Are the World, which is reputed to have sold 20 million copies.

The following year, Geldof and Ure conceived a bigger project: Live Aid. Using the fairly limited technology of the day, they would organise simultaneous concerts performed in Wembley Stadium in the UK, and John F. Kennedy Stadium in Philadelphia. The UK performance would be broadcast in the American stadium and vice versa. The show would be further broadcast on television around the world. The date was set for Saturday, 13 July 1985, and musicians signed on by the truckload. Sting, Spandau Ballet, Sade, U2, Dire Straits, Elton John, David Bowie, The Who, and more signed on in the UK. In the States, Joan Baez, Billy Ocean, Madonna, Black Sabbath, Run-DMC, Pattie LaBelle, Judas Priest, The Beach Boys, Duran Duran, Led Zeppelin ... they were all there. Phil Collins played in London, was helicoptered to Heathrow, boarded a Concord, and played again in Philadelphia. One band that perhaps raised a few eyebrows, was Queen.

By the mid-1980s, Queen were in their wilderness years. They were in their second decade of playing and many considered them passé. The music they played was firmly entrenched in the 1970s, as were many of their hits. In an interview with journalist David Wigg, Mercury had said, "We were all forming a sort of rut. I wanted to get out of this last ten years of what we were doing. It was so routine. It was like, go to the studio, do an album, go out on the road, go round the world and flog it to death, and by the time you came back it was time to do another album." However, in 1984 they'd released the critically acclaimed album *The Works*, which included songs such as Radio Gaga, I Want to Break Free, and It's a Hard Life, so they weren't doing entirely bad. Still, no one expected the performance they got.

On the day, each band was told that they had 20 minutes and no more. There were to be no egos. Band followed band in an orderly fashion. After performing two songs at around 6 pm, Dire Straits left the stage and, at 6.41 pm, Freddie Mercury and Queen walked onto the stage and no one knew quite what to expect. Well, they were outstanding. They played hit after hit, usually in a truncated form allowing them to get through more songs in the allotted 20 minutes. They played with passion and commitment. They knew what each other would do before they did it. Freddie pranced and swung his baseless microphone. Brian May's guitar performance showcased him at the height of his abilities. Roger Taylor and John

Deacon committed and played brilliantly. Watch a video of it. It's an astounding performance. After the concert, Geldof described Queen as,

> absolutely the best band of the day. They played the best, had the best sound, used their time to the full. They understood the idea exactly, that it was a global jukebox. They just went and smashed one hit after another. It was the perfect stage for Freddie: the whole world. And he could ponce about on stage doing "We Are the Champions". How perfect could it get?[10]

THE QUEEN SETLIST FROM LIVE AID

Bohemian Rhapsody
Ay-oh
Radio Ga Ga
Hammer to Fall
Crazy Little Thing Called Love
We Will Rock You
We Are the Champions

Why did Queen work so well at Live Aid? Several reasons have been put forward. First, they played songs that everyone knew. The seven songs they played were their biggest hits. They played the best bits of every song—enough to get an acknowledgement from the crowd, and then moved on to the next. Another reason was their audience involvement. They included their Ay-oh audience response song. We Will Rock You permits the audience to stamp along with them. Radio Gaga has that strangely engaging hands-over-the-head clapping. Third, they were used to each other's performance. By 1985, Queen had been playing together for 15 years. They were just off a concert tour and were slick and comfortable with their playing. It showed. And, of course, Freddie's performance was like a masterclass of audience engagement. Even younger audiences who weren't familiar with Queen's back catalogue were mesmerised.

Bugged by technical glitches and with some less-than-spectacular performances, the Live Aid concert was still fabulously successful. It remains the biggest concert experience in the history of contemporary music. Officially, 72,000 people packed into Wembley; 100,000 into the John F. Kennedy Centre. Local versions happened in the Soviet Union, Canada, Japan, Yugoslavia, Austria, Australia, and West Germany. Around the world, nearly two billion people watched it, about 40% of what was then the world's population.

Takeaway: Mercury's performance was mesmerising. Queen was right on the money. Their audience participation was superlative. They played their best songs. They were exciting and they moved. In 2005, the performance was voted as the best rock performance in history. It deserves it.

Further Reading

Probably the best roundup of experience is Pine and Gilmore's *The Experience Economy*. It's an easy read, and worthwhile thinking about from a performance perspective.

A full history of contemporary music falls outside the scope of this book. Fortunately, there are several excellent books on contemporary music that survey the entire scope of contemporary music history. The main two are John Covach's *What's That Sound* and Reebee Garafalo's *Rockin' Out*. The history of jazz is summarised in Frank Tirro's *Jazz*. Country music is covered by Bill Malone and Tracey Laird's *Country Music USA*. They are all eminently readable and engaging. Another excellent read is Simon Napier-Bell's *Ta-Ra-Ra-Boom-De-Ay: The Dodgy Business of Popular Music*. Finally, Stephen Witt's excellent account of the file-sharing revolution is entitled *How Music Got Free*.

Chapter Summary

- A musical performance is an experience.
- An experience comprises several characteristics:
  - An experience engages the senses.
  - An experience occurs at a certain time and place.
  - An experience is planned.
  - An experience is commercial.
  - An experience is engaging.
- The performance-as-experience model has existed for a long time:
  - The Ziegfeld Follies were an early, commercially successful experience.
  - Cab Calloway used movement and enthusiasm to excite audiences and generate successful and memorable performances.
  - The Beatles' performance in Washington was not an easy one to mount, but dedicated performers and stagecraft led to a wildly successful performance.
  - Queen's performance at Live Aid is a masterclass in creating successful performances.

Notes

1 Huizinga, *Homo Ludens: The Study of Play-Element in Culture*.
2 Sackett et al. "You're Having Fun When Time Flies: The Hedonic Consequences of Subjective Time Progression."
3 Santana, Santos, and Nogueira, "The Link between Local Environment and Obesity: A Multilevel Analysis in the Lisbon Metropolitan Area, Portugal."
4 Beevers and Meyer, "Lack of Positive Experiences and Positive Expectancies Mediate the Relationship between BAS Responsiveness and Depression."
5 Wegner and Flisher, "Leisure Boredom and Adolescent Risk Behaviour: A Systematic Literature Review."

6 Patterson and Pegg, "Nothing to Do: The Relationship between 'Leisure Boredom' and Alcohol and Drug Addiction: Is There a Link to Youth Suicide in Rural Australia?"

7 Pine and Gilmore, "The Experience Economy."

8 Be aware that writing of the era could use terms, acceptable at the time, but which we consider offensive. Read these in the context of the time.

9 H. H., "Mr Cab Calloway's Cotton Club Band."

10 Richards and Langthorne, *Somebody to Love: The Life, Death and Legacy of Freddie Mercury*.

2   Creating Memorable Live Performances

Being successful in a live contemporary music situation is more than simply the ability to play and write songs. Successful practitioners are also skilled in the art of stagecraft. They move. They interact with the audience. They banter between themselves. It all happens seemingly by magic. However, stagecraft is a skill that needs to be honed. Inexperienced acts will sometimes deliberately act distantly on stage in an attempt to be cool. However, a memorable musical experience occurs when the performers have planned well and are deliberately engaging, inviting the audience to share in the joy of making music.

There is a method to creating a successful live performance. Regardless of the genre or whether it's a stadium concert in front of thousands or a small pub gig in front of dozens, certain things must take place. If you've not performed at a professional live musical performance yet, or have only played in school ones, you may not be aware of these. And you need to be. If you skip in preparation or don't know what is supposed to happen on stage, your performance will suffer. Nobody wants that.

Types of Performances

There are as many types of gigs out there as there are musicians, and each gig needs a slightly different approach. Some, such as headliner gigs, focus the atten-tion entirely on you. Another type, such as the wallpaper gig, is the opposite: You don't want the audience to pay attention to you. While it is not possible to cover every type of gig, we can have a look through the main ones.

Musicians talk about a **wallpaper gig**. In many ways, a wallpaper gig is the exact opposite to the spirit of this book. It's when you, as a musician, become part of the background, a sort of musical wallpaper. You're there adding to the ambiance of the venue, but you are not the focus of the night. You look the part, you might be dressed up in a nice suit or evening dress, but you purposely try to remain unnoticed and in the background. You play softly and unassum-ingly. The venue has hired you to add class to the venue, not to draw attention to yourself. Examples might include pianists playing in hotel bars or classical guitarists playing quietly in a restaurant. Musicians often hate these gigs. An informant noted:

> When playing wallpaper gigs, it's vital to one's mental and emotional health to accept at the outset that nobody gives a flying f**k how good you are. You could be a virtuoso pianist who's trained your entire life abroad and with the greatest masters of the day. Zero f**ks given. You can play a heartbreaking song from the heart, pouring your very soul into it. Not important. Your emotions, skill, craft … it's all fodder for trampling conversation, jokes, and Instagram videos. I am convinced Eddie Van Halen could play solo guitar at a bar and people would just ignore him, roaring over him in selfish triumph.
>
> (Christopher, Pianist)

Others like these gigs:

> My experience of doing solo gigs for commercial functions—wallpaper gigs as they're called—is that I'm expected to stay in the background. I fully expect that nobody will be listening closely to me, and I have no problem at all with that. But I don't take that as a licence to play just anything. My tastes and abilities are more in the jazz and Brazilian vein and it so happens that those styles work very well as background music. Being ignored means I can play more obscure stuff and perhaps take some chances by trying a song I know in an unfamiliar key. I stay under the radar, get paid, and go home.
>
> (Rob, Keyboard player)

Some are more pragmatic. Another informant said:

> I play the gig, get paid. I use [wallpaper] gigs as a paid practice and opportunities to play stuff for me. I've been playing 44 years. Compliments and appreciation are great but neither of them has ever helped me pay a bill.
>
> (Mike, Guitarist)

Regardless, because you're typically a soloist in these gigs, these performances can pay well.

Pubs and bars primarily offer places for people to consume alcohol. They might do food as well, but probably not all the time. Sometimes a pub will offer live music as an inducement to attend, stay, and consume alcohol. These are called **pub gigs**. They can be rowdy, demand energy, and can be draining. One of our informants noted:

> Went to see a friend's trio playing at a local pub. They were killing it, sounding great. The place was packed. Twenty-somethings, closer to twenty than twenty-five I'm guessing. Nobody clapped. I can only imagine how tired

those poor musicians are going to be at the end of the gig after putting out like they were without getting anything back. Pearls before swine.

(Paul, Guitarist)

On the other hand, they can be fun as well. Another informant noted: "We play and enjoy the hell out of it and make the best sounds we can. If they don't care, I don't mind" (Kimba, Vocalist). Sometimes these gigs work and are enormous fun. Sometimes you just end up playing for yourself. In practice, you can (usually) rely on pubs and bars to do some promotion, but you should also do this yourself. These gigs rarely pay particularly well and are the most likely to try to get you to perform for free. (As a rule, don't do this, but we cover free gigs in a later chapter.)

Some venues host **open mike nights** or blackboard nights. These involve an open stage where anyone can get up and perform for no payment, so the standard can be hit and miss. They're often held on a midweek night so as not to interfere with regularly scheduled performances and musician schedules. Because they offer no financial recompense, use them only for working up new songs or practising your performance.

The next gigs we'll look at are **small venue gigs**. Every city and large town has a few small specialist venues. They're often run as small businesses offering regular live music by an owner passionate about live music. Like a bar, they will usually offer alcohol and food but, unlike a bar, the focus is actually on the music. In these gigs, people are coming specifically to see you, so you'd better fill it. The venue will have some promotion happening, but you should also promote yourself. Because profit margins for such venues are tight, they will typically seek to minimise their risk by the contract they select. These gigs are useful because they permit fans to see you in a venue designed to focus their attention on you. Venues will generally supply a small sound system and some basic lighting.

Support gigs are when your band is the opening act for a well-known band. They can have many problems, such as deliberately sabotaged sound, playing to people who haven't come to see you, and the dreaded 'buy-on', whereby support acts bid to pay to open for a well-known band. However, there are reasons to do them. You will play in larger venues than you would normally. You will familiarise larger audiences with your music and (hopefully) turn them into fans. You also potentially play for industry, which can lead to other opportunities. For example, German rock band Silbermond started by opening for Jeanette Biedermann. Queens of the Stone Age opened for Monster Magnet. Bizarre as it sounds, Jimi Hendrix opened for The Monkees. In support gigs, you do not usually need to worry about backline, as these are already in place. The promoter will take care of promotion. A support gig can wind up as a tour. You also have access to promoters and venues that you may not have. You might get little or no financial recompense for a support gig. It might cost you money. But—if you've done your work—you'll be playing to larger audiences than you normally would and your fan base could potentially increase.

Once you've done a few support gigs, and you have a reputation and a large audience, you might do some **headliner gigs**. These gigs become available because you are well known in the geographical area you're playing in. You (or more typically, your manager) have a lot more power in negotiating these gigs, as the promoter wants you particularly. Once you're at the stage of getting these gigs, you will typically be signed to a label and publisher and have a manager, so a lot of the logistics will be taken care of.

If you have a strong concept and some good contacts, you can be asked to do **corporate gigs**. These are organised by corporations when having a party or conference. To get these gigs, you often need to have booking agents with strong corporate contacts, or have these contacts yourself. You also need a very slick and professional product. You need to be exciting but sophisticated. Corporations often want something a little out of the ordinary, so don't go thinking your jazz quartet or originals band will necessarily get these gigs. Corporate gigs are often very big payers.

The **wedding gig** market can be very lucrative. If your band is a covers band (or can play covers) and can play stylish background music as well as get a crowd dancing, you might be able to get these gigs. Your principle competition for this market are DJs, who play music that the guests know and to which they can dance. However, live music, despite being more expensive than a DJ, is classier and more engaging, so some weddings opt for them. There are several ways to get these gigs. You play in markets where bridal parties might go, such as hotels. You might get recommended by previous clients or be seen playing at someone else's wedding. You can also target the market, as there are bridal magazines and bridal expos that happen regularly. You might also approach some wedding venues in your area. Typically, when you're doing these gigs, you supply the backline such as audio and lights.

Pit gigs can be extremely lucrative at a professional level, and not at the amateur level. These gigs involve accompanying musicals. To get the professional engagements, you need to have exceptionally high reading skills and work your way into the circle. Typically, they pay well because theatres are often heavily unionised. Amateur productions can pay relatively low fees because amateur companies often do not have large amounts of money. In either case, expect to have several rehearsals, calls for dress rehearsals, and then performances for the entire run.

Another type of performance is the **international hotel** circuit. Hotels in Asia and the Middle East will often hire a band to play there for several months. They can be very specific in their requirements, such as defining height, age, ethnicity, and the like. The pay is not great (often around US $1,500 to $2,500 per person, per month) but you are playing every night and the hotel usually includes meals and accommodation. Further, if your currency is low against the United States dollar, you may end up with reasonable pay. There are Facebook groups that advertise these gigs, and some agents specialise in them. You need to have a strong product to present to the hotels, as well as photos, videos, EPKs, websites, and so forth.

Another international gig is the ubiquitous **cruise ship gig**. Cruise ships recruit musicians both as bands and individuals to entertain cruise tourists. The requirements vary depending on the job you're undertaking onboard. For some of these, like the showband, you need to be an excellent reader and improviser. For others, you will get hired as an entire band and your reading is less important than the ability to entertain and engage an audience. If you have a strong product, solid charts, and a big personality, you can get work as a guest entertainer. Mostly musicians on board cruise ships get paid around the US $2,000 to $3,000 per month mark, and have changed little in the last few decades. You can seek this work through agencies such as Proship and the Suman agency.

Music is a semiotic marker of culture. If you can play the music from a particular culture, you can get gigs designed to portray that culture. We'll call these **ethnic gigs**. For example, a tourism operator might want to showcase the culture of your country to tourists, and an easy way to do that is to perform the music. A Greek restaurant might want a bouzouki ensemble to play "Zorba the Greek". Typically, these gigs are not particularly nuanced, but reference the most common songs, dress you up in obvious national costumes, and implement the most unmistakable musical and cultural features of a particular culture.

A recent innovation are the so-called **parlour or lounge gigs**. They're referred to as 'pop-up gigs' and 'the Airbnb of live music'. They work like this. Someone who is a fan of a particular musician organises a gig in their lounge room or backyard and invites their friends for a set ticket fee. They don't charge you for hosting the event, and you normally get all or most of the proceeds from the gig. You might think these may not pay very well, but if you get 40 people at a gig for $25 a ticket, that's potentially $1,000. These are very intimate gigs with a lot of contact between you and the audience. House concerts are organised by organisations such as parlourgigs.com in Australia, concertsinyourhome.org in Florida, and houseconcertsyork.co.uk in the UK. A short internet search should reveal similar organisations in different areas.

If you are religious (or at least not vocally antagonistic towards religion), **church gigs** can be a steady income source. Many religious organisations pay for their musical directors, organists, or band. Choosing to seek or not seek these gigs can be a quandary. One informant advises:

> As a long-time church musician, I have three criteria: Is the pay OK? Do they treat their musicians well? Is the theology/preaching tolerable? A firm "no" on any one of those can be a deal-breaker for me, unless the other two are strong enough to compensate.
>
> (Carolyn, Church musician)

The money paid by church gigs might not be low. There might be pressure to donate it back to the church. But it is regular and occurs at a time that is unlikely to impact other performances.

Festivals are special events that combine multiple musical performances under a particular banner. This banner might be via a genre, such as the Wacken heavy metal Festival in German, the Newport Jazz Festival, or the Montebello Rock festival in Canada. It might be a festival associated with a place, such as Australia's BigSound festival in Brisbane, the RedBull festival in the United States, or the NH7 festival in India. It might be a tourism event such as a wine festival. Managers and musicians can put in an expression of interest to play at a festival and, again, you will need to offer a slick product with marketing such as photos, videos, and EPKs. If you're offered an opportunity to play at a festival, you should probably take it. You should even seek them out. They introduce you to audiences that are interested in your genre that you may not have been exposed to before. Admittedly, they are not always the most financially rewarding performances. Almost invariably festivals pay a set fee rather than a cut of the gate, which may not be as high a profit margin. However, they are worthwhile paths for your live music career.

Finally, another way of performing and earning money is **busking**. Busking means taking your instrument out onto a city street, putting out your instrument case, and playing for the passers-by. Busking can be relatively lucrative if you are an engaging and talented performer, though sometimes you will play for very little recompense. To make matters more difficult, there are many buskers on the streets in large cities and some of them are of poor quality. The public are sometimes not particularly good at discerning the good music from the bad. Various jurisdictions will have different requirements for buskers. Sometimes you need a licence. Sometimes you can only play in certain areas. You may experience antagonism from other buskers who might feel a sense of ownership over an especially lucrative space. Busking is a useful habit to adopt, as it develops your performance skills while earning day-to-day income. However, it can also be a difficult gig if the audiences are not responding.

These gigs are the common types; however, there are others that are relevant to certain geographies. In many parts of Australia for example, local clubs provide employment to many musicians. The working men's clubs in the north of the UK have traditionally hosted live music. College gigs can be very worthwhile in parts of the world. It is worthwhile considering what other gigs are available to you in your area.

Preparing for and Playing a Performance

When you go to create a contemporary music performance, there are four stages to preparing and creating a contemporary music performance. They are:

1.   Preparation before the gig.
2.   Checks on the day.
3.   The performance.
4.   The aftershow.

Let's consider what is in each of these processes. As you read, remember that we're discussing what needs to happen and the roles that need to be in place.

We are not talking about individual people. Someone involved with the process needs (for example) to produce the show, but it could be the bass player. So, as you read, work out who, in your band, undertakes each of these roles.

Preparation and Rehearsal

Preparation is where the concept for the performance is developed, and time and money invested in making sure that the performance works. The preparation process may be specific to a performance that occurs only once. Or it may be for a performance that occurs several times, like a tour or a run at a theatre. Or it may be for an ensemble that will have many performances over months or years. Regardless, any effective performance has a preparation and rehearsal stage.

The first task in creating a performance is developing the concept of the performance or ensemble. This concept needs to be marketable and professional. Musicians rarely undertake market research before creating a band. We tend to think that the music we love will be loved by everyone. It isn't always. We think that people will love us just because we're great. They won't (necessarily). To be successful in live music, you need to approach the concept with a business mindset. Think what would be successful. Look for that gap in the local industry. Both of your authors have played in successful acts that weren't entirely to our liking or preferred genres. They have been, however, very financially rewarding, and we were doing what we love.

Once the concept is decided upon, it is developed by the person or persons undertaking the role of the producer. They decide on the genre, repertoire, and branding of the show. They engage musicians, arrangers, and bandleaders. They arrange for a professional website, social media, and associated copy, photographs, and an EPK. Where possible, they will organise video and audio recordings to be made and uploaded. Remember this web presence is where your show will look professional or not. We've both been handed too many CDs with the band's name penned on them, asking us what we thought.

Once the concept is organised and in place, the musicians are engaged, and the arrangements have been set, the project goes into the rehearsal stage. This can involve renting rehearsal spaces, potentially paying fees to session musicians, rehearsing songs, and rehearsing the performance. We will speak about efficient practice and rehearsal processes shortly, and you really need to take these on board. Time-wasting rehearsals are one reason that many musicians hate rehearsals. Don't let that happen to you.

At this point, we should have a quick word about set lists. Some musicians don't like to organise a set list. They prefer to go in the moment and change the songs with their read of the mood of the audience. However, if you think about it, this mentality is actually backwards. The purpose of having a pre-established set list it to control and shape the mood of the audience. You tell them how to feel; they don't tell you. Open your set with a strong number that grabs your audience's attention and draws them in. End the set by performing a song with a strong hook so it stays with them as they leave the gig. The intervening songs should be in contrasting keys and in contrasting tempos. They should be planned to build the response of your audience. Work out your emotional journey as you go through the performance.

The producers also need to organise backline. Backline can be the most expensive part of a performance, but they're absolutely essential. To get the most out of them, ensure that your backline knows what they're doing. If it's their first time working with you, give them a cue sheet with rough instructions on what you'd like to happen with the sound and lights. However, don't make it too prescriptive. Remember that your engineers are artists as well, and you need them to be on your good side. Respect them, and they will make you look and sound great.

PREPARING FOR A PERFORMANCE

If you do a visual advertisement on social media you can actually tell the age group of the people that are coming to see you, so I like a little bit of demographic. And if I'm getting people that are interested in the show and I know that those people are, you know, 55 and 60, I might approach it a little bit differently than I would to an audience that are 35 to 40. That's the beauty of social media now. You can actually gauge your audience. I'll often ring the venue to check as well. You know that most of your crowd for some events is going to be 50 to 60. The paying ticket crowd. It all comes down to who you're playing to. So, what is my demographic going to want to listen to? I've got an older demographic and they're not going to want to hear the latest indie rock. They'll want to hear some of the classic, softer stuff. Some of the music that was around when they were listening to music in their youth. So, preparation of the show, preparation of the set list, preparation of making sure you tailor the songs to suit the demographic of the audience, and sometimes the demographic of the venue as well. That's one thing I look at.

The second thing I prepare are screens. Imagery. I ask myself how I can create a better experience for the audience. If you're talking about a character performance, you need to make sure that the people who are coming to see the show can relate to the costumes, the lights, and the look of the show. If you're doing a particular song, there might be something that was particularly famous about that particular song. It might have been a concert that your character had certain a look in. Okay. There's no point coming out in a costume that's not relevant to the period. I've always liked to give people visual cues. The costumes. The imagery.

Preparing for the performance means making sure I'm vocally prepared, making sure that I've learnt the songs adequately enough. That I'm worthy of punters buying a ticket to see a show. That I'm across what everyone in the band are doing. So, it's not just what my performance is.

When you perform in a band you're part of a group. Part of a team. It's not just you. You have to look at the whole team. You have to understand what everyone else is doing. You have to make sure everyone is prepared and knows what you're going to do in your show. Make sure you share your ideas with the people in your band. There's a lot of great ideas floating around in a band. They're not all yours. Once you've understood all that, you're good and you're rearing to go.

I don't like to eat before a performance. I find that, as a singer, food sits on my diaphragm and I feel a bit uncomfortable and it's almost like your system's trying to process food. I like to drink warm tea. I don't drink alcohol or anything like that. I used to, but I don't anymore. I like to make sure that I'm warmed up. I do vocal exercises and then I always take a peek out from behind the curtain and see the audience, you know? That's how I prepare.

Dave, Singer.

Preparation and Rehearsal Checklist

- Do you have a strong concept?
- Are all appropriate musicians in place?
- Do you have backline organised?
- Have you prepared a document for the backline that lists the following:
  - Running order.
  - Sound cues.
  - Lighting cues.
- Have you arranged sufficient promotion?
- Do you have a professional website? Social media? Photographs? Copy? EPK?

JAZZ BANDS AND REHEARSALS

Some jazz ensembles don't do a lot of rehearsal. This is due to a few purported aspects of jazz. One is that jazz is reputedly a 'democratic' music. There is supposedly no leader, and everyone's contribution is valued. In our not inconsiderable experience of jazz, however, this is rarely true. Someone always runs the band. The second is that jazz is improvisational and spontaneous music, and too much rehearsal—jazz musicians assert— is going to make the performance stale. Tell that to the Basie band who could play crotchets like no one else. Or the enormous rehearsal time that went into the Ellington band. Or listen to the musical (and rehearsed) perfection of Ahmad Jamal's 1961 Cross Country Tour. Or Shelly Mann and André Previn playing "My Fair Lady". The third aspect is probably the most relevant: Jazz musicians are often competent readers in addition to their improvisational ability. Because of this, they have had large numbers of musicians approach them wanting them to play in their band that might not be at the same high standard. They are consequently unwilling to commit to long (usually unpaid) rehearsal periods when the success of a band is unknown.

Like other genres, jazz requires a rehearsal period to be successful. Do not skip it.

Checks on the Day

After much planning, the day of performance has come. The tickets are bought. The backline is organised. The venue is set and—except for the walk-ins—the tickets have been paid. What needs to happen on the day to ensure that the gig goes smoothly, and the performance is well-run? Well, several things. You need to get your gear to the performance, set up, and sound check. And then the fun part of the evening: Waiting for the gig to start. Let's have a look at each of these in turn.

Your performance begins with loading your gear on to the band truck or into your car. Trust us on this: Have a checklist for everything you need. Many times, we have seen musicians turn up to a gig without a vital piece of equipment: A power cable for a keyboard, or a particular fuzz box. This need is exacerbated when you're going on tour. Use a checklist and stick to it. Pack your gear so it has no opportunity to cause damage either to itself or your vehicle. The last thing you need is for poorly packed instruments to topple over and damage themselves on the way to a gig. It helps to have protective covers or (far better) road cases for your equipment.

Once you've driven to the gig, the next stage is load-in. This is where the performance equipment is carried into the venue and set up. Generally, the backline will have started setting up before the musicians arrive so you will generally have DI boxes to plug into. However, the ease of the load-in depends on the venue. Some venues have a loading dock where you can park your car or van. Other venues have difficult setups necessitating parking in no-standing zones, quick unloads, and then driving to expensive parking stations. However hard the load-in is, you have to make the best of it. A few things will help with the load-in. If you are a keyboardist, you might like to invest in wheeled equipment bags or road cases. Some of those keyboards can be heavy. If you are bringing a lot of gear, consider buying a collapsible trolley. They will reduce the number of loads you need to bring in.

Once you've got your equipment physically into the venue, you need to set it up. Speed is of the essence here. Whatever you are playing, set up your instrument quickly and get out of the way, for different instruments take different times to set up. Typically, drums will take the longest time, and the keyboard and guitar will take the shortest time. (Singers, of course, walk in, put the microphone on the mike stand, and then sit back and make comments about how long everyone else is taking.) Whatever instrument you play, however, ensure you are there for the entirety of the setup. It is a big social mistake to walk in when everyone has just finished setting up.

When you are setting up, you need to consider sightlines. This has probably been taken care of at the preparation stage, but when you perform, make sure you can see the bandleader and as many of the performers as possible. This is so that the non-verbal communication so important to performance (that we discuss later) can take place.

Table 2.1 Loading in your instrument

Instrument	Load-in notes
Voice	• You will probably supply your own microphone and cradle, but you can generally rely on the backline to supply microphone stands and cabling.
Guitar	• You will supply your instrument, cabling, and any stomp boxes or processing. You should also supply an extension cord and power strip. • Your output will go to into a DI box. Backline will generally supply this. • Some guitarists like to use a guitar wireless transmitter/receiver system to permit them movement on stage without being linked by a physical guitar lead. • Some guitarists use a guitar amp besides their monitoring.
Keyboard	• You will supply your instrument, external controls (e.g., sustain pedal), keyboard stand, and cabling. You should also supply an extension cord and power strip. • Your output will go into a DI box. Some keyboardists like to use two DI boxes to allow stereo out. Backline will supply DI boxes. • It is rare, but some keyboardists may use a keytar. In this case, all the notes for the guitar would apply.
Piano	• If you are playing an acoustic piano, you are lucky. You need to bring yourselves. Backline will set up microphones or pickups, and supply the piano.
Bass	• The rules of guitarists apply to bass guitar players. • Depending on the setup and genre, acoustic bass players may use a mix of pickup and a microphone.
Drums	• Drummers invariably need to supply cymbals, sticks, and a snare drum. They almost always need to supply their drums kit as well. • Backline will typically supply microphones.
Horns	• Horns may be miked as individual instruments or as sections. • Horn players may have their own wireless clip-on mics.

After you've loaded in and set up, the next job is the sound check. This involves setting amplification levels of various instruments with the live sound engineer so as to ensure the best experience for musicians and audience. The first task is to get the sound into the desk and ensure every microphone and DI box is receiving a signal. The level on each of the microphones on the drums will be checked first by the drummer hitting each miked-up drum repeatedly until the engineer is satisfied that the levels are right and there is no ring. They move onto the next drum and the process is repeated. Once the drums are set up, the other instruments and the vocals are sound checked. This may also necessitate adding effects such as reverb and equalisation. Next, the two mixes are set—the house mix for the audience and the stage mix for the performers. Finally, the band plays a song or two and the engineer sets the levels for the evening. (Do not treat the sound check as an opportunity to rehearse!) Note that, once the levels are set, you cannot count on them being altered unless something goes wrong, or unless you have a good and attentive sound engineer.

The venue will have notified you of a time at which the sound check must be completed. This will usually be something along the lines of "Access from 4.30 pm, sound check must be finished by 6.30 pm; doors open at 7 pm, downbeat at 8 pm". Once the sound check is over, it is time to wait. A lot of the live music industry is about sitting around waiting for things to happen. So, you finish sound check. You might get a bite to eat. (Though if you're a singer, perhaps avoid this. Nothing worse than a great big old belch into the microphone in the middle of a ballad!) If you have clothes or costumes you wear on stage, about half an hour before the performance, go to the dressing room and get into them. (Again, singers, avoid wearing costumes you're not used to, as they can affect your performance.)

You'll be excited. This is normal. But try to avoid getting too nervous. That will interfere with your playing. You'll be doing this many times in your life. You've got this.

The Performance

Five minutes before the performance, go and stand in the dressing room. One of the backline—the stage manager, lighting operator, or live engineer—will liaise with venue management. Once they get the all clear from the venue, they will signal you to start. Move onto the stage amid the lights and applause.

Once you get on stage, you need to turn on full-professional mode. Make the music and do the moves as you've rehearsed. Acknowledge your audience. Play with integrity and passion. This is the bit that presents you and your music to a discerning audience. Do it confidently and clearly and musically. That said, you can't rehearse everything. Live music is also in the moment. Your improvisations and the way you perform will be different each time. Many of the most successful bands have an easy banter on stage. Don't be afraid to talk to each other. It's part of the way that people know you are having fun.

ENERGY ON STAGE

It's a competitive world out there. Some artists give out energy, and the audience just goes, 'Yeah, whatever". And some artists give out energy and it bounces back and just increases exponentially.

Q: Can that process of giving out energy be taught?

I think there's a danger there. The basics are that if you're a musician you learn your instrument. And if you're a vocalist you learn your instrument, which is your voice. So you're practicing, you might be taking coaching lessons, you're examining what other people are doing. But then you've got to go and perform to audiences. Some basic acting skills, some basic movement skills, some engagement skills will all help with audience engagement.

There are certain things that you need to be able to do. Eye contact is great for engagement. Definition of movement is critical. Sarah Blasko has wonderful hand movement. Movement enables purpose and provides energy. If that movement is limp-wristed, it doesn't provide that energy. The focus on your audience rather than yourself—whatever kind of presentation you're doing—is one of the really important factors. It can be over-taught and then you lose the soul of what makes that person different; you don't want to do that with an artist particularly. You want the individual characteristic of the artist to come out. Miles Davis performed with his back to the audience. So don't lose yourself, but there are certain methods to holding a crowd, like how you use a voice or play an instrument. They're worth learning.

Tim, Record Executive

When you're onstage, it's important to engage with your audience. Talk to them. Get them clapping and applauding and singing. Communicate with them. Audiences attend live music to be engaged. If they didn't, they'd just put on a streaming platform at home.

ENGAGEMENT

I think the importance of engagement depends on the genre of the performer. There are genres that lend themselves to a certain dialogue and interaction between what is happening on stage and what is happening in the crowd. Like a punk or hip hop show seems successful if the audience feels like they are a part of it, contributing to the experience of the show. However, other genres lend themselves to a detachment between performer and audience, such as electronic music (techno/house) or experimental genres. Often audiences at these shows actually appear to respect a performer more if they are engrossed in creating the music rather than pleasing a crowd.

As someone who likes a lot of different live music experiences, the way I like to be engaged really depends on the genre or style of the show. I have got to say that I love audience interaction with punk/rock shows and it feels great if you go to a show and you feel like you are partying with the band, or the band appears to be having a dialogue with the audience. But I will also be happy to walk away after a techno show where the producer had their head down the whole time but engaged me by playing an awesome set.

There is also nothing worse than people breaking the flow of a performance by trying to get the audience to engage when it doesn't feel right.

Rosa, Music industry

Most importantly, have fun. Playing in a band—in a really good band, when everyone is in the pocket, the bass and drums are locking in, everyone is confident because of the preparation and everyone is playing to the best of their ability—is an intensely joyful experience. Don't be afraid to show the audience that you are having fun up there.

The Aftershow

After the performance, you will be on an adrenaline high. After decades of performing, both of us still get this. So, use it. Unless you have a super-good reason not to, go out and meet the audience. This confronts some musicians. It's not easy to walk up to a group of people you've never met and for whom you've just bared your soul, look them in the eye and say, "I hope you enjoyed the show". But that contact—that personal contact from the musician—is part of what the audience is there for. What you can do, creating music from an instrument or singing with passion and conviction, is sort of magical to people who can't. Audiences want a piece of that. Personal contact with musicians can turn audiences into fans. Even if it's just going up to them and saying, "I hope you enjoyed the show".

After this, if you're a rich and famous musician, you can then swan off and drink champagne at the afterparty. If you're not—like the vast majority of musicians—you have to set down. The backline will take care of the audio equipment, but you need to pack up your instruments. (Ensure that backline have muted the channel before you unplug your instrument from the DI Box.) Then get your car and load your gear into it.

One final word. About an hour or 90 minutes after you finish, the adrenaline will dissipate from your system. You've put an awful lot of energy into your performance, and without the adrenaline coursing through your veins, you will suddenly become very tired. If you're driving home from the gig, this is the point at which you need to be careful. You don't want to become a statistic. Pull over to the side of the road, have a micronap, and a coffee or an energy drink before you continue driving home.

Showmanship Versus Technique

One of the eternal debates in live music is about showmanship versus technique. There are musicians who think that to be an amazing musician is to necessarily have a phenomenal technique. They point to performers like Steve Vai, Candy Dulfer, Belá Fleck, Queen Latifah, or Liona Boyd. Look at these performers, they say. Look at their technique. They're amazing musicians. I want to do what they can do. Clearly performance is about technique. Others talk about the showmanship of musicians, of their engagement with the audience, of the shows they create. We have our own ideas, but we decided to take this to our interviewees.

When we did, we didn't know what to expect when it came to asking them to choose between stagecraft and technique as being more important. When we analysed the results, to our surprise, opinion was split almost exactly 50/50. Fifty percent of our musicians, audience, and music business informants asserted that musicianship and technique were more important to creating memorable performances than showmanship, and fifty percent thought showmanship was.

Technique

As a musician, I'm sure you've been to a show and been very impressed by someone's technical skills. Someone who can not only play hard and fast but musically. You might think that this is what makes a great and memorable performance because it did so for you. You're not alone. Many of our informants agreed. Listen to what they said.

- Anyone can dance and put on a show, but the technical skills shown in the musical ability will always keep fans loyal for many years. If there's no musical ability there's no show, really.
- If someone doesn't look 100% but plays exceptionally, they are held up and will probably be more noticed. If they are a 'showman' only and don't have a great musical ability their audience may be disappointed.
- Without musical ability, a performance becomes mere noise and (with showmanship) mere spectacle, and not enough about the music itself. I would rather watch musicians who stand stock still, focusing on their parts, and playing them well than a pop singer who struts about the stage amongst an entourage of dancers, with no real instruments in sight and no technical ability on display. The latter feels incredibly fake, hollow, and inauthentic. The former at least shows that these artists have put in the effort to learn their instruments and write interesting music with them.

There is a lot to be said for this point of view. Music is about the music after all. It's important to be the best musician you can be. The band has to be hot. You have to be playing at your peak capacity. Your songs need to touch people. If you're not, why would anyone pay money to hear you? Right?

TECHNIQUE AND SHOWMANSHIP

One of the best concerts I've seen was in New York at Smalls, by Johnny O'Neal and his trio. Johnny O'Neal impressed me with a performance without any weak moments. He kept the tension, and the audience's attention, while seeming completely free and far away in his own musical sphere. It was like witnessing a precious force of nature in undisturbed action. Apart from the very soulful musical performance, timing, and interplay, I was also impressed by how taken the whole audience was. I looked around at the faces of the other listeners and discovered how emotional but quiet they were—with tears in their eyes but with complete attention for the performance.

Olivia, Jazz singer and pianist

Showmanship

The other side of the coin is showmanship.[1] Showmanship is a complex idea. Showmanship describes a skilled entertainer's ability to create spectacle and to use their stagecraft (the ability to perform on stage and create an engaging stage presence) to create positive audience experiences. When we asked our informants about the importance of showmanship, some asserted that technique was secondary to the ability to create a show.

- Four chords can make a million dollars, but if no one connects with the musician then no one will hear the music.
- Something done in confidence isn't considered a mistake or 'wrong'. Showmen have confidence in spades and are there to convince the audience of their performance by communicating clearly with them where the performance is going. Someone without this ability doesn't know how to reach out to an audience and may leave themselves as uninterpreted due to poor communication.
- The average punter doesn't go "owww sick finger tapping or use of harmony". They go "that sounds cool and interesting. I like it".
- Having excellent musical skills can be handy, but if you can't create a relationship with the audience and keep them entertained, the performance will fail.

- Showmanship is what can sell your product to the world/audience. Many a band in history had little talent but still worked hard and were fantastic entertainers. The performances of technically brilliant musicians that don't engage an audience can be as boring as watching paint dry.
- Most audiences are there for an emotional hit, not technical awe.

Perhaps they do have a point. Contemporary music is, by its nature, an art form that has to be popular among the general population. Often, they're not going to be knowledgeable enough of music to really understand the finer points. So, what's the point of all that practicing if you can get away with three chords and a guitar?

SHOWMANSHIP VERSUS TECHNIQUE

What is more important, showmanship or musical performance? This depends. Both can be important and sometimes one is more important than the other. On a personal note, I will always prioritise the musicianship side. I can't picture Chucho Valdes or Paco De Lucia running around the stage to enhance the showmanship angle of a performance. They don't need to do this. Yet artists like Bruno Mars, Michael Jackson, Beyoncé, James Brown … they benefit from the showmanship angle based on expectations of other artists within a similar genre. Audio and lighting conditions have greatly improved over the years. The full package can enhance more 'frenetic' and 'uptempo' genres. Afro-Latin music genres such as Salsa, Cumbia, and Son, where styles are also based on movement and dance, can benefit from showmanship to enhance the performance.

Cesar, Bandleader, composer

What Does This Mean?

Is the music more important? Or the showmanship? In order to answer this, I want to consider the opera.

Let me give you an unpopular opinion. Opera is the bane of the music industry. And that's from someone who likes it! Now, before all you singers start sharpening your pitchforks and lighting your torches, let me tell you why. Opera is superlatively expensive and unprofitable. Almost any opera company you care to name relies on massive government handouts. In Australia, the government contributes $25 million per year to Opera Australia. Ticket prices are in the hundreds of dollars; yet the shows still operate at a loss. Performances are typically in foreign languages, and you have to crane your head to read the surtitles (supertitles in the US) if you want to have a hope of knowing what's going on. And classical music is not the most accessible music to a modern audience.

Yet, despite these shortcomings, opera is marvellously engaging. It revels in its inaccessibility. Houses are regularly sold out for entire seasons. The over-the-top costumes. The incredible scenery. The huge orchestra. The heroic stories. The showmanship. People dress up in tuxedos and ball gowns and sip champagne before the show. (This has been known to make the plot more understandable.) And they sit enthralled for hours. Technique plays a big part in this, because good opera singers are among the finest singers in the world. But ultimately, the opera is a musical experience par excellence!

Contemporary music, unlike opera, is designed to be accessible. So, it should have an advantage over opera, right? All too often though, we don't consider it as important enough to plan into our performances. Overwhelmingly, it was musicians rather than the audience or music business that cited the importance of technique. We musicians focus on our technique. We gain respect from our peers by our superlative technique, and it becomes important to us. But it's not all there is to creating a show. Technique is important, but showmanship, the ability to create a performance and engage with the audience, is also important.

Showmanship can even create successful performances independent of technique. Consider the following quote from a jazz bass player.

> Take Bob Dylan. For me, he's a great example, of success without actually a great amount of musical skill going on. Musicianship skill wise, he's very average, but when he sings a song and plays the guitar it's like just the marriage of what he has as a musician and what he's trying to give as a … maybe not a showman, but as a performer. They're just so intertwined. Even though he's not jumping up and down, it's just like, oh my god, you can't take your eyes off, and ears off it because it's just so beautifully intertwined … For me showmanship is best when it's completely intertwined and genuine with the musical message. When showmanship is an add-on, it repulses me, I can't watch it, I don't enjoy seeing that. When I see that someone like Gary Bartz, like Freddie Mercury, their showmanship is coming from every cell of their body as they're creating. It's not like I'm going to play this music and I'm going to do all those physical attributes that make people like that I'm engaging; it's the personality. When it's sort of an add-on it doesn't really sit, and it just doesn't say it's a thing.
>
> (Cameron, Venue owner/bass player)

Bel, an artist manager noted that musicians that are technically brilliant but without showmanship are boring.

> Performers on stage can be the best musicians in the world, but if they're not engaging the audience, it can be as boring as. Let me give you an example. Gabriel and Rodriguez tend to perform in black. They don't have bells and whistles on stage, don't have big blinding shows or anything like that. Technically they're brilliant, but the way they interact with each other, the way they use the stage, just builds the intensity of the music. They dress

down. They're in plain black. They're on a plain stage. But the way they use that stage just lifts it to a whole other level.

(Bel, Artist manager)

We put it to you that technique is important. It really is. Practice hard. Become the best musician you can be. Technically brilliant musicians shine. But showmanship, the implementation of audience engagement within the performance, is equally important. The planning and use of both creates memorable performances. Showmanship creates the performance; technique gives you something to say.

Songwriting

This is probably a good time to talk about the role of songwriting in your live career. Not everyone who performs live is a songwriter. There are plenty of covers bands out there. Covers bands, in a way, have the publicity made. If you decide to be an ABBA cover band, or a Red Hot Chilli Peppers cover band, people know what they're coming to see. They know the songs. You'll get an entire audience singing along to "Dancing Queen" or "Californication". Jazz, of course, relies on performing the jazz canon, which amounts to performing covers. As a covers band, you can theme your performances, wear the costumes, put up slide shows of the original band. You can arrange the songs and sub out the bass part when the bass player isn't available.

Some, however, prefer to perform their own music. There is a perceived authenticity in performing your own music in the various contemporary genres. Those are regarded as more 'real' somehow. These are your words and your experiences you are portraying, and audiences respond to that. There are advantages and disadvantages to performing your own music. If you own the copyright to your music, you can use it as an extra income stream. You can place it on YouTube, Spotify, and Apple Music, and receive mechanical royalties. You can encourage others to record it. You can perform it or have others perform it and receive performance royalties. You can place it in movies and receive sync rights. Further, you will be more highly regarded by your industry peers if you write and perform more of your own music. However, audiences don't know your music. If you perform your own music, audiences are taking a risk that they'll like your music. Further, some venues are unwilling to hire people that perform only their own music, unless they are well known. The great unknown of audience response to new songs can be a disincentive.

Ultimately, it's up to you how much you include songwriting in your performance career. At least at the start, you may need to include covers amid your own songs. Your success trail may be harder if you choose to perform your own songs rather than covers; however, the success, difficult as it might be, is also greater.

Further Reading

If you want to learn more about songwriting, can I suggest the works of Pat Pattison and Clive Harrison. These go into the technical aspects of lyrics, melody, and harmony. Jason Blume's *This Business of Songwriting* is also a good introduction to the industry.

Chapter Summary

- There are many different types of performances.
- Live performances happen in a given order.
    - Preparation before the gig.
    - Checks on the day.
    - The performance.
    - The aftershow.
- Technique and showmanship are both important to create a memorable performance.
- You need to carefully consider the role of songwriting in your live performance career.

Note

1 I acknowledge the gendered nature of the term 'showmanship'. The term originally describes the ability and flair of people mounting shows and diversions in British fairs and may date back as far as the 18th century. There is still a Showmen's Guild of Great Britain. However, the gender-neutral alternative 'showpersonship' is not in regular usage. Further, no other word quite encapsulates the concept of the required ability of musicians to create experiences. Thus, somewhat unwillingly, I will use 'showmanship'.

3 The Role of Personal Practice in Preparing for Your Performance

There's a story told of the famous Spanish cellist Pablo Casals. Though the details vary, the story appears in too many locations to be entirely apocryphal. Casals lived to be 96 and continued practising until his later life. In his 80s (or 90s) someone asked him why he continued to practise every day for several hours a day. Casals replied, "Because I think I'm making progress".

This story is a way of preparing you for a potentially startling statement. As a professional musician, you will never stop practising and rehearsing. Your technique will never be 'good enough'. You will spend tens, potentially hundreds of thousands of hours over your lifetime sitting with your instrument, honing your craft. You will spend less but still significant amounts of time in rehearsal with other musicians, getting used to each other, rehearsing songs so they are fit to perform in public or on a recording. Playing an instrument requires you to be physically, emotionally, and mentally very fit. It requires dedication and commitment as you work on that riff, transcribe that solo, or play that knucklebusting finger exercise. It demands your very best.

That's all well and good. But practice is boring, isn't it? Not always. It depends on how you approach it. The trouble is that, as contemporary music practitioners, we often don't really consider how to practise or rehearse. Classical musicians are taught practice techniques from a very early age. It might not be the best way to practise, and it might have some gaping logic holes, but they do, at least, have a model. Contemporary musicians often suffer from advice that is too general ("play it the way it feels, man!"), or too spiritual ("you have to let your inner self decide the best practice technique"). Now I'm not suggesting that there is anything wrong with general or spiritual approaches, but you also need solid, practical advice on personal practice. You need to consider how your brain works when you practise. You need to know how your body reacts. Only from here can you become effective in your personal practice and group rehearsal.

Effective practice varies from instrument to instrument and from person to person. You physically practise guitar differently to how you practise piano. Sure, you can both practise scales and the same pieces, but they are very different instruments. Even musicians who play the same instrument will have different strengths, because our brains and bodies are different. I'm a pianist. My handspan is almost an octave and a half. I've taught people who couldn't reach an octave. Thus, you and I, even if we play the same instrument, will require differ-ent routines.

There is no magic spell, no shortcuts, and no cookie-cutter approach to per-sonal and collective preparation. Your teacher, knowledgeable about the finer points of practice, can guide you, but can't be there every time you pick up your instrument to practise. Your ensemble instructor can't be there every rehearsal. We, your kind authors, can't be there as you prepare; we can only submit some points for your consideration. The only person who can develop your practice and rehearsal routine, the only person who is always there, is you. You need work on your weaknesses while developing your strengths. You need to reflect, be self-critical in diagnosing your problems, and be proactive in researching and developing exercises to develop your ability. You need to work with other people to create a remarkable music product. To prepare effectively, you need to pre-pare smarter, not harder. Efficiently, not randomly. To work with your brain, not against it.

The process of creating memorable performances does not start when you turn up at the gig, instrument in hand. It begins with the preparation. It begins with your personal rehearsal and your group practice. In this section, we're going to consider what constitutes effective practice. We're going to look at individual daily practice, the time that you spend working with your instrument on your own. We're going to consider what new research says about what works with individual practice, what it's for, and how to do it effectively.

Individual Practice

Australian music scholar Gary McPherson describes five skills essential to every musician regardless of the genre in which they play.[1] These are what you practise to be able to do, so it's worth noting them here. To be an effective musician you need to:

1. Perform a repertoire of rehearsed music.
2. Perform music from memory (learned from a musical score).
3. Play by ear (for music learned by listening).
4. Improvise in both 'stylistically conceived' and 'freely conceived' idioms.[2]
5. Sight read music from notation that has not been previously seen or rehearsed.

Musicians of different genres will approach these differently, with different strengths dictated often by their genre. Classical students rarely have the ability to effectively improvise. Contemporary musicians often struggle with sight read-ing. However, to become the best musician you can be, you should be able to do everything on this list as well as you can. This is a lifelong struggle, but it's part of the musical journey.

Classical students have a tradition of practising music that has been passed on from their teachers, which will be passed on by them to their students in turn.

While there are some issues with the classical approach to practice and rehearsal, it has some good points. It gives them a beginning structure from which to work. Does this sound familiar?

- Practise one hour a day.
- Start with scales and technical exercises.
- Work through your pieces. Start at the beginning, then play down to the bit that your teacher has earmarked. Then start at the beginning again.
- Once you've played through your piece, go on to the next one. Check the clock and manage your time carefully so you're not going to go over time.
- Watch the clock until one hour has passed, then go back onto Netflix or have a beer or do whatever.

You might think that's farfetched. Probably it is for many musicians. But when I was an undergraduate at music college, it was a badge of pride to say you practised for four hours. As if the time actually mattered.

While it shares some similarities, contemporary music practice is also different to classical practice. The best contemporary music practitioners, the Eric Claptons, The Alison Krausses, the Dizzy Gillespies, are/were masters of their instrument with technique as good as classical musicians. This mastery is developed in manners similar to classical students such as scales, technical exercises, perhaps playing pieces in the classical tradition, and so forth. However, as contemporary musicians, we also need to be able to improvise. Thus, improvisation studies need to form a part of our individual practice regime.

As a professional music practitioner, you need to practise every day. Sometimes you will be in the zone with your practise, and it will barely seem like practice at all. On other occasions, you will struggle. And that's okay. It's the nature of music. Musicking is a wonderfully human activity, and humans are variable. However, by deciding to practise every day, you are closer to being a successful performer.

Your daily practice routine will fall into six categories. You may not do all of these every day, but together, they will form part of your practice:

- Daily Technical Practice: Scales, exercises, practice designed to keep your chops up.
- Daily Solo Practice: Practice for your own solo work. This might include learning new pieces, learning to play your transcriptions, working on solo licks and so forth.
- Daily Sight Reading Practice. Not every musician does this. (Yes, guitarists, I am looking at you!) But it is important if you are ever going to become an expert in your performance.
- Transcription: Classical musicians don't have to do this (lucky sods!) You, on the other hand, need to transcribe regularly.
- Solo rehearsal: Rehearsal for the ensembles in which you find yourself. This is important. Musicians that have actually done the work and learned their music are very intolerant of those who have not.

- Free Exploring: This final piece of the puzzle is often neglected by regimented classical music practice, but it's an important piece of the puzzle. You need to be free to explore and reflect what you're doing and how you're doing it.

As musicians, we've all had teachers who tell us "you must practise for an hour every day". When you're starting out it sort of makes sense. Practising every day for a set amount of time creates a regular and habitual practice. However, it's not effective to watch the clock. Consider the maths homework you did at school. Imagine your maths teacher had said to you "Okay, class, I want you to go home and do 20 minutes of the maths problems on page 29 of your homework book. If you finish, go on to page 30 through 34. Thanks". Do you think, given this approach, you'd finish your homework, or just sit there doing the bare minimum? Setting (usually large) time limits on practice ignores two factors. First, human brains are not designed to focus on high intensity tasks such as music practice effectively for four hours at a time. Second, it asserts that practising for some random number of minutes each day will produce results.

Now we're not saying that you don't need time spent at your instrument. To become an expert, you certainly do, and a lot of it. You might have heard of the '10,000 hours rule'. This was popularised by Malcolm Gladwell in his book *Outliers*[3] in which he argues that you need 10,000 hours of work to become exceptional at something. It's worthwhile quoting the work that this is based on, that of Swedish psychology professor K. Anders Ericsson who argued that

> it takes time to become an expert. Our research shows that even the most gifted performers need a minimum of ten years (or 10,000 hours) of intense training before they win international competitions. In some fields the apprenticeship is longer: It now takes most elite musicians 15 to 25 years of steady practice, on average, before they succeed at the international level.[4]

Ten years or 10,000 hours. If you think about it, 10,000 hours over ten years is actually something like 2¾ hours a day. Every day of the year. No days off. No Christmas. No birthdays. What ten-year-old is going to want to do that? That said, to become that expert you want to be, that technically gifted musician, you need to spend regular time at your instrument.

Your practice must also be effective. While there is evidence that the most skilled musicians have had more time to practice (simply because they started younger), the picture is different for students playing at the same level. Musical competence and motor skills are about effective practice, not merely practising ineffectively for a set time. Two recent studies[5] found that effective practice was not concerned with time spent on a piece, but how effective the practice was. As you get better and better, you end up practising more and more, but not because you know you have to practise four hours a day. You practise because you become fascinated with the idea of getting better and better. When that happens, the hours fly by. That becomes your motivation and your passion.

Gamify the (Practice) System

You've probably heard of the term 'to game the system'. The concept comes from computer science originally and describes an attempt to use rules designed to protect a system to instead manipulate a system to a different outcome. Basically, it applies game design and theory to other aspects of life. For example, your music practice. One of the accepted rules of music practice is that it is intended to be a negative and potentially boring experience one must go through to become a better musician. In this way, you achieve enlightenment through struggle. If this is what you believe, then you need to manipulate that rule to change the music practice system towards a more enjoyable end. If you think of gaming the practice system as a challenge, you might find yourself enjoying it more. How you do this is largely up to you, but if you think about it and watch your practice, you can come up with some innovative ideas. It's worthwhile thinking about this.

One of the ways to do this is to make it easier. In the 1980s, there was very limited technology available to music students like your authors. However, now your phone, your tablet, your computer, and often your instruments can assist you. While it is not the object of this book to recommend certain software apps (indeed a pointless task considering how many apps are released each day) a few categories are useful.

- Metronome apps: Obviously this is one of the most basic but also one of the most useful. Particularly useful for slow practice.
- Notation apps: There is a lot of music that is downloadable free, either in creative commons or in the public domain. There are apps that will display music on a tablet and allow you to mark it up, circle it, and create interactive scores.
- Audio recording apps: Regularly make recordings of yourself and save them. Not only does this act as an ongoing archive of your performance, it permits you to see how you are practising on a day-to-day basis.
- Practice logs: Practice logs are vital. They permit you to note difficulties you experience, tempos of pieces or exercises, and other notes. You can keep them in a notebook or get an online practice log.
- Slow down software: In the 1980s, if you wanted to transcribe a piece and were having difficulty hearing that tricky passage, you'd play the record on 16rpm rather than 33rpm. Of course, that changed the pitch. Now there are applications that slow music down without changing the pitch. They are a godsend, and of incredible use during the transcription process.
- Tuning apps: Unless you are a pianist, you should develop the skill to tune from a piano. However, tuners and tuning apps can also be useful.
- Backing apps. There have been Aebersold backing tracks for years. However, with the development of Band in a Box and RealBookPro, backing tracks have moved far more into your control.

I cannot emphasise too much the advantage of keeping daily records. Your teacher has probably told you to do this, but it is easy to get out of the habit. Keeping records will help you come back to your practice the next day knowing where you left off. It also provides documentation of your practice over time.

Reward is a big part of gamification. Video games (unsurprisingly) are masters of this. When you kill off a boss or achieve a goal, there is some form of recognition. Perhaps a little fanfare, perhaps a cut scene about how awesome you are. Use the ideas of rewards in your daily practice. Somewhere, perhaps at the start of your practice book, write a list of rewards for yourself. These can be small (a cup of coffee after your practice) or large (an overseas trip after a significant performance).

Finally, if you're finding your practice dull, change it. There's a reason boss fights don't go on forever: because they'd get boring. If you find your repertoire dull, change it. If you are not being challenged by your technical work anymore, move onto other scales, other patterns.

Daily Technical Practice

McPherson's five music skills are reasonably high-level skills. They tell you what you should be able to do as a musician. Underneath this are underlying skill sets. Things such as an understanding of music theory, knowledge of your instrument, interpretive skills, and so forth. One of these base abilities is essential to all performance: technical ability. Coordination and fine motor skills are a fundamental of being a performing musician. Such attributes are developed using technical exercises such as scales, finger exercises, held tones, and so forth depending on your instrument. Technical exercises are therefore one of the most important aspects of your daily practice. However, contemporary musicians often struggle to include this in regular practice. It seems so much more fun to shred on guitar or solo over "Autumn Leaves". However, if you want to take your playing to the next level, technical exercises will form a regular part of your practice regime.

Every instrument has standard technical practice exercises. Piano has Hanon, Pischna, and Czerny. The drums have Stick Control and Progressive Steps to Syncopation for the Modern Drummer. The bass has Simandl. The trumpet has Arban. You get the idea. And even apart from these classic texts, there are all sort of scales, arpeggios, held notes (for wind players), and so forth. Your instrumental teacher will have even more ideas themselves. The choices can be overwhelming. Your teacher can help guide you, but you will also know your weak areas. This is where you need to be thoughtful and honest with yourself. Identify your technical strengths and weaknesses, seek exercises for these, and work on them every day.

Saying this, do not discard the humble scale. Scales are useful as they improve your motor skills within keys and add deep music theory knowledge.

AN INDIAN TAKE ON PRACTICE

In my final year at music college, when I was in my last two semesters, which were part-time semesters because I had already finished a chunk of my studies, I took the entire summer off just to practice. Indian classical musicians do this thing called *Chilla*. For 40 days they lock themselves in a room. I practised for 40 days non-stop. You don't even skip one day. And you practice a minimum of six to eight hours every day.

Tarun, Drummer and music educator

Daily Solo Practice

This book does not aim to tell you how to practice the trumpet or piano or drums because (as we've observed) not only is every instrument practiced differently, but every musician practises differently. You practise differently. Only you can really come to grips with your practice style. But there are some common features of effective practice. It's a term we've used a few times. Regardless of your instrument or what genre you play, seek to make your solo practice time effective and efficient. There's no use doing an exercise or working on a piece unless it is contributing something to your playing. Thoughtful, analytical practice strategies result in bigger improvements in your performance. Effective practice has a few common features. It:

- Is demanding.
- Is aware of mistakes.
- Is smart practice.
- Focuses on outcomes rather than working to a clock.
- Utilises increasing tempos from slow to fast.
- Listens to models.
- Is willing to divide, reassemble, and repeat
- Is thoughtful practice that holds you to account.

One of the musician sayings from the trenches goes (if you will excuse the expression) every musician has his ass handed to him on the bandstand at some stage of their life. I have. Waldo has. Your teacher has. You have or will have. That's because what we do is demanding. Your fellow musicians have spent years honing their craft and often have little time or patience for mistakes that unnecessarily prolong rehearsals or result in train wrecks. Thus, your preparation for performance should be demanding. When you're practising, you need to strive for absolute perfection, even if you don't make it. Play your scales, your exercises, your songs, and your improvisations as close to perfect as you can. On the bandstand, you sometimes need to let mistakes fly past. You don't in rehearsal.

You need to watch your errors in practice. When you're first learning a piece, you inevitably make mistakes. Being aware of those mistakes in the early stages will govern how much work you have to do to master the piece. Ukrainian-American pianist Alexander Liebermann used to say, "practice doesn't make perfect, it makes permanent". Effective practicers do not play the entire piece robotlike from beginning until the finish, then turn around and play it again. Efficient solo rehearsal concerns the identification and rectification of errors. When an error is repeated early in the learning process, it becomes a rote part of the performance. The more times you repeat the error, the more difficult it is to fix. When you make a mistake, stop and play the erroneous material until you can get it right. Then play it in context, a few bars on either side, then incorporate it into the greater work. It sounds obvious, but that burning attention to detail will pay big dividends in your final product.

Effective practice is smart practice. It works with the brain rather than against it. A lot of studies have been conducted on musicians learning instruments. One of the key findings from these studies is that musicians are more likely to be effective with regular breaks than sitting at their instruments and playing for hours. Practising for three one-hour sessions is more efficient than one three-hour session. However, how you want to approach your practice time will be up to you. Some people prefer to study for several short periods over the day. Others practise over a period with regular short breaks. (You might like to read up on the Pomodoro technique.) Whichever way you choose, work to your amazing brain's advantage and don't ask it to do things it wasn't designed for.

Developing your musical technique can seem an elephantine task. You want to be a better player, but it seems like such an enormous job. Well, you know how to eat an elephant? One plate at a time. Every day. Each time you sit down to practise, you need a manageable goal. A single plate of elephant. Don't sit down to master the collected works of Horace Silver. Work on "Strollin'". Get the chord changes down, learn the melody, then work on improvising over it. Or learn the lyrics and structure to that Dixie Chicks song. Work on these eight bars, work on these scales, or this exercise, or this mode. Work until you are satisfied with this small thing. Don't worry about the time. If you are practising effectively, you will become fascinated with the details of getting this tiny task done. Do small tasks repeatedly you'll get through the elephant.

One of the best tools you have in your practice repertory is varying the tempo.[6] A drummer friend, an amazing teacher, used to say to me that anyone can flail away quickly at the instrument, but to truly master the drums is to be able to play things perfectly slowly. Use your metronome. Effective practice uses a metronome and begins practice at slower tempos and increases slowly until eventually the performance is at the requisite tempo. Get the song, exercise, scale, improvisation, or whatever, played correctly first, slowly, and then build the speed up.

Being thoughtful in your practice involves a certain amount of self-awareness and honesty. You know your weaknesses better than anyone. Better than me. Better than your teacher. Better than the public. Because only you inhabit your brain and your body 24/7. When you're practising, don't practise what you're good at. Practise what you're bad at. Be aware of what you're trying to do and take your time. Your results will be better. The one thing about practice, no matter how much you do, you need to do it every day. Every single day. Even on the weekend. Even if it's just touching the instrument for ten minutes. The more you get to love your instrument, the more time you will want to spend with it. You'll notice that if you go away on holidays, it takes time to get back into the instrument. You also might lose the habit and have to work to get it back. Unless you are practising every day, as a student or as a professional, your skills will not improve or maintain themselves at a professional level.

PRACTICING WHAT YOU LOVE

There are universities that conduct exams in Indian classical music all over India. I did my exams through that, but I was never really a classical musician. I could never connect to it. As a kid, my mother would force me to sit in practice every day for half an hour, just like happens to all children. My mother would be like, "Oh, you must practice. How will you become a good singer? Blah blah blah". Then I would practise, but my heart was always into Western music. I was introduced to Western music in my school. I was a part of the choir for maybe a year or two, and then part of the school band. I was introduced there to rock music. All the 60s influence. There were rock 'n' roll song sounds when I was growing up, Backstreet Boys and Boyzone. That's where I sort of picked up Western music.

Ipshita, Blues singer

Practising Improvisation

Practising your improvisation is probably one of the most contentious issues for contemporary music practitioners—and usually completely opaque to classical musicians. You need to practise your approach to improvisation. Improvisation is personal and every teacher, every great player has a different idea on how to improvise. Contemporary music, no matter what genre you play in, be it rock, jazz, pop, Latin, country, or whatever, is at least semi-improvisatory. You don't customarily play contemporary music in the same way as classical, from notes. But the nature of improvisation is to express one's own individuality in the moment. Alice Coltrane improvises differently to Patricia Barber and Abigail Washburn. With all these variables, how then can we learn and practice improvisation?

First, we should define improvisation. If you're thinking that improvisation is confined to jazz, to the improvisation section of a head arrangement, you're probably looking at it too narrowly. Similarly, if you're thinking of a guitar solo, you probably need to broaden your definition. Whenever a musician plays music that they are spontaneously creating without reading all the notes on a given sheet music, they improvise. Comping on a guitar or piano is improvising. Playing a cover of "Day Tripper" is improvising. Creating the groove and feel of a newly written song is improvising. Improvising is the de facto performance mode of contemporary music.

Popular music is a relatively new addition to the academy. Jazz, however, joined tertiary music programs in the 1960s, and jazz does have a history of teaching improvisation. Of sorts. Historically, there have been several approaches to teaching jazz improvisation, all more or less relating to chord-scale theory, an idea that suggests that certain scales can be linked to chords. For example, over a G major seven chord, you can improvise on a G major mode on a G lydian mode. Jamey Aebersold's famous books, that provided tracks to practice along with a range of jazz standards, sold in the millions. Other books such as Coker's 1964 *Improvising Jazz*, Baker's 1983 *Jazz Improvisation*, and Paul Berliner's 2010 *Thinking in Jazz: The Infinite Art of Improvisation* took a more intellectual approach to improvisation. These books provide a solid intellectual grounding in jazz improvisation and, with a teacher's guidance, can develop solid jazz improvisers.

Contemporary music, however, includes more than jazz. A body of work that addresses improvisation in traditions outside of jazz simply does not exist. Improvisation classes in contemporary music courses consequently tend to have a jazz underpinning. This is fine if you're intending to be the next Carla Bley or Brad Mehldau; if you're planning to be a rock guitarist, however, perhaps learning the lydian dominant scale may not be the best grounding. Further, because of jazz's focus on chord-scale theory, there is a tendency to produce performers whose improvisations can sometimes sound more like a set of scales than an improvisation. And uniformity is not what improvisation is about.

So, what can we apply from existing jazz improvisation practice and teaching that applies to contemporary music more broadly? Well, there are a few things.

Teaching jazz improvisation is predicated on gaining basic technical skills before you develop an individual voice. So regardless of the genre you play in, work on your technique to improve your improvisation. Play your scales and exercises. Your brain conceives your improvisation and your hands implement it, so ensure there are no technical problems that impede the passage of ideas from your brain to your hands to your instrument.

All the jazz improvisation books are theoretical. To become a better improviser, work on your theory. Improvisation is applied music theory. It's not enough merely to know that we call this chord a C major seventh. You need to know why it works, why it fits into the tonality, and what notes sound good and bad over it. If you don't, your improvisations will always rely on intuition rather than understanding. The result will be a sameness about your playing. You want to control your music, and the key to that control is applying the music theory that you learn.

A regular staple of jazz improvisation training is transcription. Transcribe the music of your heroes! Then play your transcriptions! Then analyse them to find out what they're doing. (We go into this more below, but it's worth mentioning here.)

The Thorny Problem of Sight Reading

A while ago, I was talking to a colleague, an excellent working guitarist. He expressed how he wanted to learn to sight read but didn't really see the point. Unless he was working in venues that had an accompanying house band, he just wouldn't use this skill. This same musician in the same conversation was saying how much he'd like to cut down his day job to concentrate more on music. Do you see the logical fallacy here?

Every working musician should be able to sight read. Pianists, singers, guitarists, bass players, drummers, you, me. Everybody. I'll tell you why. The professional music industry is vastly competitive. Think of the best players in your city, who are called to every recording session and pit gig. Once you leave the hallowed halls and ivory towers of your institution, these people are your competition. For gigs. For recordings. For everything. You simply cannot afford to cut yourself out of any gig. Every gig lost is an income stream lost. The simple industry fact is that musicians that can sight read are sought after because they are more efficient than non-readers in certain circumstances. They require less rehearsal. They can fit into a band more quickly. Some gigs are completely closed to non-readers. Work on your sight reading.

That said, sight reading is one of the most difficult things a human brain can do. When you're sight reading, your brain is working at the very edge of its capacity. It's processing an incredibly complex notation of a musical performance, interpreting it, and seamlessly performing it in real time. Sometimes this occurs while other musicians are also performing. Sight reading involves taking notated music and playing it without rehearsal as close to note perfectly as you can. The way to get better at it is to do it every day. There is so much music available for legal download now. Every day, try to read something you don't know. It will make your sight reading so much stronger.

Transcription

Transcription is the process of listening to a solo (or a lick) and writing it down in music notation. It is regularly touted (especially by jazz musicians) as the way to learn to improvise. However, in practice, it is the bane of contemporary music students. In my teaching experience, it is difficult to get contemporary music students to undertake transcription. Perhaps this is understandable. Transcription is hard. It involves time spent listening to a solo over and over again. Further, the process of writing it down means that students have to become very familiar with music notation, which not all contemporary music students are. The benefits, however, outweigh the temporary pain. When you transcribe:

- You develop aural skills (the ability to hear music).
- Your music theory skills improve (as you notate and analyse what you hear).
- You build your improvisational vocabulary by studying the licks of your music heroes.

- As you play along with the recording (or with a backing track) your technique improves.
- By writing a solo down, you can analyse the notes your musical hero is playing.
- The process of transcribing a solo makes that music a part of you. Musicians who have transcribed a solo can still play that solo many years later.

The process of transcribing a solo has three steps: Writing, singing, and playing. When you transcribe a solo, you listen to a recording by an artist you admire over and over again in small bursts, sometimes a bar at a time, usually slowed down, and you notate what they play. This includes the notes they are playing as the solo and the chords in a sort of modified lead sheet. Second, you learn to sing the performance, which helps internalise it. Finally, you then learn to play that solo or lick, initially slowly, then slowly building up in speed. Each stage will take dozens of repetitions but, by the end of it, that solo will be in your head. And you'll be just that bit closer to playing like your musical heroes.

No matter what genre you play, if you want to be a great artist, study the great artists. Identify your musical heroes in your genre, get hold of recordings of them, and find out how they play. By transcribing you're taking apart their musical approaches to improvisation. You can see what they are doing on the page. That is the beginning of understanding how they think and perform. Once you do that only then will you play as well as them. You can't get that from a book of transcriptions or tablature of famous rock solos. By transcribing the music of your heroes, they become a part of you.

Solo Rehearsal for Your Ensemble

The last thing you want to do is to go to a rehearsal unprepared. If there's one thing professional musicians hate, it's wasting time in rehearsal. Whenever you're in a rehearsal, always go prepared and knowing your parts. This means that another part of your individual practice will be rehearsing for any ensembles in which you find yourself. If you have sheet music from a band, look through it ahead of time and learn any tricky parts. If you're not using sheet music, learn the songs. (This is where programs that create backing tracks such as iReal Pro or Band in a Box come in handy.) Make tracks from what you're doing in rehearsal, or play from sheet music, learn the material, and get off the page.

However, not all bands are completely organised. One of the time-consuming parts of playing in an ensemble is when you have to learn performances from recordings of the band's performance. It's fairly common, but it is annoying to have to do, particularly if it's for a one-off performance. If you're running a band that sometimes has to use subs, always try to have charts—even rough charts—to save their time and energy.

Free Exploration

Finally, explore different areas in your rehearsal. Not all of parts of your practice time has to be completely targeted. Explore different traditions. Listen to Spotify. Be reflective in your solo practice. Consider your weaknesses and try to work out ways of fixing them. Record yourself and write things down. You're a creative, so be creative in your rehearsal.

BUSKING AS PRACTICE

In discussion with Cameron, he mentioned that he spent a year busking in Holland to expand his performance abilities.

I got really used to being a performer who was playing concerts where people were paying money to come and see you play. And you were playing repertoire that was fresh and new, so you knew that your audience were there to see you perform at that gig. That's a very different vibe to just walking up to a bunch of people in a bar or a café in foreign country, and just setting up and playing. And what we're doing with that too was that you come and you don't play repertoire music, you play original music. You play the standards, you play songs that they're hopefully going to know from the classic jazz ensemble. And so doing that, I learnt a lot of songs. And I learnt how to perform without edification on a street with a saxophone player and maybe a guitar player, or I had a percussionist sometimes. And to just engage people who were just sitting there, having their beer or their coffee, where you're sort of throwing entertainment at them. And it's a very different way of approaching it.

When you're performing it's like you can't just be in your own bubble. I always would sort of visualise myself being really centred in whatever spot that I'm in and expanding my energy, like outward and imagining my sound doing the same thing. My sound on the bass became creative, moving outwards, and would hopefully be attractive to people coming towards it and meeting that sound and that energy. I've always cultivated that idea in the practice room, and I've always cultivated that before a show when you're on stage and people are paying money to come and hear you play. You sort of go, okay, it's not just me here. I need to fill this entire room with my presence. And I need the other musicians to feel my presence, so that they know that I'm there for them. And I need the whole room to feel my presence so they know that I'm there for them too. And that way I feel like the sound that you create emanates with an intention to connect.

When you're on the street that's the same thing. It's like you're not forcing anything. It's just like a centredness. And to create a groove, like a soul and a feeling in the air around you. When you're out in the open too with lots of things going past, it made it way harder. There's a lot of distraction. I actually really enjoyed that challenge.

In Amsterdam, it was also a survival thing. I got myself in a situation where I had no gigs, so we needed them. We would go out at 10 o'clock in the morning and sometimes I wouldn't come home until 12 o'clock at night. We would busk for 10 to 14 hours a day. We made good money so I could afford to go on trips, travel off around the European neighbourhood.

Cameron, Venue owner and jazz bassist

Further Reading

There are several excellent books on the market that teach you about practicing. If I had to choose one, I'd recommend Madeline Bruser's amazing *The Art of Practising*.

If you want to learn more about improvising, check out the jazz books mentioned: Coker's 1964 *Improvising Jazz*, Baker's 1983 *Jazz Improvisation*, and Paul Berliner's 2010 *Thinking in Jazz: The Infinite Art of Improvisation*.

Chapter Summary

- Solo practice is an essential process for successful musicians.
  - However, contemporary musicians often do not have a practice routine. Classical musicians have one, but with some issues. But they do have one.
  - You need to undertake solo practice regularly to be a successful musician.
  - You can gamify the practice system to make it more enjoyable and trick your mind into engaging with it.
- Your solo practice should include:
  - Daily technical practice.
  - Improvisational practice.
  - Sight reading.
  - Transcription.
  - Solo rehearsal for your ensembles.
  - Free exploration.

Notes

1 McPherson, "Five Aspects of Musical Performance and Their Correlates."
2 Stylistically conceived means improvisation within a genre of music, like jazz improvisation, or a guitar solo. Freely conceived means improvisation that doesn't necessarily belong to a particular genre.

3 Gladwell, Outliers: The Story of Success.

4 Ericsson, Prietula, and Cokely, "The Making of an Expert."

5 Duke, Simmons, and Cash, "It's Not How Much; It's How: Characteristics of Practice Behavior and Retention of Performance Skills"; Hallam, "What Predicts Level of Expertise Attained, Quality of Performance, and Future Musical Aspirations in Young Instrumental Players?"

6 Donald, "The Organization of Rehearsal Tempos and Efficiency of Motor Skill Acquisition in Piano Performance"; Braun, "Effects of Differentiated-Tempo Aural Models on Middle School Orchestra Students' Attitudes and Motivation toward Practicing"; Cecconi-Roberts, "Effects of Practice Strategies on Improvement of Performance of Intermediate Woodwind Instrumentalists."

4　Rehearsing in a Group

As musicians, we love what we do. When others go to work, we go to play. We get together with friends and engage in that oh so human activity, musicking. But that love and enjoyment and passion and camaraderie at a rehearsal can easily come unstuck, and you end up sitting around chilling, listening to music, having a few beers, and then doing a half hour's rehearsal getting nowhere. When you get together in a group to prepare for a musical performance, you need to remain focussed and collectively work as efficiently as you can.

One of the greatest challenges new musicians encounter when entering the profession is learning how to rehearse with others. An effective rehearsal requires a burning focus on maximising your collective efficiency for an extended period. Nothing annoys professional musicians more than time wasting. That can be someone showing up who does not know parts, or who can't cut the gig. It might mean a lack of organisation by the bandleader. There are many factors that influence the efficacy and quality of rehearsals.

This doesn't mean a joyless experience. Waldo regularly plays salsa. Rehearsals in this genre (in his experience) typically begin with an hour of *maté* and talk before getting into the rehearsal. Some rehearsals are democratic ventures where everyone has a say, and the rehearsals reflect this. Others utilise a more tense and combative way of conducting rehearsals with a social structure comprising bandleaders and sidemen. It's difficult to achieve a unifying balance.[1]

The more an ensemble plays together, the more you get to know each other's performance and the less rehearsal you need. The Beatles learned to play with each other by performing every other every night in the Hamburg Reeperbahn. The Count Basie Orchestra "played new arrangements and repeated them every night in a new town, fine tuning all the moving parts—a rehearsal in motion".[2] That doesn't mean you can stop rehearsing. Despite the Basie band's success, they still rehearsed every week when they could.

Group rehearsal is a significant step in preparing for a memorable and successful gig. This is where you really start imagining and creating your performance. And when you're doing it, it simply isn't enough to sit down in the practice room and channel Van Halen, or Ella Fitzgerald, or Floyd Cramer, or Gloria Estefan. In this section, we'll consider the role of group rehearsal (as opposed to individual practice) in creating a performance that turns people from passive consumers into active fans. If this is what you want, you need to rehearse effectively and with the performance (not just the music) in mind.

I've often heard the line that being so focussed on the performance and the industry is being too commercial or selling out. Listen up! If you want to be successful in the industry, you need to embrace the industry and be professional. Let me ask you something: Who do you think the richest jazz musician in the world is? If you look it up, it's Tony Bennett, estimated to be worth $200 million. Bennett is 92 and widely regarded as one of the finest singers in the world. He's also the only jazz musician to make it into the top 100. Along with everyone else in that list from Paul McCartney (#1, $1.28 billion) to John McFee (#100, $50 million), Bennett listens to the audience and prepares accordingly. He once said: "I'm still learning about music. The best way to learn is to listen to the audience. When you listen to the audience, they will tell you what they like".

There are three things to consider in rehearsal, and we'll deal with each of these. To rehearse effectively, we need a philosophy of music rehearsal. We need to consider some overall principles that will guide our rehearsals. If you remember these, your rehearsal techniques will already be better. Second, you need to consider the best and most effective ways to rehearse the music, for we are first and foremost musicians. Third, you also need to consider how to rehearse the performance. Consideration of these three points will lead to better and more efficient rehearsal for successful and memorable performances.

Philosophies of Music Rehearsal

The first point we will make is that the rehearsal procedure depends on the performance for which you're preparing. There are four approaches to rehearsals as there are four broad types of gigs: Reading gigs, improvising gigs, rock gigs, and folk gigs. An example of a reading gig is a theatre pit gig. In these, you perform notated and very set music in the pit of a musical theatre. There is an enormous amount of material to get through, along with very set musical-hierarchical roles (a set bandleader/conductor), improvisation may or may not occur, and reading ability is paramount. The second is an improvising ensemble rehearsal, such as a small jazz ensemble. This gig emphasises soloing, working together, and the memorisation and performance of a canon of accepted repertoire. The third is typically a performance in the genre of rock/pop and related traditions. In this gig, sheet music and notes are less important than improvisational skills. The notations used are typically chord charts. The last type we label a folk gig because it does not use music at all, relying on oral transmission, as performances by the British/North American/Australian folk traditions might. These are not discrete categories, and different gigs might draw from different traditions. A small jazz ensemble (where the focus is on improvisation) might also use charts and thus draw from the first category. A rock gig that performs funk might draw some of its improvisational approaches from jazz traditions. Table 4.1 shows these different rehearsals, makes some notes, and gives some advice for dealing with them.

Table 4.1 Types of Rehearsals

Type of Rehearsal	Description	What Is Required	Rehearsal Features/Advice
Reading gig e.g., theatre pit, cabaret, big band, classical or semi-classical performance, cruise ship showband, movie or TV recording.	A group of musicians get together and rehearse from notated music. This music is often imposed by the performance. The line-up is defined by the instruments written for by the composer and/or arranger.	Excellent sight reading ability is a prerequisite for this gig. Ability to blend with other musicians and work with a unit with little rehearsal. Work within the very structured approach of formal rehearsals. Concentration and discipline.	Reading gigs have a defined bandleader who is responsible for running the band. Unless the band is playing there is absolutely no noodling.[3] These rehearsals are far more formal than others[4] and have designated formal roles for conductors, section leaders and so forth that are drawn from the classical tradition. **Advice** Come to the rehearsal with your part prepared. If you are going to undertake these gigs, ensure that your sight reading is up to par. These gigs are useful to you if you intend to participate mainly in the first two types of performance. Undertake as many as you can.
Improvising gig e.g., small jazz ensemble, rock orchestra.	A group of musicians get together to play from the corpus of standards pieces. Sometimes 'originals' (newly composed pieces) might be introduced. Participants are generally divided into rhythm section, horn players, and singers. These rehearsals may play from 'lead sheets'.[5] However, emphasis is on memorisation of an accepted canon[6] of music.	Excellent improvisational ability. Ability to sight read lead sheets. Memorisation of the common songs contained in the canon.	Improvising gigs tend to be more democratic than reading gigs. The leader will count songs off and may choose some of the songs. If you don't know a song, don't try to fake it, but let people know.[7] **Advice** If you are currently at university, take those song lists you have to learn seriously. This is the canon. Maintain sightlines with everyone. This has lots of benefits. It maintains a collective approach to music. It is how you know it is your turn to improvise. It allows the bandleader to control the band.

(Continued)

Table 4.1 Continued

Type of Rehearsal	Description	What Is Required	Rehearsal Features/Advice
Rock gig e.g., rock band.	These rehearsals play from chord charts. Participants may or may not be able to sight read.	Good genre-specific improvisational skills. If you're a rock band, or a country band, or a Latin band, be able to improvise in that genre. Memorisation of the songs in the set list.	This form of ensemble is fairly common in the industry. It is the rehearsal for the majority of commercial gigs. **Advice** Learn the music before you come to a gig. Work on your improvisation.
Folk gig	These gigs do not use any form of music, but rather are taught by an oral tradition. One person teaches another person the music.	Ability to play from memory. Good listening and memorisation skills.	This form of music is rarer in the industry as traditional folk music is not usually a commercial music. The folk music we are used to in the commercial music industry is a form of folk-rock. Think of Bob Dylan. You will not typically use sheet music in these rehearsals.

Music rehearsal prepares for two aspects of a musical performance, and they're both contained in that term: Musical performance. Undeniably the musical aspect is important. You can't be a successful musician if you cannot play the music. However, the music is only one aspect. You also need to rehearse the performance. This means considering the staging, the movement, the lighting, the set list. Who is going to solo? How are you going to groove? These things are also important.

> ### REHEARSING AND SUCCESS IN PERFORMANCE
>
> A successful performance is a performance that meets several characteristics. Being well prepared and rehearsed with the music, being familiar with the music and style you are performing. This makes a high-level performance that not only brings satisfaction to the musicians in the band but also to the audience attending it. It's very important to connect with the audience on an energy level.
>
> Alex, Drummer, bandleader, composer, educator

One of the most important common principles of successful music rehearsal is that everyone should show up knowing their stuff. A rehearsal is not the place to work on what you should work on in your private practice times. To do so is not only disrespectful to every other musician on the bandstand who has bothered to learn their music, but it is enormously time wasting and likely to get you fired from the gig. If you're on a reading gig, ensure you can sight read or, at the very least, practise the material before you show up. If you're on an improvising gig, ensure your improvisation is up to par and you know the repertoire. If you're on a rock gig, listen to and learn the material before you come to rehearsal.

When you're planning a show, give thought to the set list. We've all played in bands that have a huge amount of songs and where the singer or bandleader turns around to tell you what song to do next. They often resist any efforts to organise a set list because they tell you they can "read an audience" and "know what song to do next". The result of this is usually one or two minutes of dead time while everyone prepares to play the song called. Perhaps the bass player doesn't know the song. Perhaps the pianist can't find the lead sheet. In the meantime, your performance has lost momentum. The big gigs—the Bruce Springsteens, the Diana Kralls, the Shania Twains—use set lists. You should too.[8]

Be realistic in your rehearsal timeframe. Don't under- or over-rehearse. If you are seasoned professionals doing a covers gig, you might only need one or two rehearsals. Alternatively, if you're starting out and writing your own music, it can take months or even years of intense rehearsals to build up your songlist and find your sound.

Don't waste time in rehearsal. Being in a rehearsal space can be expensive in the real world of the music industry. Sure, your college might have rehearsal spaces. You might have a garage or tolerant neighbours. But get out into the professional music world and you'll be spending money on rehearsal spaces. Be friends with your fellow musicians. Enjoy the hang. But from the moment you enter that rehearsal space, you need to be completely professional.

Finally, rehearsals are not times to play it safe. Push the boundaries. Try different ways of playing songs. If you wrote the song, ask for constructive criticism and don't be precious about it. Try to get everyone to contribute to the band. Push each other as musicians. If a song isn't working, come back to it.

Rehearsing the Music

To get the greatest musical benefit from a group rehearsal, you need to plan effectively. It sounds obvious, but in practice it's a rarity. The vast majority of rehearsals are either disorganised and careless, or formulaic. Everyone shows up, runs through the music until they get bored, and then goes home. Or, if they're planning for a particular show, they run through the music as quickly as possible, and then head to the bar. Effective planning of your rehearsal in advance can assist the outcomes. So, sit down and work out what you're going to rehearse.

It is hard to be prescriptive about rehearsals because each ensemble rehearses differently. Consider a pit orchestra versus a band rehearsing up new songs. A pit orchestra needs to get through a lot of notated music quickly. There is no room for musical development, as they have to just play what is on the page. It is very intense with little margin for error. By contrast, a band that is developing newly written songs takes a more relaxed and organic approach. They may spend time playing with the groove and the arrangement. They may work intensely but may not get through as much music. Despite these differences, there are a few common areas that every rehearsal must undertake.

A rehearsal must have a single clear musical purpose. There is nothing more demoralising than rehearsing for no reason. We've both been in this situation. Learn a new song. Work on your vocal harmonies. Whatever. But have a purpose and make sure that everyone knows what it is.

A rehearsal must have a leader. In an ideal world, all musicians would have equal input into the music and the band. However, in the trenches of popular music rehearsal, that's rare. Someone needs to take charge. Perhaps it's an appointed leader or conductor. Perhaps it's the lead singer. Perhaps the producer. Perhaps people take turns running different songs. But regardless, if one (organised) person takes charge, the rehearsal will run smoother and be more effective.

A rehearsal must be planned. Before you go into rehearsal, know what you will do and how long you will spend on it. If you don't, you can end up running out of time and leaving music unrehearsed or badly rehearsed. Write a running order before you go into rehearsal.

A rehearsal must be as pleasant as possible. An unpleasant rehearsal experience will not be effective because people will focus on getting out as quickly as possible. Ensure that rehearsals are in as pleasant an environment as possible and are conducted professionally and courteously. If you think the bass player can't play, the rehearsal is not the time to bring that up.

A rehearsal aims to get the musicians working together and sounding good. I've worked in bands where I (as pianist) could play the same hits as the drummer and bass player, even though we hadn't planned that out ahead of time, almost like ESP. The more you play together, the more you get used to each other's sound and musical decision-making processes.

A rehearsal aims to learn the music. A rehearsal seeks to learn the constituent parts of the song. This means learning the harmony, melody, and lyrics. You'll have done some of this before the rehearsal, but you'll do it again in the ensemble rehearsals. This is important if you're learning a new song. A rehearsal allows musicians to learn their parts. While you need to practise your parts beforehand, there is no substitute to playing your parts in an ensemble. A rehearsal seeks to establish the groove and style of the song. The groove can be many things, but here, it's the aspect of the music that fits it into a style. How a Bossa Nova grooves is different to how a bluegrass song does. There are simple default styles for performance. Perhaps you're playing a standard rock or jazz song. Once you know the style and groove, this becomes easy. Or perhaps there are nuances, individual and unique approaches to the song. Perhaps you're like Postmodern Jukebox, applying styles in an unexpected fashion. Or perhaps you're playing it exactly how the original performers played it. Whichever, the purpose of rehearsal is to ensure all musicians are on the same page with the groove and style. A rehearsal aims to learn the arrangement of the song.

A rehearsal aims to foster trust between musicians. If trust exists between musicians in a band, if musicians know they can rely on each other, there will be less anxiety on stage. Everyone knows that they have their back. The more you rehearse together, the more you will trust each other.

A rehearsal (usually) aims to get you off the page. In most situations, it's better that performing musicians play without written music. It enables us to better engage with the audiences, to make eye contact, and to make them feel special. There are some genres that this isn't appropriate for: Pit gigs, big bands, classical ensembles. But whoever is the focus of the performance should use as little music as possible. Think of the best performers in your genre, the ones you admire the most, and consider what they do. You'd never see Blondie play from sheet music.

Some other rules about running the rehearsal:

- Turn up on time. This is important. Arriving late is expensive (if you're paying for rehearsal space), frustrating for musicians, and disrespectful to your fellow performers. Nobody cares about traffic or your horrible day or whatever. They care that you're late. In this there is no compromise. Always, always, plan to arrive early.
- If you don't have to bring equipment (singers, horn players), help the poor drummer who has to bring an entire kit.
- If you are adding to your repertoire, don't rehearse over two or three new songs at a single rehearsal. Learning new music is demanding. Trying to do more than this will be counterproductive.
- Ensure you practise with health in mind. Singers need water and cannot scream for as long as guitarists can shred. Horns, particularly lead trumpeters, can damage their lips by practising for too long. Set limits to what you can do and take short breaks when necessary.
- It can help to schedule a rhythm section rehearsal before you get together with a singer. They will probably require less formal rehearsal.
- Rehearse eye contact. All members of the band must be able to see each other at vital parts of the song. This is especially true at the beginnings and endings of songs, and the beginnings and endings of solos. It is also particularly true between the drummer, bass player, and band leader.
- Record your rehearsals on a video camera. For preference, use a good recorder such as a GoPro or a Zoom Q4 or Q8. These will pick up your sound, but will also pick up your image, which we'll consider in the next section.
- Warm-ups are rare in popular music for some reason. But they're worth considering. Play something you all know. Perhaps a blues. Or a simple song in your repertoire. This enables you to check the levels, the singer can warm up their voice, and you're set for rehearsal.
- Rehearse until the song is absolutely right. This will often take more than one rehearsal, See the quote by Tim below.

- Only people in the band are at rehearsals. Anyone else is distracting. No family, no friends, no exceptions.
- Be quiet. Don't noodle between songs. Don't be the loudest person in the band.
- Do not turn up under the influence of alcohol or drugs. Believe it or not, you do not sound better when you're drunk or high. You just annoy your (sober) bandmates. After the rehearsal is the time for such shenanigans.
- Be critical but make your criticism creative. Remember, being an artist is about baring your soul. Any criticism is going to hurt unless it's given carefully and in the right spirit. It's very difficult to replace musicians.
- At the end of the rehearsal, review what went right and what went wrong. Take notes so your next rehearsal can start effectively. Disciplining yourself to do this will increase your rehearsal effectiveness.
- An obvious one. Never point a microphone at a speaker!

PRACTICING UNTIL YOU CAN'T GET IT WRONG

Before you play the songs in a live situation, you're going to have to practise together for eight weeks and get tight. You're going to have to learn your stuff, man. You know, you're going to have to put time into it. You're going to have to invest time into this if you want to be good. And if you do, you'll get the results, man. And it's just an opportunity, you know, to shine. Where else do you get an opportunity to shine in music? Every weekend, kids shine in their sport, man. But we try to shine in music. And the way to do it is to practice, practice, practice, practice till you can do it in your sleep. That's the only way to go at it with confidence. Until you can do it and not fail, you haven't practised enough. It's not practising until you get it right, it's practising it until you can't get it wrong.

Tim, Guitarist

Rehearsing the Performance

Large acts, the headliners you see at big venues, not only rehearse the music that they will play, but they rehearse the way they play it. They'll book out a large rehearsal space for a couple of weeks, bring in the backline, all performers, and rehearse the show. Now, booking out a large stage might be beyond your budget (or your college's rehearsal spaces) but that doesn't mean you can't take a dive into the big performers' bag of tricks and rehearse your performance. If you truly want to make your performances memorable and successful, you have an imperative to do so. One of our respondents noted that "non-musical audiences respond to visual aspects and body language on stage more than a sick string skipping arpeggio. A person's charisma and stage banter with the crowd makes for a more enjoyable experience that people will talk about". You'll achieve these visual aspects and body language more if you rehearse the performance.

Your rehearsal is a simulation of your performance. Consider: If you are learning to fly a plane, they don't just give you some books to read, put you in a captain's uniform, and wish you bon voyage. You spend hours in a simulator, learning how your plane responds to any condition before they entrust you with passengers' lives. Rehearsing your performance is the same. In this simulation, you are trying to recreate the same conditions as you will face in your next performance. You rehearse lighting, banter, effects, progressing quickly between songs, engaging with an imaginary audience, and as much as you can to make it like an actual performance. Think about the things you are likely to encounter at your next performance and try to include them in your performance rehearsals.

A word of warning. When musicians rehearse the performance, sometimes they make stupid mistakes. That's normal. Don't chastise yourself. You're now not only concentrating on the music, but on other things like the set list or the technical aspects. That's why you rehearse them. Once you get confident dealing with the distractions, your music will improve again.

First, and most obviously, rehearse the set list. Go from one song to another. Do you have three ballads all in C major (or E major for guitarists)? Then you should swap them around. Does the order in which you play your songs take your audience on the journey you want? Does it capture them and make them want to stay until the end of the performance? Or are you musical wallpaper, creating a pleasing environment, but not much else. Can you move quickly from one song to the next? Rehearsing as a simulation helps you spot these errors and address them.

CREATING A SETLIST

To create a really strong set list, start with the songs. Choose songs that suit your show's theme that work best for you. They need to showcase what you do best. Make them the best songs you can. Be mindful of your audience's—your demographic's—expectations when you're choosing your material. Then put them in a deliberate order. Begin and end strongly. At the start, you need a strong song to capture their attention. At the end, you need a strong song to stay in their memory. Between, take your audience on a journey, and watch your narrative. But you won't really know how successful you've been until it's been performed.

Annie, Singer

Second, consider your movements. This doesn't mean that you'll do a can-can, but every movement you make has impact and it has intent. Every movement says something to the audience. Are you going to stand straight? Sit on a stool? Run around the stage like a madman? Consider what that says about you and the performance. If you're worried about movement, watch the video recordings of your rehearsals with the sound turned off. You'll quickly note any issues.[9]

MOVEMENT

It's essential that an artist communicates with their audience by any means possible—including verbal and non-verbal communication. Movement creates energy and must come across with ease and purpose to be effective. We've all seen acts that are awkward on stage and this unsettles the audience. Movement must appear natural. Remember, it is a part of your communication and it is essential in audience engagement. Movement, any movement, if used effectively will enhance your act and allow you to shine.

Bel, Artist manager

Consider your staging. Staging presents the biggest visual impact because it's how your entire band is set up, and you need to think about how you want to present your ensemble to the audience. Where will the drummer go? What about the horns? Will the singer move around and where to? You want to have the best visual impact you can. However, you also need to set up for the best sightlines. Can you all see each other? If the pianist is directly in front of the drummer, they won't be able to see the drummer's cutoff. You can fix these in rehearsal.

Technology is great, but boy, when it goes wrong, it goes wrong. That's why you need to rehearse the technological aspects of your performance. Most performances rely heavily on technology and it's the thing most out of your control in performance and the most likely to cause issues. So, rehearse it. If you're using backing tracks, rehearse with them. If you're using video screens, rehearse with them. If you are changing patches on a keyboard, or effects on your guitar, practise this change in real time. Try to develop guidelines for equalisation and effects on your vocals for the backline. Leave no technical aspect to chance.

Performances, as we observed, occur within a certain timeframe. If you go over, it will cost the venue money in extra salaries for staff. If you go under, you'll have the venue owner in your ear demanding you play more. For this reason, rehearse the duration of the performance in real time to a stopwatch. If you need to cut songs or add songs, do so.

Finally, consider your spiel. Almost every performance has on-stage discussion for the benefit of both the band and the audience. It's part of the fun of performance. Unless you are actors or putting on a certain type of performance, you shouldn't script your performance. This can make the delivery feel stilted. If you're not bantering, have a reason for it. Perhaps you're playing a soft, meaningful song and banter would be counterproductive. Fun repartee on the stage creates a fun, easy atmosphere that is very attractive to audiences. Talking to the audience engages them and allows them to feel a part of the performance. Both of these are very desirable in performance.

ONSTAGE BANTER

Our on-stage banter evolved quite naturally. I had been a professional theatre sports player for a few years and, as a result, I was confident with improvisation. The reaction the members of the show had on stage when I improvised provided great entertainment for the audience and always kept the show fresh. The cast of the show soon realised how the improvised 'banter' became a unique characteristic of the show and gave them the ability to put on a show that was adaptable to any audience. As a result, eventually each member of the show now participates in the unscripted moments of the show. No two shows are ever the same, and this is a result of the improvised 'banter' and the skill of being able to read an audience and adjust the comedy and 'banter' as applicable.

Anthea, Promoter and singer

Further Reading

There are two books in particular that will offer further insights. Garwood Whaley's *The Music Director's Cookbook* offers insights in rehearsal and planning from the point of view of music educators. John Colson's *Conducting and Rehearsing the Instrumental Music Ensemble* talks about rehearsal from a classical perspective.

Chapter Summary
- Rehearsing as an ensemble before a performance is important.
- Rehearsal will vary depending on the ensemble.
- All members of an ensemble need to arrive at rehearsal prepared to rehearse, with their parts learned.
- At the scheduled rehearsal time, be prepared to play, with instruments set up.
- Be realistic in your rehearsal timeframe.
- The rehearsal is the time to experiment and push the boundaries—not the performance.
- Rehearse the music first. Ensure that you can play the music as close to perfect as possible.
- Once you have the music rehearsed, rehearse the performance.

Notes

1 Söderman and Folkestad, "How Hip-Hop Musicians Learn: Strategies in Informal Creative Music Making"; Pulman, "Popular Music Pedagogy: Band Rehearsals at British Universities."
2 Green, *Rhythm Is My Beat: Jazz Guitar Great Freddie Green and the Count Basie Sound*, 104.
3 'Noodling' is playing music (either from your part or general practice) between running through songs. It is a bad practice that interrupts the flow of rehearsals and makes it difficult for musicians (and the bandleader/conductor) to talk. It is also distracting. Avoid it.
4 When I was having my first orchestral piece conducted by the august and formal John Hopkins at Sydney Conservatorium in the 1980s, I made the mistake of addressing the orchestra by saying 'Okay guys'. At my elbow, Hopkins quietly and discreetly at my elbow murmured, "I think you mean ladies and gentlemen".
5 A lead sheet is a piece of music that shows the melody and the chords.
6 A canon is a collectively established group of pieces that are considered 'worthy' and regularly performed. While it applies mostly to classical and jazz genres, rock, country, and folk also have songs that is are played more than others, and musicians that are considered more 'worthy' than others.
7 It is worth remembering that we are trying to create memorable performances. Regularly, the middle category—improvising gigs—are 'jam sessions' where there is no rehearsal. Sometimes such performances can be paid. Musicians show up, talk between songs working out what songs everyone knows, and then they perform them. Such performances have the capacity to be musically satisfying. However, because such they do not consider the performance, they are probably the least likely to be memorable.
8 That said, you can sometimes break the rules. In the 1985 Live Aid concert, Queen opened with their biggest song, "Bohemian Rhapsody", and continued through a set of high-energy and inclusive songs like "Crazy Little Thing" and "Ay-oh" and finishing with "We Are the Champions". The quiet song, "'Is this the World We Created" ' wasn't played until the later concert finale. So, the below rule on pushing the boundaries in rehearsal also holds true here.
9 Jazz musicians in particular are terrible at considering their movement. Jazz pianists (myself included in the past) hunch over the piano. The saxophonist looks off into the distance, implying nobility and soulfulness. The singer sings to the band rather than not to the audience.

5 Your Audience

The audience. The punters. The people that come out to listen to you play. Whether by ticket prices, or by consumption of alcohol and food, these people pay your salary. They come into venues, sacrifice their hard-earned cash and, more importantly, their precious free time just to hear you perform music. They will make or break your career. Ignore them or condescend to them at your peril.

In every interview, our informants, the successful music industry members, performers, and educators we spoke to, all hammered home the importance of the audience. For example:

> You hear a lot of performers who are self-indulgent. They'll perform what they think you want to hear. There's a danger in that because your audience is your client. They are the one that are there listening to you. You have to be mindful of what an audience wants and make it as special as you can.
>
> (Dave, Singer)

Or here's another:

> I don't like this fixed distance between the bands and the audience. You know what I mean? I don't want this line to be drawn between the people playing on stage and the crowd or whatever. I want them to be a part of the band and for the band to be part of the crowd, a kind of partnership. It's very important for us also, because the energy is always radiating from the audience to us. We deliver them something, and they respond in return. Their response matters to us. If they're going mad and crazy, it's a plus for the next song.
>
> (Mithy, Singer)

Or another from a venue:

> We've found many a time with many of our bands, those who put on shows or have interaction with the audience will do a lot better than those that get up and play their instruments and then pack up and walk away again.
>
> (Regional Australian Venue)

Successful live music isn't created by you. Or by a venue. Or by a promoter. A successful live music event is a collaboration between musicians, the music industry, and consumers of live music. The audience are not passive participants. They do not sit down and meekly consume your music. They are active partners in the experience. They listen. They dance. They mosh. They leave reviews on Facebook or Google. They buy your merchandise. They do all these things … or they don't. If you want your performances to be an artistic, experiential, and financial success, you audience needs to be at the top of your mind in planning your gigs.

In this chapter, we will consider your audience. We will talk about them in performance and discuss how to turn the public into audiences and audiences into fans. It's important, so listen up.

Considering Your Audience in Performance

What is an audience? Well, the answer to this depends on who you ask. To media studies folks, audiences are those who tune into television or (much more frequently now) stream from various streaming services. To them, the experience of immersing themselves in the latest televisual feast from HBO or Netflix is escapist and diversionary; but it is easy to access. All people need is a smart TV (or a computer) and an internet connection.

For we musicians, audiences are a little different. For starters, they aren't numbered in the millions. When you begin playing, you might perform to audiences numbered in the dozens. As you get going, they might be numbered in the hundreds. Eventually, you might play for thousands. But you will never play for the figures that your average Netflix episode will tune in for. However, in contrast to the people that sit and watch television, live music audiences are active rather than passive. They don't just sit at a television in their underwear drinking a cheap beer and compliantly watching the latest tales from the seven kingdoms of Westeros. They get dressed up. They jump on public transport and physically go to a venue. They pay the cover charge. They buy drinks. They are active in seeking their entertainment, and your performance has to be that much more engaging than the telly. Third, live music audiences are seeking an experience as or more engaging than the Westeros sagas. They don't want to sit down and be bored or disappointed. They are putting their hard-earned cash and time into your performance. They want you to succeed. They want you to have a fantastic performance. But they'll condemn you if you don't consider them!

Historically, contemporary music didn't have to worry much about engaging its audience. Of course the audience was engaged! It's rock and roll! It's jazz! It's country! It's salsa! People go crazy for music! Audiences bought records, CDs, and cassettes. They attended live concerts in droves. They bought t-shirts emblazoned with Metallica or Madonna or Miles Davis. Record companies invested enormous money in a select few artists that were carefully chosen and coached by talented A&R managers, marketed, promoted, recorded, and sent on tours all over the world. The executives of music labels (mostly) knew what they were doing and consequently made enormous amounts of money. They sometimes even shared this bonanza with the musicians.

These days, things are a little different for two reasons. The collapse (and slow rebuild) of recorded music means that the gatekeepers of contemporary music—A&R executives—no longer have control over the industry. Anyone can go out and buy a guitar, learn three chords, record an album, set up a WordPress site, and call themselves a musician. Tadah! Let's start raking in the bucks! The consequence of this for you is increased competition, sometimes by musicians who aren't as good as you, but might be as committed to their industry. To cut through, and to develop and sustain your career, you have to focus on your audience, on your performance, and on your business.

Live music has competition for attention. Sure, people go out and hear live music. Sometimes. But there are many more diversions, and whether or not we like it, this is eating into our audiences. One of the biggest threats to performance is the rise of streaming media. In 2018, Netflix generated an income of US $4.19 billion. Instead of going out, potential consumers stay home, turn on Netflix and binge-watch the latest series. Even if potential audiences are engaging with music, they are more likely to ask their smart speaker to stream Spotify than they are to go out and hear an actual gig. But it's not all doom and gloom. The evidence is that people do create successful careers at all levels of the industry, from regularly gigging musicians to international mega stars. However, there are two things that these musicians do well: They focus on their audiences, and they maintain a professional industrial approach. They know that their audiences are paying for them to perform and they craft musical experiences to engage them. If you're going to have a chance at dragging audiences away from their television sets, you're going to have to do that as well. You need to engage with your audience, make them feel connected, perform well, and always, always consider them.

Engaging With Your Audience in Performance

Audiences want to feel connected to you. They want to understand what you're singing about and to feel that you're only singing to them. If there's one performance art you always need to work on, it's how to connect with the audience. This can be tricky. Depending on the venue and the size of the lighting rig, you may not even be able to see your audience. You may not even see the first row. So you may need to learn to connect with an audience that you can't see, but still make it so that each one of them thinks you are singing to them. Easy, right? Well, perhaps not. When we talked to the masterful performers that formed our interviewees, they made a few suggestions for engaging with your audience, and I offer them here for your consideration.

The first thing they said was that where you look is important. Humans take in a lot of important information about the world through their eyes. If you're not looking at the audience, you don't make that connection. Face your audience. Don't fix your gaze. Move it around. Do a Taylor Swift: Stand at the front of the stage and just look out at the audience, moving around. Taylor probably can't see many of them, but because she moves her gaze, it gives the illusion of contact. Ultimately, that contact in performance is what you want your audience to experience.

Moreover, your eyes aren't the only sense you have on stage. You might not see your audience over the glare of the lights. But you can hear them. When you hear the audience, when you hear someone say something, like a laugh, or a reaction to a song, play to it. Talk back to them. You're trying to acknowledge your audience. Do it in any way possible.

Remember that your audience is visual, but also encultured. We in the West associate strong movements with confidence, so it pays to consider your movement. Strive to make your on-stage persona (and thus your movements) strong, confident, and decisive. Think about what your movement says. Think about what an excited type of movement, such as running around the stage, says about your music compared with standing in the middle of the stage without movement. They both have their place, but you should choose them intelligently. Are your movements wishy-washy? If so, what can you do to counteract that?

Direct engagement with audiences is a great idea. It's not always possible, but if it is, after a few songs, pick your radio mike off the stand and get out and into the audience. It helps to have a follow spot (or, if the venue is small, a sound engineer with a very bright torch). But directly engaging with your audience within the performance makes it just that much more memorable.

Your set list is also a big part of your engagement with the audience. Pay attention to it and craft it well. Each and every song you play has a different dramatic intent. Slow, fast, quiet, loud, major, minor, acoustic, electric—they all mean different things. Slower, quieter songs draw people in. Louder, faster songs excite people. You need to take people on a musical journey. Craft it well. Revise it after performances.

Think about how you introduce each song. Sometimes you'll segue from one song into another without speaking. Other times, you'll talk about the song before it starts. You might talk over an introduction, talk over a vamp, or have the pianist noodle softly while you introduce the next song. You might say what this song means to you. You might tell the story of how you came across it, or how you came to write it. Plan what you'll say beforehand, but make your introductions seem spontaneous. Remember that musical performances are about smoke and mirrors. While everything has to seem authentic and spontaneous and fun, in reality, there's a lot of planning that has to happen if you want your audiences to remember your performances.

When you're playing, it's easy to get caught up in how great it is … even how great you are. In performance, be authentic and humble. Most audiences want honesty in performance. We've talked about this, but it's worthwhile returning to.

Be authentic. One performer known to us used to begin his performance by standing in the centre of the stage with his arms spread waiting for applause before he'd played a note. Agents and bookers who observed this behaviour recounted how they were reluctant to book him again. I advise you to watch how the big performers interact. They are enthusiastic, brash, fun, talented, but rarely do they fail to appreciate their audiences.

The physical and sonic environment you're playing in affects your performance and affects the audience. Good venues are designed with great acoustics, and with great audience sightlines. However, these are rare and specially designed for live music performances. They're also probably very expensive to rent out and perform in. The greater proportion of live music venues fall into one of three categories. Some of them adopt existing spaces from previous purposes, such as banks, restaurants, or strip clubs with little or no alteration. Just put a stage up, hang a few lights, and put in a thousand-dollar sound system all designed by their cousin. Other venues adapt these spaces by some minor rebuilding. Sometimes, venues are temporarily erected and torn down afterwards, such as at a festival. Each of these scenarios mean that you need to allow for less than perfect environments. Sometimes you won't have good audience sightlines. Sometimes the audience won't hear you distinctly. But with humour, and good backline, you'll be able to counter this.

Employ and plan for audience participation. Queen were masters at this. Plan ways to get the audience singing. Get them chanting back. Get them clapping. Use songs that have audience-participation sections. Make sure they feel they are part of the performance, not merely passive consumers. Encouraging audience participation empowers an audience to create energy and join in the joy of performance.

Enjoy yourself. We keep coming back to the joy of your performance. It's an important one for your audience. If you are enjoying yourself on stage, if they see you enjoying yourself on stage, they will interact. This is where the seemingly unplanned banter comes up on stage. Where the goofy joyful grins appear. If you don't look like you're enjoying yourself on stage, the audience won't either!

THE RECEPTION OF THE AUDIENCE

A successful performance deeply touches and inspires the audience in some way. This might be in terms of their mood, courage, balance, or his/her understanding of life and of him or herself. For me, the performance is not only about the "product", the music itself, but also includes the background/reasons/motivations for why the performer is performing his/her music in the particular way he/she does. For me, it's not enough for someone to perform simply because he or she likes to be on stage. I want to witness music giving their life a deeper meaning. I think that a performance is successful when every audience member feels special and touched individually, when they like to think back to the atmosphere of the concert and remember the ways in which it inspired them.

Olivia, Jazz singer and pianist

Developing Your Audience

The process of audience development establishes a relationship between musicians and consumers of live performance. Once you get audiences to your gigs through good promotion, you need to keep them coming back. Audience development is about turning casual audiences into fans.

Do you think you have a good relationship with your fans? Classical music critic Greg Sandow has five questions he asks to consider whether a performer has a successful relationship with their audience.

- Are your gigs full? Do you sell lots of tickets?
- What is your audience response? Do you get applause at the appropriate time?
- Is your audience engaged and commenting online?
- Are you selling merchandise?
- Is there a buzz about you in whatever genre you perform?[1]

If you can answer yes to each of these questions, congratulations. You're probably developing your audience pretty well. However, it's more likely that you need to work on one area or another. Large organisations, record labels, opera companies, and symphony orchestras have personnel and departments dedicated to audience engagement. You probably don't have that luxury.

Audience development revolves around several areas. You need to consider these when you are planning your performance, your brand, and your music. And you need to keep returning to it as the industry changes and new methods of reaching audiences develop. Fundamentally, you need to ask yourself:

- Who are my audiences? (Demographics)
- Why do they come out to hear me? (Audience motivation)
- How do I increase my audiences?
- How do I keep audiences coming back to see me? (Fan development)

Let's consider these in turn.

Demographics

Before the 1950s, contemporary music was marketed to the whole family. Everyone from grandparents to parents and teenagers to toddlers would gather around the radio to hear Frank Sinatra doo-bee-doo-bee-doo. Then rock and roll emerged, and with it the realisation that there was a market for music specifically created for young people. This had literally never occurred to the music industry before. Young people became the key demographic that contemporary music targeted. In the early 1960s, young men and women such as Bobby Vee, Connie Francis, and Neil Sedaka sang industry-approved songs of romantic love created for young people. The Beatles played to young people.

The Rolling Stones, David Bowie, Madonna, these successful musicians knew precisely who they were singing to.

To be successful in an industry, you have to know your audience. Are you performing to 30-somethings? Teenagers? Gen Y? Baby boomers? Super-successful performers know their audience. They write and perform to them. We're not suggesting you take surveys after gigs, but you need to be aware of who you're playing to, because it affects everything about your musical performance. You need to know their age, their listening habits, where they are from, what kinds of venues they attend, and what might prevent them from coming out to gigs. You need to know how to get in touch with them. Facebook or Instagram? Loud posters wrapped around telegraph poles in the inner city, or quieter notices in shop windows? Naked skydiving on fire while tailing a large fluorescent sign about your gig or a few lines in a church newsletter? Knowing your target demographic will enable you to target your branding specifically to these people.

Audience Motivation

The reasons people give for attending a performance are called the audience motivation. Somewhat surprisingly for one of the main methods of consuming music, we know little about why people attend live music performances. We know why people attend music festivals (from tourism studies), and some things about why people attend theatre or museums; however, few people have undertaken studies into music attendance. And this is important because unless you know why they come, you won't know how to get them to come.

So why do people come out to hear live performances? Let's look at two studies, one that is broad and one that is pragmatic. A 2012 study on audience motivation in the theatre[2] posited that people attend theatre for five broad reasons.

- They attend for spiritual reasons, such as escapism, immersion, reflection, aesthetic appreciation, and pleasure.
- They attend for sensual/sensory reasons, such as the visceral response to the performance.
- They attend for emotional reasons, such as empathy with the performers or getting an emotional response to the performance.
- They attend for intellectual reasons, such as wanting to be challenged by a performance.
- They attend for social reasons, such as spending time with friends and partaking in a live experience.

Theatre, like music, is about the creation of experience, and these broad categories are worth considering in your performance. Plan your performances around these. For example, in this study, audiences need aspects of escapism. So how do you incorporate escapism into your performances? Where do you take your audiences for them to escape from their everyday lives?

Another 2001 study[3] was perhaps a little more pragmatic and directly related to live music. It cited seven specific positive reasons for attending live music:

- Because of curiosity and to listen to the music performed at that specific concert.
- To experience the joy created in live music attendance.
- To sample the music of an unknown musician without great commitment.
- To worship their musical heroes.
- To access opportunities for uninhibited behaviour.
- The social aspect, hanging out with friends in a laid-back atmosphere.
- To experience the ritual of live music performance.

Live music has changed since 2001 from an auxiliary to the core of the industry, but many of these reasons remain. Look at the keywords here: Curiosity, experience, sampling music, worship, uninhibited behaviour, social/friends, ritual. These are the concepts you need to consider.

TALENTED RECORDING ARTIST, DISAPPOINTING LIVE PERFORMER

Not that long ago I went to see [name redacted] and was completely disappointed with her because I thought she's such a talented girl and a talented songwriter. I loved what she was writing. I loved her music. I listened to it all the time. Then I went to see her live, and it was like she was just not interested in the audience at all. It was like she was going through the motions, it was like, "I really want to just record and sell my CDs". She was in with her band and there was nothing for the audience. I've never been so disappointed. She didn't interact with the crowd. It was like she didn't want to be there … almost like performing was just the last thing she wanted to do. She gave me nothing. And that came through in the show. It was almost like we were schmucks having paid money to come and see her. That's what it felt like. Like they were almost having a bit of a joke at our expense.

Anthea, Promoter and singer

How Do I Attract New Audiences?

One of the ongoing arguments with venues is the process of promotion. Venues expect the band to do it, and the band expect the venue to do it. The result is that promotion is often not done at all. However, playing devil's advocate here, why would you trust the relationship between you and your source of income to someone else? Why leave promotion to venues? Don't get me wrong, I'm not saying that venues shouldn't promote their upcoming gigs. They should. Venues have their target audiences and they benefit from gigs as well as you do. I *am* saying that you should also promote yourself, your gigs, and your performances to your target demographic, to your audience and to your fans.

We will deal with promotion techniques in a later chapter. Promotion of yourself and your performances is a significant manner in which you will attract new audiences. However, it's not the whole package. Any opportunity you have to interact with your target demographic is a significant opportunity. Think about when and how you might promote your music and performances.

An obvious opportunity is at music festivals. Festivals are (usually) fun. As a performer, you get paid. (Sometimes not a lot, but that's okay.) You get to see other acts and see what other acts are like. You also get to sell merchandise. But, most importantly for your career, you get to encounter new audiences. Not only do you perform for them, you can talk with them in person, and create the relationships needed to make them fans. One of our informants noted:

> I travel the world to festivals, purely to discover new acts. Festivals engage audiences with their headliners, but also introduce new acts to the punters there for the experience. I also believe the merch aspect of acts at festivals functions strongly in engaging audiences with new markets.
>
> (Bel, Artist manager)

In short, get as many festivals as you can. It will pay more than financial dividends; it will increase your fan base.

Regional and rural areas are often starved of quality entertainment. One of our informants from a remote town in Australia noted that he would have music several times a week, but he couldn't find the musicians. Regular touring is a way to increase your fan base in other geographic locales. Regional areas are good because there may be less competition with other bands. Other urban areas also reap dividends because there are greater population bases that haven't heard of you and your music. This will be easier in geographical areas such as the UK or USA where urban areas are close together, and more difficult where they're spread out such as Australia and Canada.

How do I Keep Audiences Coming Back To See Me?

An audience member has seen you at a performance at a venue, or a festival. Your performance has been memorable. How do you keep them coming back to see you? How do you turn them into fans?

Developing fans out of audience members is about a relationship. When a new audience member walks into a gig, they don't know what to expect. They may have heard about you from a friend. Some slick promotion may have attracted them. They may have just wandered in for a beer. Whatever. An audience's relationship with you is a transaction. They invest time and money into coming to see you. You deliver an experience. Voila. The transaction. At the end of that experience, everyone goes their separate ways, hopefully to meet again in the future.

If your relationship with your fan base is going to flourish, it needs mainte-nance. You need to interact with your fans in ways that resonate with them. Fortunately, there are multiple methods and opportunities to interact with music consumers in the early 21st century. You might use social media to interact with lots of people at once. You might use email or direct messaging to build personal relationships with consumers. You might talk to them after gigs or at festivals. Use any opportunity you can to engage with audiences.

The easiest way to maintain relationships with your fans is through the regular contact of social media. In the olden times of BSM (before social media), art-ists used mailing lists. You'd go to a gig and, if they could, they'd sign you up as you were leaving. Or you'd stumble across their webpage and subscribe to their newsletter. You could then expect a solid stream of messages in your inbox tell-ing you when the band was coming to your area, what gigs were on, what songs were being released and so forth. These days, the many and varied forms of spam mean we ignore most emails that aren't related to work, friends, or family. But the idea was right. If you're going to turn casual audiences into fans who follow your performances, you need to engage them between gigs.

These days social media is the preferred manner of engagement. We'll go into the processes of social media later, but we should consider why we do it. The big acts have multiple social media presences. If they do, you should too. Take American jazz singer Patricia Barber. She's great. Go and have a listen. Patricia has a Twitter account (@pbjazzmusician), Instagram (@patriciabarbermusic), Facebook (www.facebook.com/PatriciaBarberJazzMusician), and a YouTube channel. She lists her upcoming gigs on Facebook events, posts stories from her Twitter account, and videos on her YouTube channel. She knows that engaging with fans is part of the job. That's how she gets fans. Result: Patricia Barber plays all the time. She tours the world. Her entire job is being a musician.

You need to do this too. I know, I know, social media is a drag. You'd rather be practising or writing songs, or in the studio or performing. Well, listen up. The business side of the industry is as much a part of your music career as the music. You need to be engaging with your audience. Don't set up social media accounts and forget about them. Or feel guilty about checking in once every two months. Set up social media accounts on Facebook, Twitter, and Instagram at least. Link to them from your webpage. Set aside time every few days or every week to update them. I mean it. Put this book down for ten minutes and do it now. Create con-tent. List gigs. Create videos for YouTube and link to them. Email or send direct messages to your most ardent fans. Use technology to interact smarter and faster with your audiences. (Just don't spam people!)

Social media is easy, and you can engage with a heap of people. However, social media can't beat the in-person touch. After gigs, go out and talk to people. I know it's tempting to just hang with the band afterwards talking about how awesome you were. But the awesomest awesomeness doesn't necessarily make

Figure 5.1 Patricia Barber at the stage at Victoria Teater in Oslo in 2017. Lineup: Patricia Barber (vocal/piano), Patrick Mulcahy (double bass) and Jon Deitemyer (drums). Source: Tore Sætre.

people fans. Personal contact with audience and fans does. People will remember the musician that was honest enough and confident enough and cared enough to walk out and talk to the audience.

Your audiences and fans want you to succeed. They want you to have great gigs. They want to love your music, go and hear you play, buy your merchandise, and listen to you on Spotify. But to really maintain them for months or years, you need to have a consistently high-quality musical product. You're only ever as good as your last gig. Good gigs maintain your audiences and fans, but bad gigs actively lose them. Work to build a consistently great product, then work on developing relationships.

Finally, a word of caution while you're focussing on building new fans. Don't neglect your existing ones. Keep talking and writing to your existing fans. They're the people who adore you. And there's a hundred other musicians wanting them to come and hear *them*, buy *their* merchandise, and listen to *them* on Spotify.

The Hard Word

Here's some hard truth. If audiences are not coming to your show or not reacting when they do, it is not their fault. It's yours. Sometimes, after a bad performance, you might hear one of the musicians blaming the audience for not responding to the music. Shouting that they are all proles and don't understand the art and hard work the musicians have put in. No attitude in the music industry is less professional and more likely to sink your career. If the audience doesn't respond to your show, if they don't come, if they ignore you, even if they heckle you, it is always, always your fault.

Now, we're not talking about if you're not being booked. There can be mitigating reasons for that. Perhaps you need to work on your promotion. Sometimes industry politics can enter into it. Perhaps you've annoyed a booker around town. Perhaps your act is being sabotaged by rival acts. Sometimes you need to reconsider your business approach. These are things you can deal with.

An audience, however, is different. When an audience doesn't respond, it's time to take a long, hard look at what you do on stage. Play back some recordings of performances you've made. Ask people to watch them. Ask people who've seen you. Sometimes you can misread an audience, if they're quiet when you're performing or not responding as you want them to. This happened to me this week. I played a gig when they were quiet, but absolutely effusive after the show. But when you play to no applause, and after the gig everyone avoids you, you've got problems.

However, if you're reading this, you're likely talented, passionate, and reflective enough to see what's going wrong with your performance and revise your approach. Keep going!

Further Reading

There is a fair amount of work in fan studies, though relatively little on music. Still, there is some good further reading. There is some great work on popular music performance spaces by Robert Kronenburg. Denis McQuail's *Audience Analysis* is a little old, but still a useful introduction to audiences from the perspective of media studies. Bob Harlow's *The Road to Results* is a tome of useful information on audience development and promotion. It's targeted at large arts organisations, but you can also pick up some terrific ideas.

Chapter Summary

- Your audience is all important in planning your musical product and your career.
- Successful performances are a collaboration between musicians, the music industry, and audiences.
- Music audiences are:
    - Relatively small.
    - Active (not passive) in seeking their entertainment.
    - Pay your salary.
    - Want you to have a successful performance.
- A significant problem is that there are so many people trying to garner an audience in the industry that it is difficult to be heard above the white noise.
- In performance:
    - Where you look can engage audiences.
    - On-stage interaction when you see or hear audiences can engage them.

- How you move on stage is important.
- Getting out into the audience with a radio mike can make a performance memorable.
- Think about how you introduce songs.
- Audiences demand authenticity and honesty.
- The performance space and sound can affect audience reaction.
- You also need to develop your audience between performances.
  - Know the demographics of your audience.
  - Know why people come to hear you.
  - Attract new audiences.
  - Turn audiences into fans
- If audiences aren't responding positively, revise your musical product.

Notes

1 Lehrman, "What is Audience Engagement?"
2 Walmsley, "Why People Go to the Theatre: A Qualitative Study of Audience Motivation."
3 Earl, "Simon's Travel Theorem and the Demand for Live Music."

6   Working as a Musician

There are two different requirements to working as a live musician. The first requirement is to cover the gig. That's obvious. Covering the gig means playing technically well, practicing your work, rehearsing well, arriving at the performance on time, playing well and engagingly, and accepting the collective responsibilities of the gig. The other requirement of being a live musician is equally important. You must get on with people. It's said that there is a 60/40 rule here. Forty percent of being a successful musician is about covering the music. Sixty percent is about not being a jerk. As a musician, you must get on with all kinds of crazy people. Despite the popular perception that musicians are aggressive and unpleasant, in reality, musicians that have a long career tend to have a very long fuse and get on with people. They are not prima donna singers, aggressive guitarists, geeky and unsociable keyboardists, dark, moody bass players, or meathead drummers. They are just normal people making music. We are all in this together. Being a good hang is part and parcel of being a good live musician. Musicians with poor social skills who grate on their bandmates don't last long.

In this chapter, we'll take a long, hard look at your fellow musicians. (It's actually better than it sounds.) We'll look at what musicians need to perform, and how to get on with them.

Different Musical Roles in a Band

When you perform solo, you undertake all roles in the band; however, in an ensemble there are a range of different jobs, all of which need to be undertaken if the band is going to succeed. In practice, there are four main roles for performing musicians in bands:

The person in the leadership role of a band is the bandleader. They often represent the band within the industry. They typically run rehearsals and performances.

The person who leads the in-performance engagement with the audience, who is the star performer, and who is in the spotlight, is called the frontperson. They often represent the band in the minds of the public.

Other members of the band, who perform as a part of the band, but who do not front the band nor take leadership roles are called bandmembers.

Musicians who perform with a band but are not part of the band are called sidepersons.

Let's consider the role of each of these musicians.

Bandleader

In any group of people, you will have someone who is a leader. Sometimes this is the lead singer. Billy Joel, Elton John, Shania Twain, Dolly Parton, Michael Bublé: These people are headliners as well as bandleaders. Sometimes the bandleader is someone other than the headliner. Guitarist Brian Jones or bass guitarist Bill Wyman (depending on who you ask) led the Rolling Stones through their most successful period between 1962 and 1968. Organist Jon Lord ran Deep Purple. And what about Jimmy Page and Led Zeppelin? Go into jazz and you find the Basie band, the Ellington band, Diana Krall, Miles Davis, Alice Coltrane, Nina Simone and more. I can keep going. In country, you've got The Charlie Daniels Band, Alison Krauss, and Union Station. Even when bands are democracies with everyone having a say, someone usually graduates to a de facto leadership position. No matter what genre, what style, what music you're playing, if you aspire to running a band, you need to have to undertake certain jobs.

First and most importantly, bandleaders are consummate professionals. Despite the popular portrayal of musicians as being disorganised party animals that booze too much and are just too creative to exist in the real world, in reality, it takes enormous amounts of knowledge, discipline, business acumen, hard work, and down-to-earthness to make it in the modern industry. Most of these responsibilities fall on the shoulders of bandleaders. It is their responsibility to schedule and prepare rehearsals, organise shows, deal with industry, promote performances, and present the band in a positive, professional light. They cannot do this if they are in the corner with a beer and a cigarette.

THE RESULTS OF DISORGANISATION AND UNPROFESSIONALISM

I played a couple years ago in a small venue where we had a rehearsal before the performance that night. All the musicians and people from the tech team were late (the band leader was the latest). Not to mention, there were at least five key changes and an arrangement change thrown in at the last minute. It was so embarrassing performing because you could see how unorganised the whole night was. Also sounded shit too.

Anita, Guitarist

Bandleaders have to be extraordinarily patient. Getting a band to where you want them to be takes time and energy. You need to prepare, practice, rehearse, and organise until the band is ready for just the right moment. And you need to recognise when that moment is, when all your ducks are in a row, and then strike quickly and in an organised fashion.

Effective bandleaders are invariably respectful and open-minded. Every musician in a band brings their own experience and talent. Bandleaders need to value and encourage that. If one person is making all the decisions about a band, you have the creative output of a single brain. If everyone in the band feels empowered and permitted to contribute, you have the creative output of several brains. That will result in a better and happier band. Respect everyone's contributions and make allowances for different ideas. Try to see things from different people's creative and musical points of view.

Bandleaders keep an eye on the big picture. Even though bands can change in the short term, even though circumstances can alter, the leader keeps their eye on the big prize. They know where they want to be. Yet, bandleaders are also masters at the little details, and don't let things fall between the cracks. It's hard to maintain both, yet good bandmasters manage it.

Bandleaders have to be decisive. They're confident and quick in their decision-making. As a bandleader, you might be faced with two equally good options. You'll have to choose. But which one? A good bandleader makes their decision and then sticks to it.

If you're working as a bandleader, you need to give people the room to be creative. Micromanagement is a curse for bandleaders. You need to encourage people to give their opinions. Sometimes you might even have to run with an idea you don't agree with. If you do, your bandmates are more likely to invest in the band. Treat everyone, the band, the backline, management, venue staff, everyone, pretty much as you'd like to be treated.

Finally, bandleaders are self-aware. They acknowledge that they are not flawless. They need to toe the line between guiding and control. Effective bandleaders are rarely control freaks; they allow people to run with their ideas and opinions. They empower rather than control. They treat everyone associated with the gig in a friendly, professional fashion.

Frontperson/Lead Singer

Before we get into this next role, I should make a comment. The industry term for this position is the very gendered 'frontman'. 'Lead singer' also describes the role, which is fine unless the role is being performed by someone who is not, or is not exclusively, a singer. Not wishing to exclude female performers who wish to front a band, I've gone with the gender-neutral 'frontperson'.

The frontperson and their personality often defines the band to the public. Think Peter Garrett in Midnight Oil, Chrissie Hynde in The Pretenders, Brian Setzer in the Stray Cats, Debbie Harry in Blondie. They interact with the audience and form the focus of attention. The lead singer often, but not always, takes the role of the frontperson. It is possible for a band to have more than one frontperson. Lambert, Hendricks & Ross worked together as frontpersons. So did Sam and Dave, The Runaways, and The Doobie Brothers.

The frontperson may be the official spokesperson for the band. This involves representing the band to the public and the press. However, this is not always the case. Angus and Malcolm Young were the official spokespersons for AC/DC, but the lead singers were Dave Evans, Bon Scott, Brian Johnson, and Axl Rose.

If you are the frontperson, it is your job to engage the audience in the performance. Talk to them. Engage them. Dance around on stage. Sweat. Sing to them. The frontperson acts as the conduit between the band and the audience. They may introduce the band members to the audience. They may appear to control the music (even if they don't). They perform with the force of a thousand-watt bulb no matter how they feel. If your dog has just died, your partner has left you, and your car has just been repossessed, you still need to go out and give the audience a show.

Bandmembers

Bandmembers are permanent members of the band. However, they are not bandleaders and they are not frontpersons. They will play in every performance of the band. They may have their moments to shine, particularly when they solo. However, they should let the frontperson do what they do and play to the audience. This doesn't mean that you sit or stand motionless when you're playing. Move around. Engage with each other. Even engage with the audience. Just remember the frontperson is typically the conduit between the band and the audience.

Not all musical entities use bandmembers. Sometimes it's just the frontperson and a collection of contracted sidepersons. Ed Sheeran, Taylor Swift, Beyoncé, Justin Bieber, Elton John, Billy Joel, Madonna, Michael Jackson, Michel Bublé, Lee Kernaghan, and many others use sidepersons rather than bands. It is much easier to deal with a truculent and troublesome musician to terminate a contract than it is to legally move them out of a band.

Sidepersons[1]

Sidepersons are the musicians that play with the band but are not legally or actually part of the band. But they may be as talented. Ever heard of Earl Slick? He's David Bowie's guitarist who played with him for decades. What about Bernard Fowler? He's been a backing singer for the Rolling Stones since 1989 and has also worked with Duran Duran, Michael Hutchence, Alice Cooper, and Herbie Hancock. Kenny Aronoff is a drummer who has toured with John Fogerty, Smashing Pumpkins, and Joe Cocker. How about Wendy (Melvoin) and Lisa (Coleman) who were key members of Prince's band in the late 1980s? There are a lot more. The best-known bandmembers of Nirvana were Kurt Cobain, Krist Novoselic, and Dave Grohl. Between 1992 and 1994, they also toured with sidepersons John Duncan (guitar), Lori Goldston (cello, 1992–1993), Melora Creager (cello, 1994) and Pat Smear (guitar, backing vocals). Sidepersons are so significant that in 2000, the Rock and Roll Hall of Fame introduced a 'sideman' category.

A sideperson is to the live music industry as a session musician is to the recording industry. They may perform at gigs or on tour with star performers. They rehearse up a show, play on stage, and appear as part of the band. But they are outside of the legal entity of the band. They are basically employees or contractors to the band. Once the gig or tour is over, the band has no obligation to continue to use them. Consider Bruce Springsteen's E Street Band. Springsteen used the E Street Band from 1972 to 1989. In 1989, he informed them he would not be using them for the foreseeable future, and the band went their separate ways. However, none of them were as successful on their own as they had been in the band. In 1999, Springsteen reunited with the band, but in late 2018, he announced new music that did not feature the band.

If you are working as a sideperson, you need to become invisible. You are there for your musical abilities only. Your number one job is to make the frontperson and (if they exist) the bandmembers look good, sound good, and feel good. You need to get on with everyone and just make music. You need to be a capable player and a good hang. Earl Slick once said: "If you've got an ego to satisfy you're in trouble". It helps to have a musical connection with the star. You also need a good work ethic, as often you need to learn an entire setlist in a few days. The frontperson may become a close friend over decades. Or they may use you for one gig only. Always remember, though, that this is a business relationship.

FLORENCE AND THE MACHINE AND THE PERFORMANCE ENERGY

I remember we were trying to break Florence and the Machine when she played The Metro in Sydney. It's an interesting one because now she's a really big artist. Her success seems a forgone conclusion. But at the time, a very senior person in the organisation I was working for said she had the worst record that he'd ever heard in his whole life. Someone else senior commented that radio would never play her. So while it seems pretty obvious now, it wasn't at the time. One of the key tipping points in terms of wanting to back her financially for what we were doing in this market, was when she played The Metro. You could just feel the energy coming back off the audience to her performance. She was giving energy out in the first place. It told me that this was one to back.

Tim, Record executive

The Difference Between Bandmembers and Sidepersons

The difference between bandmembers and sidepersons can be a little blurry. You could argue that because Springsteen was so easily able to discard them, the E Street band were sidepersons. Kurt Cobain was founder and lead singer of Nirvana, and Krist Novoselic and Dave Grohl were bandmembers. It would have been difficult for Nirvana to exist without Novoselic and Grohl. Before she started her own bands, Tal Wilkenfeld toured with Jeff Beck for several years. Jeff noted, "It's interesting to have some amazing players in my band like Tal, who is about, you know half, a quarter of the age of either Vinnie or me. She's a genius. She will pick up mistakes that we, even Vinnie and I, miss. So she's a great anchor as well".[2] Rob Hirst, Jim Moginie, Martin Rotsey, and Bones Hillman were part of Midnight Oil for decades: They weren't the frontperson, but they certainly weren't sidepersons. The difference is usually legal. Bandmembers are legally part of the band and they may contribute songs. Sidepersons are not. They are contracted for a set number of performances that may be renewed or extended, but the frontperson is under no legal obligation to do so.

Communicating on Stage

Normally, in performance, a show will run smoothly. You've rehearsed and practised, and everything will go fine. However, sometimes things will happen that you need to address on stage. Perhaps a song is started too fast, or an ending needs to be coordinated. You can't yell across the stage without upsetting the flow of the music, so such adjustments and direction need to be done with physical communication. Even if an entire show is tracked, you need to watch the bandleader or the frontperson as they can require adjustments, If you are a sideperson or bandmember, you will need to understand the flow of on-stage communication. This is why on-stage sightlines are so important. When you set up, ensure that you can see everyone. As a pianist, sometimes I may have to turn around to observe the drummer, but when I perform, I can see everyone on the stage fairly easily.

Every bandleader or frontperson will have their own signals. I used to have a frontperson lean over and hiss things as me such as 'cocktail!' when he wanted me to play piano high and sparse. However, there are some reasonably common physical signals:

- The tempo before a song's start can indicated in a number of ways:
  - The bandmaster can silently conduct or tap two fingers together.
  - The drummer (who may be the only person listening to the click track) can click his sticks together four times.
- The bandleader can conduct changes to tempo using standard conducting methods.
- An increase in tempo can be indicated by a raised index finger moving quickly in a circle. This can also indicate that the band is to repeat a passage.

- A decrease in tempo can be indicated by a raised index finger moving slowly in circle.
- A decrease in volume can be indicated by the bandleader's hand moving gently downwards.
- A solo is indicated by watching either the bandleader or the person who is soloing. They will look at you and nod.
- A rallentando or held ending is indicated one of two ways:
  - The bandleader raises their arm to show that the ending is held. They will then drop their arm quickly to indicate the ending.
  - The drummer moves their sticks and body to indicate the ending.
- A cutoff can be indicated by the bandleader holding his hand open and closing it quickly when he wants the band to finish.

Figure 6.1 Australian bassist Tal Wilkenfeld playing with Jeff Beck in 2009. Source: Guillaume Laurent.

Conflict in the Band

Any group of people who spend enough time together will inevitably have some conflict. Add to that the pressure cooker of long rehearsals, live performance and touring, of passion and excitement and ego, and you have a situation that has the potential to lead to full-on pitched battles and flying instruments. Plenty of bands have ended through conflict. ABBA, Guns N' Roses. The Fugees. Oasis. Rage Against the Machine. You don't want to join their ranks. Musicians are strong, opinionated people. By the nature of the job, we're passionate. Passion is good. It's what keeps us writing, recording, and performing. But it comes with a belief and a commitment that your way is the best way and everyone else is wrong. Hopefully, your disagreements can be kept fairly minor. Hopefully, most of the conflicts you experience in your career will be minor ones. Alas, sometimes they may not be. Disagreements between band members have a way of spiralling out of control and suddenly this great group of people that actually like each other most of the time are flinging snare drums and bass amps and going their separate ways. And there goes not only the lost potential of the band, but possibly years of hard work. For what? So someone can be right? You need to plan to overcome conflict so that it doesn't affect your ability to make music.

To do that, you need to develop a thick skin and empathy. This isn't always easy for we artists. Any band needs a certain amount of tolerance towards each other. Sometimes you don't like a bandmate. Sometimes you may not have chosen to be friends with them outside of the performance scenario. That's okay. It happens. But you need to respect them and listen to their opinions. I may be telling you something you know already, but among the legions of happy, well-adjusted musicians, there is the occasional oddball. As professionals working in a band, you need to develop a healthy immune system for everyone. If a fellow-musician grates on you, that's fine. Don't hang out with them outside the band. But get on with them in the same way you would get along with an unpleasant colleague.

Other problems can rear their heads. Sometimes a band might have a problem with a particular bandmember. One day, because of unforeseen circumstances, someone will have to miss a rehearsal. Perhaps they might even miss even a gig (though they better have a very good reason for this!) Small and infrequent issues can be given a pass. Occasionally though, a pattern develops. Perhaps there is repeated poor or unprofessional behaviour from a particular band member. Perhaps they're failing to attend rehearsals. Perhaps they consistently run late. Every band member is responsible for their own action towards the band, so you collectively need to change this behaviour. It may be a good idea to organise to approach this bandmember collectively. Maybe you need to identify consequences for the actions. If the bandmember persists, you may have to resort to firing them and finding someone new. Avoid this is you can, though, because it is difficult. There is no endless stream of amazing musicians.

Sometimes, the issues in a band run deeper than that and affect multiple players. Sometimes there is an undercurrent of disenchantment in the band. This can be poisonous. If you're the bandleader, you must act. Identify the root of the problem. Do bandmembers feel that they have no creative control? Is it about money? Does someone feel disempowered? Is someone experiencing personal issues? These are fairly common in the live music world and fairly easy to manage once they have been identified. You need to encourage people to be open and honest in their communication. The situation left unresolved will fester until the aforementioned snare drums and guitar amps are flying.

So what do you do when there's conflict in the band? Like any group of people, a band needs a process for working out conflicts. There can be several methods for this. Perhaps someone is appointed peacemaker. Perhaps the leader intervenes. Perhaps you get an outside arbitrator. If your band is experiencing repeated conflicts, you need a way of dealing with it. Don't leave it until it affects the music. Deal with it now. If you can't come to a final solution, you might just need to agree to disagree and work out a compromise solution. This is not an ideal resolution, but it is professional. What you want to do is avoid a permanent split above all else. If you keep your professionalism—for you are professionals after all—you can run your band like a business and leave the emotions out of it.

Working With Other Artists 101

Working with other musicians can be a lot of fun. And it can also be a lot of not fun. Creating music is an intense and euphoric experience. We make friendships with our bandmates that last a lifetime. However, that doesn't mean we musicians are always easy to work with. We are driven and perfectionist. The process of making music (in particular our own songs) can cause insecurities and anxieties. The fear of public failure in front of an audience and in front of our peers terrifies us. The insecure nature of the work can besiege our mental health. Problems in interpersonal relationships have reigned destruction on more bands than nearly anything else you can think of. Fundamentally though, most musicians you play with want to work with you. We want to make awesome music, hang out with brilliant people, and to feel satisfied with what we do. So how do you do this with your happy band of musical malcontents?

Let me first talk about trust. Trust is important to making music. There are three kinds of trust it takes to be a live musician: Professional trust, social trust, and musical trust. Professional trust is the trust that each different person in the ensemble is an experienced and skilful musician. You might know the other people in the band by reputation. Perhaps you have mutual friends who speak highly of your bandmates. Perhaps you'd not met them before you started working with them. Whatever the reason, that professional trust is the first step along the road. It is the knowledge that the people you're working with take their job seriously, are reliable, and will honour their musical and financial obligations. The second trust is social trust. This is the trust that not only are the musicians you're working with good musicians, but they're also good people. This takes time spent in each other's company. As musicians, this happens in the trenches of the rehearsal room, or in the venue, or on the road. It means becoming friends as well as bandmates. The third trust, musical trust, can be described as a sort of musical extrasensory perception. When you're playing or improvising, your bandmates will automatically understand what you're doing and adjust their playing to accommodate. It is unnerving when it first happens, but it's the most rewarding of the three types of trust. It means that this band you have is working effectively and to your musical capacity. This only happens with all three types of trust.

Let me tell you a rock story to illustrate a point. In 1982, The Clash were having difficulty dealing with success. They were an edgy punk band that had suddenly become mega-stars when they released "Rock the Casbar", and they didn't really know how to cope. Worse, everyone wanted to go in a different direction. Guitarist Mick Jones was exploring hip hop, bassist Paul Simonon was interested in reggae, and frontperson Joe Strummer wanted to return to the core values of punk. In 1983, they kicked Mick Jones out of the band and used replacement guitarists until 1986. Nothing can bring a band unstuck more quickly than different visions for what it's trying to achieve. Perhaps the singer sees the band as a vehicle for themselves, whereas the rest of the band wants it to be a collective. Perhaps the drummer wants to tour, but the bass player wants to stay at home with their children. Maybe half the band wants to exclusively record, and the other half wants to exclusively perform. How do you know that you're all on the same page unless you discuss these things? When you first work professionally in a band, ensure that you have a discussion about what each of you wants. Write it down. When you bring someone new into the band for whatever reason, ensure that they understand what the band is about and why. This will ease problems down the track.

Allow people to be moody. You'll be working closely with your fellow musicians, and we're all human. I've got some news for you: People are temperamental. You can be temperamental. There will be times that someone in the band is not in a good mood. There'll be times when people have events happening in their lives that you'll be unaware of. As musicians, you need to respect people's space. If someone is curt with you, most of the time it has nothing to do with you. Just move on. As much as possible, don't get frustrated or offended. Just get on with rehearsing, playing, or whatever is going on. If they have an issue with you or something you've done, they'll tell you.

WHEN TO LEAVE PEOPLE ALONE

Years ago, I was working in a band in Miami. It was a pretty good reading band, but the saxophonist got sick and we had to find someone else for a couple of months. We got in an awesome alto player. Brilliant player. But my god was the man moody! In two months, I don't think I ever saw him smile or volunteer a comment. Usually he looked sour and unpleasant. But he was a good player and it was only for two months. One night after a gig, I saw him backstage looking darker than usual. I asked him if anything was wrong, and he exploded: "I wish to fuck everyone in this band would just leave me the fuck alone!" I backed off real fast, and never asked him again. Never did find out what his story was.

David, Pianist, author of this book

The ability to criticise is an imperative for musicians. We are all in this together, and we're working towards creating something superlative. Everyone's advice and critique is important to the product and no one can be left out. In a band, we need to have the freedom to criticise what our fellow musicians are doing. However, there are two caveats with this freedom. First, criticism must be constructive. It's not enough to say that some guitar solo was terrible. You need to articulate why you thought it was terrible. Second, you need to separate criticism of what someone is doing musically with who they are as a person. We musicians draw a lot of our personal identities from being musicians. Do not remove that from us. Unless you can do these two things, you will never be able to criticise musicians effectively.

Understand the difference between destructive narcissism and normal ego. Everyone that plays on a stage before an audience has a certain amount of ego. You don't seek the spotlight unless you do. However, when that ego and that sense of self-importance becomes extreme, it also becomes destructive. You might have worked with people who can never take criticism, even the smallest amount. Who treat others—who treat you—like servants there to cater to their whims. Who lie, cheat, and manipulate with no sense of remorse. These are the people you really don't want to work with. If you come across them in the industry, run!

Chapter Summary

- There are different jobs in the band:
  - Bandleaders represent the band to the industry and direct the band in rehearsal and performance.
  - The frontperson leads the in-performance engagement with the audience and is the face of the band. They may be a lead singer or play another instrument.
  - Bandmembers always perform as part of the band. They are usually legal part owners of the band.
  - Sidepersons are musicians who perform in the band but are not legal owners of the band. They are typically musical contractors. They may perform with a band for many years.
- It is important to understand non-verbal communication on stage.
- Inter-band conflict needs to be managed.
- All musicians need to know how to work with industry.
- Working with other artists is a skill unto itself. You need to work at it.

Notes

1 The industry term here is usually the gendered 'sidemen'. However the term 'sidepersons' is not without precedent. I've opted to use that term.
2 Moore, "Rocker Jeff Beck Returns to Australia."

Section 2

Making the Money: The Business of the Live Music Industry

In the second section, we look at the industry. If you're going to be a live musician, you have to learn about the live music business, how it works, and how to maximise your earning potential within it. Let's dive into the seamy underbelly of the live music industry!

7 The Players in the Live Music Industry

How often have you been told that the music industry is dead? Well, consider this. Of the 20 biggest tours of all time (calculated on gross and adjusted for inflation) 13 have occurred since 2011. (Wasn't the music industry supposed to be coughing up blood by then?) Only one was before 2000 (the Rolling Stones *Voodoo Lounge* tour of 1994–1995). The biggest completed tour of all time was U2's 360° tour of 2009–2011, which played 110 shows to 7,272,046 people, and earned a staggering $736 million (or about $820 million in 2019 dollars). In 2018, Ed Sheeran generated more than a $1 billion in a single year from touring but, at the time of writing, he is still on the road. By contrast, the biggest show of the 1980s was Pink Floyd's *Momentary Lapse of Reason* tour which earned $135 million ($272 million in 2019 dollars). Live music has come a long way. This is partly due to the rise in ticket prices, partly due to larger venues, and perhaps because more people are seeing live music. The recorded music industry has struggled for the past two decades, but there is certainly no evidence that live music is dying.

Different people undertake different roles within the live music industry. These roles are essential to the efficient operation of live performance. Sometimes one person undertakes a role; sometimes a group of people undertake one role. But each of these jobs is important. Each of these jobs need to be done if you're planning for a successful performance. A newly established band is likely to have the roles of music producer and bandleader and musician all undertaken by the same person. Perhaps they may also take on the role of the sound designer, lighting designer, manager, and promoter. In other, larger performances, specialists undertake these roles. Sometimes there are overlaps. But regardless of who does the jobs, it is essential that someone undertakes these roles for every performance. As a live music practitioner, you need to understand how these jobs integrate with each other and work together to create the beautiful, slick, oiled machinery of the live music industry.

As you become experienced in the industry, you will meet and learn to trust certain people. You'll end up with an audio engineer you work with regularly. Or an agent who is trustworthy. Maybe your manager will become a friend as well as a business colleague. You might also meet people you don't want to work with.

The bass player might be a great hang but can't show up on time. A sax player's intonation may be terrible, they can't solo, and can't cut the gig. You should always balance friendship with business. If you're to succeed in the music industry, by all means work with amazing, inspiring people that you like, but make sure they share your industrial approach to live music.

The People that Run the Industry

Let's have a look at the jobs that run the live music industry. These jobs occur in productions ranging from stadium events in front of thousands to small clubs with a couple dozen people in attendance. The six main roles of the live music industry are the producer, the performers (including the bandleader), the manager, the agent, the promoter, and the venue. However, there are myriad other essential

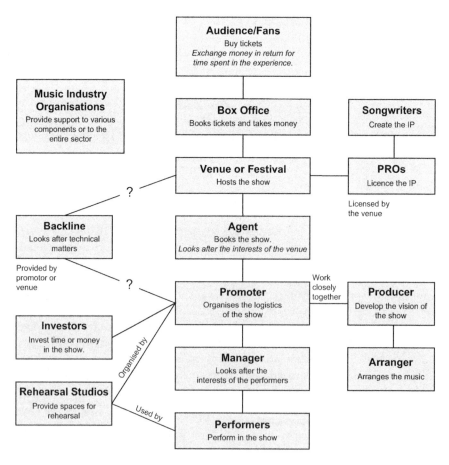

Figure 7.1 The main players in a live music performance.

personnel, such as the producer, songwriters, arrangers, backline, festivals, music industry organisations, and the like.

Producer

Historically, the music producer was the person who oversaw the production of a record. Now they also work in the live music industry. The music producer combines the theatrical and film role of director and producer. Their role is to oversee the production and development of a performance. That could be a nascent band you are developing or the latest Kylie Minogue dance extravaganza. In the early planning stages, the director will choose repertoire, establish the set list, and decide on the branding for the performance. They may develop staging. They may put up the money and/or time to develop the show, or they will find it from investors. They find musicians or arrange for them to be found. They may create or commission arrangements. The producer has the overall say on the direction of the show. They 'own' the performance.[1]

Performers

This is (probably) you. As live musicians, we are paid for our ability to create an engaging musical performance. As we've said, that requires musical ability, but also the ability to create an experience. As a musician, you have several responsibilities. You must turn up on time to rehearsals with the music learned. You must interact effectively and professionally with the other musicians. You must turn up on time for the sound check. You must take direction from the producer and bandleader and work effectively to realise their vision for the show. You may be a bandmember, frontperson, or a sideperson. You need to create the product in a musical and efficient way that aligns with the needs of the ensemble and industry.

Bandleader/Musical Director

There's a Romanian saying: Only one sword can fit a scabbard. The sword is the person of the musical director, and the scabbard is the leadership of a band. Bands may not particularly want to have bandleaders. Some prefer a homogenous and easy way of working among the musicians. However, in practice almost always one musician, whether by strength of musical ability or force of personality, will emerge as the bandleader. In some bands, for example theatre orchestras or name bands, the leader is imposed. In others, it may develop organically. But to be effective in the industry, one person needs to run the show.

If you are the bandleader, it is your responsibility to direct the other musicians and ensure a smooth and flawless preparation process and performance. You will typically run and organise rehearsals and run the band on the bandstand. You may count in numbers. The bandleader acts as a conduit between the role of the musicians and the role of the producer. This is important if the producer does not have musical skills. Here, it is the bandleader's job to interpret their intent and advise what is possible and what is not.

Artist Managers

As a musician, bandleader, or a producer may not have the business acumen, contacts, or the will to deal with the business aspects of the industry, the need for an artist manager comes in. A manager works with a band or musician to safeguard their business interests. They are there to create opportunities for you to perform your music in public and thus generate revenue. They are typically a professional businessperson rather than a musician and their involvement lets musicians get on with the business of songwriting, performing, recording, and whatever else they may do. The manager will deal with agents and venues and try to get you work. You pay them a commission for their work, which may vary but is often around the 10% mark.

You don't need an artist manager at the start of your career. Once you reach a certain point however, it's time to find an artist manager. Bel, an established and successful artist manager, observed:

> A musician should engage an artist manager when their time is taken over by the management side of their career. If they're spending too much time dealing with industry, record labels, agents, applying for funding, festivals, and gigs, it inevitably takes over from the creative process. It takes over from music making, songwriting, performing, recording, which the job of a musician. At that time, they need to find a good artist manager.

The trouble is that good artist managers are difficult to find. Good ones can be swamped by musicians who want to work with them. If you can find one, a dedicated and capable artist manager will increase your business by over their 10% commission (or whatever you negotiate). They will promote your work through their music industry networks to agents, record companies, publishers, venues, and to festivals. A good artist manager will keep you on the steady road of getting better while increasing your marketability and thus your profitability and ability to generate a career. This is a relationship worth developing. Artist managers deserve every trembling penny you pay them.

Booking Agents

The booking agent is the individual who connects an artist with paid performances at a venue. Some of their roles overlap with the artist manager's; however, whereas a manager's first loyalty is to the band, an agent's is to the venue. It's an important difference. This is not to suggest that agents are not the friends of musicians. Musicians are their product. They get into the industry to support live music. They love hanging around them. However, in a business sense, their first loyalty is to the venue.

Agents are completely involved in the live music industry. They don't get paid from the sale of recordings or from songwriting: Just from live performance.

They negotiate the fee a venue is willing to pay a performer for a performance, and check that the performers are willing to play for that. Sometimes this might involve a bit of back-and-forth negotiation. They might organise tours. They might organise television appearances. As the performers get bigger and more successful, they might coordinate available live performance dates with the manager and the record company to fill as many paying dates as possible—and check that the artist is willing to perform.

Like artist managers, agents work on commission. They are paid a percentage of all fees for performances they organise. Generally, venues pay the agent, then agents pay the artist manager, and then the artist manager pays the musicians. (If there's no artist manager, agents pay the musicians directly. The artist fee is usually around 10%.) Some agents will reduce their fees for major acts and larger tours because even small percentages on this kind of booking can generate considerable commissions for them. Agents who book small venues may charge higher than 10% to make it worth their while to handle lower-paying engagements.

Artists can be exclusive to agents for their performance bookings, meaning that there is only one agent that represents the artist for live performances. Some agents insist on regional exclusivity. Thus, a musician or group of musicians may be only able to book through one particular agent in a state or territory. This is not preferable and you should avoid it if you can. If you have an artist manager, they will deal with agencies for you.

THE PROBLEMS WITH AGENTS

An agent makes a couple of phone calls and then they think they deserve more money than the musicians do. That upsets me because I know that there's rooms that would have booked us back but they think we're too expensive because they paid too much for us. And they did pay too much for us. And I've seen it happen where a venue has come in and asked me to consult for them and they've shown me the acts that they've had in the past and what they paid for them. And I've nearly died because I know for a fact that those acts get half of that amount of money and I've just been horrified. Or where they give the venue a rider and they say, "Now you have to supply a bottle of scotch, a bottle of red wine, a dozen beers, fruit platters, cheese platters", the whole thing. And the venue's like, "Well, we can't afford to do this". That's terrible. I don't know about you, but the average person that I know, they go to work and nobody gives them a three course meal and alcohol while they're sitting at their desk doing their work.

> Q: So how do we get around that? Is there a way around it?
>
> It's hard because this industry has been run for a long time by certain groups of people. I've slowly sort of found a little niche. It's weird because being a female for a start, is a different thing. There's a lot of men in this business. They're learning now to deal with me because they sort of have to. I've got too many venues. I just genuinely want to keep this industry alive and I genuinely want to see people continue to work. I hate the idea of talented people having to, you know, go and work in a job that kills their soul because they can't get any work doing what they actually are good at doing.
>
> Anthea, Promoter and singer

Promoters

As the artist becomes well known and builds a sizeable fan base, the artist's booking agent will seek concert promoters. These will contract the artist for a performance or series of performances in a particular market. The promoter pays all the costs of producing and marketing a live performance and take all the financial risk. The promoter creates a budget, leases the venue, contracts with performers, hires local labour, leases all necessary production equipment and expertise, purchases all permits, pays all taxes and fees, pays for all marketing expenses, and supervises all aspects of the event. The specifics of these activities have the prior approval of the artist manager, and the tour manager has the final say on behalf of the manager on the day of the show. When the show is over, the artist and promoter are paid proportionally according to the contract. This proportion is known as the split point. It is divided from the remainder of earnings from the performance after everyone has been paid.

Venues

Venues are performance spaces that host performances. They range in size from huge stadiums holding tens of thousands of people to small clubs that might hold a few dozen. Typically, a venue employs an agent to find acts. Smaller venues may deal with band managers or even directly with the bands themselves.

Most venues are commercial enterprises. Local and city government may run some and make them available for hire. Others may be multipurpose, such as a bar that's primary purpose is serving food and drinks but may host performances to entice people to the venue. Others are primarily venues for performance. However, when dealing with venues, always remember that they are commercial enterprises. They are there to maintain profitability. You are there to assist them maintain that profitability. If they don't believe in your band, they won't book you no matter how awesome you think you are.

THE PRIVILEGE OF PLAYING AT A VENUE

Recently I've noticed a trend amongst club owners. The clubs/venues I've spoken to are seemingly trying to brainwash musicians into thinking that it is a privilege to appear there. I think this is symbolic of a problem. This brainwashing is what has created the concepts of playing for exposure, freebie first gigs, and the obscene "pay to play". Don't fall for this. If you have talent that you know has value and will attract customers/patrons to any venue, take back your turf. A gig is a mutual arrangement between a venue and an artist, where both should agree to a mutual risk if it doesn't work, as well as a mutual benefit if it does. That's show business, as well as the club business.

If you run into a venue that attempts to convince you of what a privilege it is to play there, politely quote your credentials from past successful gigs, and your terms for a performance. If they won't talk business with you and persist in their fantasy that they are doing you a favour, walk. You've lost nothing, and have done your part to help extinguish these practices once and for all.

Finally, on a positive note, for every venue that treats musicians this way, there is at least one other that genuinely respects what you do and the value you bring, and will deal with you decently and fairly.

James, Guitarist

Arrangers

Arrangers are specialist musicians who create arrangements. All songs performed in a live environment need arrangements. Arrangements define the way the songs are performed, the feel/genre, what notes are played, where the solo comes in, and so forth. Traditionally, great arrangers such as Quincy Jones and Nelson Riddle created scores and parts for musicians to read and rehearse from. (Or at least had professional music copyists write these.) These days, arrangers can undertake this role; however, they might also have other roles in creating your performance. An arranger might create five entire backing tracks for the performance. Such recordings may be created using live musicians in recording studios, music samples that are played into a Digital Audio Workstation (DAW), or a combination of both. A good arranger is a great asset to your band.

Sometimes musicians take on the job of arranging. They can default to the easiest arrangement. In jazz, this is the head arrangement where everyone plays the head of the song (the melody), then people take it in turns to solo, then the head is played again, and then they finish with a rote formula such as a Basie ending. In popular music, it might be the arrangement that the original band used. But arrangements can be so much more than verse/chorus/verse/bridge/chorus.

Songwriters/Composers

Songwriters and composers create the intellectual property of the music industry. Musicians and venues use this intellectual work to create performances. Songwriters need to be recompensed for that work. There are two ways that this can happen. Most commonly, songwriters are members of performing rights organisations (see below) who licence venues and distribute the resulting proceeds of exploiting performing rights. The alternative process is the exploitation of what we call grand rights. These are paid by the producers and directors to composers for live performance of music in a theatrical context. They are directly negotiable with the copyright owners.

Backline

Backline is the technological and logistical help you need to mount a performance. This can include sound and audio operation and design, and stage management. Sometimes the venue supplies backline. At other times you organise backline as part of your fee. The sound and lighting techs usually run small businesses and will bill you or the club. Good ones are worth their weight in gold. Bad ones will make your performance a living hell for you, the audience, and the venue. It is therefore essential to get the best backline with the best gear you can afford. Venues usually supply the lighting themselves and may supply the audio rig, or you may supply that yourself.

Backline includes stage managers, roadies, and stagehands but these are typically only used in high-end performances and tours.

THE IMPORTANCE OF BACKLINE

It's really important to have good backline. I learnt that the hard way. When I first started, I was hiring production, sound, and lighting on a budget. Comparing two different people and saying I won't get this guy because he costs this much when I can get this guy for this much. But you get what you pay for. I didn't realise how important it was to have good sound and lighting. They can make or break a performance. You could have the best voice in the world, but if a bad sound guy stuffs up what you sound like out front, that's all the audience hear. They don't think that it's the sound guy, they just think you sound shit. I remember doing a gig once and we had this sound guy and we came out and started singing, and he didn't even have my mic on for halfway through this song. And even the audience were going up and yelling at him and he couldn't even hear it. When I got home, I turned the computer on and got an email from a random punter. They said, "I just wanted to say I saw you guys tonight. You're brilliant musicians, brilliant vocalists, fabulous show. Do yourself a favour and sack your sound guy". That was my turning point.

So now the sound and production crew make more money than anyone else in the band. I have regular backline, I actually have put my foot down because we get so much work now that I actually say to my guy, "I don't care what you're doing, I don't care what family things you've got on. If you can't do the gig I want somebody else as good as you". And that's what we're down to now, because occasionally when he hasn't been able to do one and I've got someone else in, sure enough it's the difference between me having an effortless gig and me having a stressful gig. I've actually turned around and said, "I'm not going on stage if this doesn't get sorted". And that's not being a diva, that's just self-preservation. You see some of these live gigs where big performers can't hear themselves when they're on Superbowl or something. And they just completely humiliate themselves because they're singing off-key. It's not their fault, because they can't hear themselves.

Anthea, Promoter and singer

Backline can make you or break you. My advice is to get great backline, then get on their good side. Do whatever you can, make them feel like the most important person in the world, because they'll make you sound even better. Anger them, and they'll do a mediocre job or may actively make you sound terrible.

Music Industry Organisations

There are multiple industry organisations available to assist you in your live performance career in whatever area you are in. They might be musicians' unions. They might be live music offices. They might be professional organisations. Whatever they are, join them and use their resources. Go to their networking events. They exist to help you develop your resources.

Investors

Every single show costs time and money to put on. Even if it's only the money required to hire rehearsal spaces. Putting on a show takes time and, as anyone with an MBA will tell you, time is money. Every moment you're rehearsing a show, you're not doing other stuff that would have earned you an income. Thus, we can posit that every show needs an investor or investors. Investors put up money for the show. While this formally happens in only large performances, it is worthwhile noting that every performance needs money and time invested to be successful and someone needs to invest it. Just like an actual formal investor, you need to be ensured of getting a return on that investment. For some that is the actual joy of playing. However, to be a professional musician, you need a financial return.

Rehearsal Studios

If you're at music college at the moment, you're lucky. Not only do you have dozens, maybe hundreds, of talented, creative, passionate fellow students around you, not only do you have access to brilliant, successful teachers to inspire you, not only are you directed to insightful, well-researched and reasonably priced textbooks (like this one), you have access to free rehearsal studios. Your rehearsal studios will (probably) be clean, well-lit, treated for sound, and comfortable.

However, if you're no longer at a music college, you need to lower your standards and be prepared to pay. Basically, you have two options: Rehearsing in commercial rehearsal spaces and rehearsing at home. Commercial rehearsal spaces are regularly linked with recording studios and are used to offset losses incurred by the downturn in commercial recording. Because of noise issues with residents, commercial venues are often in industrial areas. Rooms are often small and indifferently soundproofed. Trying to work up an indie folk band while next door a Metallica covers band is in full swing brings a challenge to your rehearsal. You will generally pay by the hour and can expect some backline to be set up already. The alternative is to practice at home, in which case you need to consider your neighbours, keep the sound down, and consider the hours you are going to rehearse.

Box Office

The box office is a term for the people who actually manage the bookings. They are a textbook unto themselves. There are several types of organisations.

The simplest box office is operated by the band at the door. People pay for tickets by cash or (sometimes) credit cards. At the end of the night, the amount made on tickets sales is the amount of money that it in the till, so make sure you trust the person who is on the door!

An in-house box office is operated by the venue. Here, the venue takes bookings, takes payments (online or at the door) and remits money to the band according to the contract. The amount of money the venue takes is set by the contract you have with them. If you are on a set fee, the venue takes all the money from the ticket, and pays you a set fee regardless of how much money you make. If you are on a door deal, the venue will typically take a set fee per ticket. If your ticket is $10, the venue might take $3. This is to recompense them for the administration of selling tickets. If you are using this, you can put a clause in your contract about having access to the ticket office, and counting ticket receipts, and have a representative observing ticket sales. Many venues in the industry are scrupulously honest. Some are not.

A ticketing company is specifically dedicated to ticketing. There are different ones in different parts of the world. In Australia, there is Ticketek, which has exclusive contracts with several large venues. Eventbrite provides ticketing options in the US, London, Ireland, Holland, Germany, Australia, Argentina, and Brazil. There are many others depending on where you are. Using these companies makes ticketing easy. They monitor the number of tickets sold so you don't overbook and take online bookings. They provide a web link you can embed in your website and Facebook event. However, they charge for their services. Further, they are clever at masking additional fees until checkout. The more expensive the ticket, the less they charge, but you can expect to pay a minimum of 4–5% for these services, and sometimes (with low ticket prices) up to 20%.

There have been two serious problems in ticketing in recent years. One has been the production of counterfeit tickets. So, a member of the public buys a ticket in what is called the 'secondary market', such as an online auction site. But when they show up to the show, they discover their ticket is invalid. Perhaps it was sold twice. Huge disappointment for the fan and some shady character has got away with their hard-earned cash. Given the prevalence of eticketing, it is difficult to stamp this out entirely, despite its reputational damage to the industry.

The other issue is ticket scalping. Ticket scalping is the process of purchasing tickets for a show that is likely to sell out and reselling for inflated prices. It is not rare for some concerts to sell out in moments. Scalpers can set their automated scalping bots to log in to the ticketing website and buy as many tickets as they can. They then offer these for sale through the secondary market for inflated prices. If the concert sells out, scalped tickets can increase exponentially in value. In 2015, literally minutes after pre-sale tickets were made available for purchase to an Ed Sheeran concert in Brooklyn, 4,000 were made available on a secondary market website. Different jurisdictions have different approaches. In parts of Australia and Canada, ticket scalping is illegal but hard to enforce. In other parts of the world, it is entirely legal. In the US, because of outdated laws and varying approaches across different states, ticket scalping is a $5bn business.

COMPLIMENTARY TICKETS

Complimentary tickets (or 'comps') are always tricky. I know promoters who refuse to give out comps under any circumstance. Others give them out like water. There needs to be a middle ground, and there is. It's one of purpose.

For every comp, you need to ask yourself what the purpose for this comp is. Every comp you give out is a missed opportunity to generate income for yourself and the venue. It affects the viability and profitability of the performance. Our advice is to give comps out only if there is a solid reason to do so. Give comps to industry, to reviewers. Offer them on radio stations to promote the gig. But giving them to your mum's friend's dog sitter may not be such a good idea.

On the other hand, sometimes ticket sales are down, and giving out some comps the day before a gig can be worthwhile. If you're not going to sell the tickets anyway, wallpapering the room with friends and family will create a better performance than the soul-grinding agony of playing to two people drinking at the far end of the bar. Plus, it will look better to reviewers and the venue/promoters.

Hypothetical Event

So, let's follow the money trail of an event. For the sake of argument, we're going create a band. This band is an originals indie rock band from Des Moines called Five Odd Goldfish with lead singer Karen. By prior negotiation, Karen takes an extra 50% share for her work as producer/promoter and she also writes some songs. Other members of the band are Natalie (guitarist/songwriter), Phil (bass), Elijah (Drums), and Lex (Keyboard), who get a single share each. An extra share goes into the band fund. They have a manager named Chad, who is on a 10% deal of gross with them. A year ago, they recorded their second album, which has been doing reasonably well on streaming services. They also have a cassette version (more as a keepsake than for playing), which they sell as merchandise for $9 at gigs. They also have a T-shirt featuring the album.

Five Odd Goldfish have been working together for a while and have established a good following. They will put on a performance in their hometown at The Inkstand, a 600-seat venue. They're pretty used to playing together, but in order to brush up for this gig, they rehearse for a total of seven hours in The Warehouse, a community-run rehearsal space, which costs them $30 per hour, a total of $210.

Chad negotiates a guarantee plus percentage deal with The Inkwell who are confident with this band, having worked with them before. Five Odd Goldfish have a guaranteed $2,000 with 50% of the ticket sales after they reach $3,000. Tickets are $20 if bought online and $25 on the night. The Inkwell takes 7.5% of ticket sales in administration for both tickets. In the run-up to the gig, they sell 410 tickets, just over a two-thirds house, so they release a few comps to local radio stations. They arrange a local backline company to run sound and lights which costs them $800.

Their backline arrives at about 3 pm and starts setting up. The band arrive and set up by 5 pm for a 6 pm sound check. After this they wait for the performance. A further 67 people show up at the door adding to the house.

The performance goes well. They have asked Phil's sister to attend the merchandise desk and will pay her $60 for doing so. They sell 89 cassettes and 31 T-shirts.

Their costs for this performance are Chad's 10% management fee, the backline, the rehearsal space, and the costs of attending the stall.

Table 7.1 Ticket Sales

Ticket Price	$20/$25
Tickets Sold Prior	410
Tickets Sold at the Door	67
Gross Ticket Sales	$9,875.00
The Inkwell Box Office Fee	$740.63
Net Income	$9,134.38

Table 7.2 Band Profits

Guarantee	$2,000.00
Percentage of Door	$3,067.19
Cassette Sales (89 @ $9)	$801.00
T-shirt Sales (31 @ $20)	$620.00
Total Band Profits	**$6,488.19**

Table 7.3 Band Costs

Management Fee	$648.82
Backline	$800.00
Rehearsal	$210.00
Costs of Stall	$60.00
Net Band Profits	**$4,769.37**

Table 7.4 Performance revenue

Karen	$1,100.62
Singer/Producer/Songwriter, 150% Share	
Natalie	$733.75
Guitar/Songwriter, 100% Share	
Phil	$733.75
Bass, 100% Share	
Elijah	$733.75
Drums, 100% Share	
Lex	$733.75
Keyboard, 100% Share	
Band Fund	$733.75

After subtracting the costs from the performance profits, each member of Five Odd Goldfish is left with $733.75, except for Karen who gets $1,100.62. A full share also goes into the band fund.

While Five Odd Goldfish are not going to be megastars in the short-term, this is a single performance. If they report the songs they performed, Karen and Natalie are going to be earning income from their Performing Rights Organisation. Further, if this is part of a small tour, they can count on other performances. All in all, this is a reasonably successful performance.

Chapter Summary

- Players in the live music industry include:
  - Producers.
  - Performers, including the bandleader or musical director.
  - Managers.
  - Agents.
  - Promoters.
  - Venues and festivals.
  - Arrangers and songwriters.
  - Backline.
  - Music industry organisations.
  - Rehearsal studios.
  - Box office.
- As a performer, you need to know your industry well to understand the money flow.

Note

1 Some musicians collectively act as producers. This particularly occurs in the democracy of a jazz ensemble. In this case, you are all responsible for the jobs of the producer. This means a lot of meeting and thinking if you are going to have a strong brand with strong performances.

8 Earning an Income in the Live Music Industry

Whether you're Bruno Mars selling out a stadium gig in Philadelphia, a jazz trumpeter gigging in Glasgow, a small venue in Vancouver, or a band just starting out in rural Queensland, the live music industry comprises the same basic principles, the same money routes, and the same groups of people doing essentially the same jobs. The difference is one of magnitude. Bruno Mars concerts attract more of an audience, generate greater revenues, are more expensive to mount, are created by extremely professional people, have higher-end back line and equipment, are held in bigger venues, and generate greater revenue for copyright owners (in this case, probably Bruno himself). But the Glaswegian trumpeter, the Vancouver venue, or the Queensland band all play by similar rules.

If you perform in public, know as much as you can about your industry. Your performance will engage, excite, and move people. It will make them want to move to the music. It will make punters part with hard-earned money to join in. But it is very important that you also treat each performance as a business event, and your career as a business. Failure to do so will lead to reduced opportunities, reduced income, and reduced exposure for your songs. It doesn't matter how good your songs are, how skilled a player you are, or what genre you play, there is a truth you need to learn: If you don't treat this as an industry you will fail.

It is hard to get a true depiction of the size of the live music industry. Figures released by the International Federation of the Phonographic Industry (IFPI) stated that, in 2018, the global music industry generated about US $19 billion, of which performing rights contributed 14%, or US $2.4 billion. IFPI figures (reasonably enough, given their name) concentrate on recorded revenue and do not take into account performance fees and merchandise fees. For comparison, the top 25 tours of 2018 grossed $ 3 billion not included in the IFPI figures. That's not including the other hundreds of thousands of smaller tours and local gigs. Nor do they take into account the various other contributions of the live music industry, such as the travel to a concert, food, drink, accommodation, ticketing, salaries, and so forth. To discount the figures from live touring is to discount a large amount of the music industry. Live music makes up a large percentage of the music industry's revenue and profits.

SKINNY MARGINS

I think really there's a lot of money in live music. But the margins! Live music is a skinny margin business. That's particularly so if you're promoting big acts and/or they're taking a big proportion, 70, 80, 90, 100% of the bill. Smaller acts are cheaper to work with, particularly at festivals. But live music is still a skinny margin and a high-risk business. If you agree to front the artist 80% of the sold-out earnings and you don't sell out, that's where your before gross comes in, then you take a bath. So yeah, so if you're a promoter and you're in this, you're playing these high-risk stakes which promoters do, and it's becoming a bit more corporate these days. But a bunch of them are still sole traders. It's their money. They've got to want to know that your artist can perform.

Tim, Record executive

Sources of Income in Live Music

As a musician, you need to maximise your income streams. You'll record original songs and place them on streaming services. You'll write soundtracks for advertisements or films. You'll teach. However, live music is in there. In a big way. A recent survey[1] of how professional musicians earn their living showed just how big. If you are a rock, pop, country, Latin, jazz, or other popular music performer, your biggest income stream will be that of live performance (40% for rock, 37% for jazz). Session work is around the 10% mark. Income from compositions (e.g., performing rights fees and mechanical rights) amounts to 8% for rock musicians and about 3% for jazz. Those recordings you have slaved over and put out into the online streaming realm generate 10% of rock musicians' income and 4% of jazz. Teaching contributes 24% for jazz musicians and 13% for rock musicians.

While we are artists, we need income streams. Without income streams, we do not have the time or energy to dedicate to our craft. There are, in fact, three main sets of income streams for musicians in the live music industry. The first are performance fees (our 40%/37%), or the fees paid by venues to musicians for performing in their venue. There are several ways that this fee is calculated, such as a flat fee or a percentage of the door and bar. Another is performing rights fees (8%/3%). These are fees paid to songwriters for the use of their intellectual property. The third source of income is merchandise (4% for rock/1% for jazz).

Let's consider each of these income streams.

Performance Fees

The performance fee is money that the producer, promoter, or venue pay for you to perform. Your talent on your instrument, your ability to build a rapport with

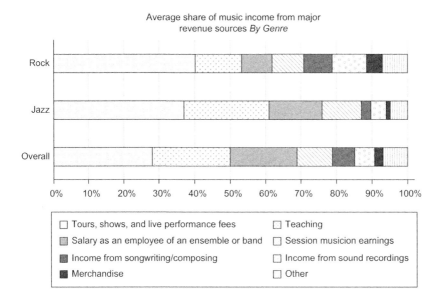

Figure 8.1 Sources of income for contemporary musicians.

the audience, your knowledge of how to move effectively, how to sound, how to interpret a song, how to create an experience ... this is your value. This is what people pay money to the venue to see, which the producer, promoter, or venue passes on (a part of) to you.

How much the venue and you share in what the audience pays (and the risk if they don't come) depends on the contract that you sign. There are five basic models for performance fees, though there are myriad options within those setups. Each type of performance contract comes with risks and benefits, advantages and disadvantages for the band and the venue. Both musicians and venue/promoter want to minimise their risks to take a financial loss and maximise their ability to make a financial profit. Thus, the performance deal is negotiable. Some venues firmly stand on one type of performance fee and refuse to budge. They may miss out on acts but, they reason, there are always more people willing to play (though they may get a lower standard of musician). Other venues may be more amenable to different options. How you negotiate that is up to you and (potentially) your manager. It is important for you to know what the different performance fees are so you can craft a performance contract to maximise your income and minimise your risk.

The first performance fee is the 'set performance fee' or 'guarantee'. Here the musicians are paid a set fee for their performance no matter how many people show up to see them. For the band, this is the lowest-risk model. It allows for easy budgeting. The manager or band leader knows how much they will get and can budget appropriately. The venue guarantees individual musicians and a certain amount of backline. However, if the gig is a sell-out, the band does not share in these profits. The set performance fee is riskier for the venue. If ticket sales do not at least cover the band's fee, they might end up losing money. But the sell-out gig means they increase the profitability, which may offset less profitable gigs. This seems to be the default position for many performing musicians as it guarantees a base amount with less risk for the band.

The reverse is called a door deal—technically a 'percentage of gross' deal. In this deal, the band receives a percentage (or the entirety) of the gross profits (profits before costs are deducted) from ticket sales. This is low-risk for the venue, as it is the audience, not them, who are directly paying the band. If few people come, they are not necessarily out of pocket. However, it is high-risk for the band or promoter as a poor performance (or a poorly promoted performance) can leave them in a precarious financial position. This is especially the case if they have to pay for backline, rent equipment, and pay for ticket sales support. However, this deal gives them the maximum opportunity to generate a profit. This deal is used by the most powerful musicians (who can be sure of ticket sales and wish to maximise their profits) and by those just starting out (as these leave the band with all the risk and the venue with next to none).

A hybrid option is the guaranteed fee plus a percentage of the door after a break-even point. In this, a band receives a certain amount, but when ticket sales reach a point, they begin to share in these profits. This is the most desirable option for the musician as they can budget, but if the concert is popular, they still receive a percentage of that. It's probably the least appealing for the venue, as they still have a risk if the performance fails, but they lose part of the profits if the performance succeeds. Venues use this to entice established acts to play at a venue.

A fourth performance fee is the 'net participation fee'. If you can negotiate these (and have a sound contract), they can be very fair. In this deal, the net profits (not the gross income) from the night from all sources—ticket sales, bar, merchandise—are split between the musicians and the venue/producer. So if the bar makes $3,000 (after paying bar staff), the ticket sales are $2,000 (after paying ticketing fees), and the merchandise is $500 (after paying someone to attend the stand), if the band has negotiated a 50/50 deal, they would get 50% of $5,500 or $2,750. However, this contract is more complicated because you need to decide what is deductible from the gross. Bar wages? Ticketing fees? The band rider? Further, you need to have a very careful accounting and clear documentation of deductibles for the gig. It can be a good option, but you need to negotiate and monitor things carefully.

A four walls deal is where you rent the space from the venue owner. You are responsible for everything else that is associated with the performance. Depending on the contract, this can include staff, bar, catering, backline, insurance, the whole gamut. In this scenario, the venue adopts no risk and the performers/promoter adopts it all. However, the performers/promoter also receive all the net profits.

A TIP FOR MUSICIANS

In Toronto, almost no bar pays more than $250 total. In most (Toronto) venues we use a tip jar and make decent money. The concept has never made it to Hamilton (home), so a cover charge and/or low pay is the current standard (other than having three to five bands on a bill and thus no money to spread around). Tip jars are essential musician-survival tools in *many* places. There is no reason for dissing them when they are one of the only ways to fair remuneration as a musician.

'TubaJay', Tuba player

A sixth option—you wouldn't really call it a performance fee—is the notorious pay-to-play option. Since the 1990s, this has become a fairly standard procedure in some venues and regions. Basically, you pay a venue money to play rather than them paying you. Weird, right? Many industry people advise against ever making such deals with venues. It's understandable. The preferable way to work is to be paid for your performances. You value your music, and so should the venue. You can't pay your rent in 'exposure'. However, while we advise you to be very, very cautious in paying to play if you have a solid reason to lose money on a gig, such deals can occasionally work. If you are playing to much larger crowds than you would normally because of the gig, and if you're sure you can impress the crowd, you might consider it. It may increase your fan base. In the real world, there are plenty of bands and venues that do this. However, I advise you to be careful in making these deals. Only make them if you can quantify exactly what you are getting out of the performance.

Other options include playing for free (or nearly free) or playing for tips. Unless you are just starting out, playing for free is never recommended. Not only are you selling yourself short, you are making it harder for every other performer. Venues can get very used to having to pay nothing to have bands play. This has happened in several parts of the world. Always, always get something for your music.

Performing Rights Fees

The other income source from live performance is performing rights fees. If you would make money from performance, you need to get under the hood and examine the engine of the live music industry. Songwriters are paid for live performance rights through the action of performing rights. Performing rights are the collection of rights of the creator of a piece of music to perform that music in public. Performing rights are enshrined in the Berne convention. Technically, only the performer can perform a work that they have created in public.[2] That's clearly unworkable.

The way we get around this is the work of PROs or Performing Rights Organisations.

A performing rights organisation is a commercial body or governmental agency responsible for collecting monies for performing rights. Songwriters, lyricists, and music publishers licence the performing rights in the music that they own to the PROs. The PROs collect money from organisations that use music in public. This includes:

- Recorded music played on radio and television, played in places of business such as department stores and hairdressers.
- Live music played in venues.

This money (less a small amount for administrations) gets returned to the songwriters, lyricists, and music publishers.

This system eases the need to seek permission directly from the copyright owner to perform a song. Without being licenced by PRO, a venue or performer leaves itself liable to legal action and significant fines from copyright owners.

Any venue that performs live music needs to be licenced by the PRO for that region. Thus, if a venue is in Germany, it is licenced by GEMA. If a venue is in Canada, it is licenced by SOCAN. Confusingly, if a venue is in the United States, it has to be licenced by ASCAP, BMI, and SESAC. All these organisations have reciprocal rights, so that if a New Zealand song is performed in the UK, the rights are collected by PRS for Music, remitted to APRA, and paid to the copyright owner.

If you are a songwriter, the money you get from performing rights can form a regular income. If you perform your own songs, or know others that do, let the PRO for your region know. If your songs are performed in public regularly, it can add up to a regular side income.

Merchandise

Merchandise (merch) are band-branded objects sold at performances. They comprise three groups of things: Recordings, mementos of the performance, and items that display allegiance to the band. They are usually created by the producer and sold at performances. They may be sold behind the bar, or by a specialist stand set up by the band or promoter.

Recordings are not as popular as they were previously. Fewer people own the capacity to play CDs, preferring to stream their music. CDs are thus less likely to be sold at events or are cheaper than they once were. Cassettes and vinyl records are sometimes sold for their nostalgia value, but they are more souvenirs than actual recordings. DVDs of performances exist, but even this is now being impacted by Netflix and YouTube. Despite this, if you have a physical CD or DVD that you have pressed, always include it at your events.

Mementoes of the performance are more common on large tours. A T-shirt with an album on the front and tour dates on the back is an example of such memorabilia. A DVD or physical recording of a live concert on tour is another example. It marks that an audience member was there at that particular time.

Items that display allegiance to the band are items—often clothing—featuring the band and form an interesting range of merchandise. They might be mementoes of the performance, or they might be general T-shirts featuring the band name, photo or CD cover. Large bands are more likely to have these, but small bands with an interesting and well-designed logo can sell a few too.

Experiences as memorabilia are not uncommon, even if they're not normally regarded as merchandise. A fan might talk to a musician. They might take a photo with them. At a certain level, this is just good practice—a way of ensuring that your fans keep coming back to see you. However, at high-end concerts, you might see paid meet-and-greets. Want a photo with Miley Cyrus? That'll cost you a neat $1,000 please. Now, you might not quite (yet) be in that category, but taking a photo, smiling as you talk afterwards with the fans, takes time and energy after a performance too.

Merchandise is a useful side-earner for live musicians. If you have the capacity, it's a good idea to have a few items for sale during or after a performance.

Contracts

As a performing musician, there are several types of legal contracts you will come across in your career. The most common type is a live performance contract. This is a contract between you and the person who is mounting the event: A venue, agent, or promoter. However, there are also band contracts, artist management contracts, agent contracts, and backline contracts. In this section, we will outline common clauses in the different legal contracts you will end up signing.

I'm going to stop here and give you rule number one. Never sign a contract unless you read and understand it thoroughly or have had your lawyer check it out. Some contracts, say a live performance contract, can be pretty standard. You're going to be signing these for performances you organise directly, and venues do them every day. Others, such as artist management contracts, are written very specifically and I strongly urge you to have it checked by a lawyer, even if they pressure you to sign it on the day. You should avoid entirely verbal contracts where possible. While they technically carry the same legal weight as a written one, they are far less enforceable in practice. Even an email which outlines the below information is preferable to a verbal contract.

I should note it that in discussing legal issues with contracts, I am discussing broad concepts. I am not a lawyer. Each jurisdiction is slightly different, and you should seek help from a lawyer, music union, or industry body in your jurisdiction who will have advice specific to the laws of your country and region.

Live Performance Contracts

A live performance contract is also called a booking contract. It outlines the conditions under which a performance will take place, the rights and responsibilities of each party (the venue/booker and the band), and how financials are to be acquitted. It lays down the rules for, but isn't always not limited to, promotion, ticketing, production, performance, payment, and band riders. By signing a booking contract, both the venue and the band understand their obligations and expectations. It minimises potential conflict over how the gig should proceed. Unless you are using a manager or an agent, every time you do a gig you should use a booking contract. Often the venue will supply a pro-forma contract. Your ability to negotiate a contract will be impacted by how much the venue wants you to perform.

Common terms of a booking contract include:

- Times: Both parties should agree on load-in, sound check, performance, and load-out times. A late band can impact performance times and load-out times. Licencing restrictions may also be impacted. The contract can stipulate penalties for delays and late performances.

- Payments: This section outlines the way the band is to be paid. It defines which of the five types of performance fees will be applied here. The contract will outline any deposit required by the band and agreed to by the venue.

- Backline: Venues may insist that the band use their in-house backline for the show. The venue or the band may bear the fees for this. Sometimes, the venue will permit or require bands to bring their own engineer. Here, the engineer will earn more by providing their own gear but will also be more used to the band's sound.

- Travel and accommodation: If the gig is out-of-town, the band will need to travel to the venue and may need to spend the night somewhere close to the gig. These costs can eat into band's profits and be a disincentive for doing a show. A band playing out-of-town should try to increase their fee to cover these costs or arrange for the venue to provide accommodation.

- Promotion: This is one of the long-running sources of friction between bands and venues. Venues may expect the band to bring a crowd and do minimal promotion themselves. The band may consider themselves artists and expect to turn up to adoring throngs. In reality, the most successful performances are a combination. The band (with their manager) does promotion with their mailing list, their website, their social media, and so forth. The venue does their promotion with posters, signage, advertising mailing lists, website, social media, and so forth. This clause is where these arrangements are set in stone. Sometimes venues request that bands provide them with gig posters to be placed around the venue in the lead up to the show. Be very careful that you are able to fill the required promotional arrangements.

- Cancellation and termination: Sometimes life will intervene and the band or the venue may be obliged to cancel before the performance. This clause outlines what happens here. If the band cancels, do they owe a cancellation fee to the venue? Or vice versa. Occasionally you will have what is called *force majeure*. This means that the performance was cancelled or stopped by situations outside the control of the band or venue. This might include weather, power blackouts, or civil unrest. Both parties to the contract will detail how any costs associated with the cancellation are shared and paid by each party.

- Insurance: This clause will outline what insurance the band will bring to the event. It will typically include a certain amount of public liability and require that the entire band be covered.

Band Contracts

Bands generally start out pretty happy. A group of friends are getting together and playing music. What could be better? They might even write a few songs. Perhaps those songs are successful and start getting some airplay and streaming. They might make it onto a Netflix series. Some other bands might cover the song. Perhaps the band moves from small venues to doing festivals, support gigs, and then even a headline here and there. Suddenly, there is money involved. How does the band split that money? You might say that's easy, we'll split it evenly. We're all friends here. Sadly, it rarely works that way. It is far easier and more efficient to sort these things out amicably with a band contract negotiated in the earliest days of performing. Different types of bands may need different band agreements.

Covers bands probably have the simplest way of operating. Typically, one person will own the band, and everyone else is contracted to play as a sole trader. This is a very simple arrangement for covers bands where there is no intellectual property that is collectively generated. The only agreement between the band is an understanding to continue using the same people where possible. It is difficult to replace members of working bands and is generally avoided where possible.

However, this situation may not work if the band is producing intellectual property. Several people may contribute to these songs: The guitarist may write the chords and melodies, the singer may write the lyrics, and the bass player and drummer may contribute the groove. In this situation, a band may form a partnership. A partnership is the legal relationship between a group of people who intend to work together to create a profit. It is considered a legal entity in many jurisdictions. A band that becomes a partnership may share the profits from performance, songwriting, and recording at a negotiated rate between all partners. Thus, our four-piece band may decide on an equal split for performances, but may decide that profits from exploitation of the performance, mechanical, sync and other rights of songs will be split with 40% to the guitarist, 40% to the singer, and 10% each to the drummer and the bass player. Or whatever. A partnership is generally formed through the signing of a legal contract that outlines everyone's responsibility and the profit share. The partnership then becomes a legal entity for taxation and legal purposes. The partnership can open accounts and pay people as they have outlined in the partnership agreement. Note that different kinds of partnerships have different liabilities. In some of these, you may be personally liable for any debts and legal actions taken against the partnership. Check with a lawyer and accountant when setting up your partnership.

Rarely, a band will form a company. This is very involved and differs from jurisdiction to jurisdiction. However, a company has the advantage of being completely separate from the members of the band. A company can sue, be sued, buy, sell, hire, fire, and buy out existing members all by itself. Each musician in the band will have an agreement with the company to provide musical services. Any profits are distributed among the shareholders (bandmembers) in the form of dividends. Generally, the hassles of creating a company far outweigh the benefits. In different regions, there may be tax reasons for forming a company (companies usually pay less tax than individuals). If you are even considering going down this road, talk with your manager, your lawyer, and your accountant.

Artist Management Contracts

The relationship between you and your artist manager is one of the most significant you will have, second only to the relationship between you and your fellow musicians. In almost all situations now, managers are not a formal part of the band, but are a separate business retained for their services. They are very rarely paid a salary but receive a percentage of the money you make. Occasionally, someone in the band may act as the manager, particularly in the case of someone who owns the band.

A management contract is typically written up by a lawyer. However, as always, if you can prepare a few points before you go to your lawyer, you will save some money. Ask yourselves these questions:

What is the scope of management? What services will the manager undertake? This might include getting gigs at venues and festivals, getting a record deal, any number of things. Artist managers are responsible for all industry-related activities of the artist. The management scope will be necessarily wide to ensure their work can benefit a wide range of the artist's output. They might manage your performance, recording, songwriting, sponsorship, and anything that generates a profit.

The division of labour outlines which jobs are the responsibility of the band and which ones are the responsibility of the manager. It also outlines whether the business manager can sign on behalf of the band.

What is to be the management fee? At first, you might think you want this to be as little as possible. It's your money. However, a manager on a higher management fee will also have more incentive to work for your band and achieve greater success for both you and them. The industry standard is between 10% and 20% of your earnings.

What business expenses can they claim? If a manager travels to specifically promote the band, should they pay for this, or should the band? Can they claim phone calls or office expenses?

Most artist managers will require exclusivity, at least in a certain region. This means you cannot sign with another artist manager for the term of the contract.

The term of the contract length is covered in the contract. This is often 12 months with an extension possible with the consent of all parties.

What happens in case of breach? Breaches define what happens if either party does not perform the jobs outlined in the contract. This can involve cancellation of the contract or financial damages.

When you begin negotiations with an artist manager, remember that they are not the enemy. It is their job to increase your profitability and thus the amount of money that you make. They can be your most useful business contact if you let them.

Booking Agency Contracts

A booking agent has certain similarities to an artist manager. However, whereas the artist manager tries to create performance, recording, and songwriting opportunities, a booking agent receives requests for performances from venues and pitches musicians to the venues. It is possible, even likely, that a musician will have both an artist manager who deals with an agent to get work. An agent may even work as a de facto manager for some bands. Agents engage a band for a single gig or for ongoing work.

Booking agency contracts share many similarities with artist management contracts. In negotiating a booking agency contract, you need to consider the following aspects:

- The duties of the agent (what they will do for you).
- The rights of the agent and of the artist.
- The commission paid (usually about 10%) and from what income it is drawn.
- How the agent is reimbursed for expenses.
- The agent's authority to act (this says that they can accept bookings on your behalf).
- The term of the contract.
- What happens in case of a breach?

Backline Contracts

A backline contract is organised when you bring your own engineers in to an existing gig. It will generally outline:

- The time of load-in (usually before the musicians arrive but dictated by the venue).
- What equipment they need to bring.
- The downbeat.
- What time the load-out must be completed.

These are probably the least formal contracts and may comprise an email only. However, it is important to have something written in case of dispute.

Running a Live Music Business

You and I are, first and foremost, musicians. We play music. We are gifted at notes and at words, at creating memorable experiences and playing in the studio. We are creative and flexible and talented. What we may not be good at is the business side. Don't get me wrong. Some musicians are born very good at this. Others become so through hard work, the experience of working in the industry, and determination. Others never gain more than a passing understanding of it.

Being a performing musician in the 21st century means being a small business. All the different aspects of your career—teaching, recording, writing, and performing—may form part of your music business. But it is a business, and you need to treat it as such. The way this works varies from jurisdiction to jurisdiction, but unless you are treating it as a business, paying taxes, invoicing (and chasing up invoices), you will not generate the income that permits you to devote your time to musical pursuits.

Live music performances are cooperative business ventures within the creative industries. They are typically organised by either a venue or a promoter who 'owns' the performance. The venue/promoter may have employees (such as hospitality staff, administrative staff or in-house backline) that may be employed full-time, part-time, or casually. Each of them serves a purpose in the construction of the experience. Bartenders serve drinks. The box office sells tickets. Musicians such as you and I create the musical performance that is the focus of the experience. However, we are not usually employed on an ongoing basis, but are employed for a single night. The easiest way to employ us therefore, is to consider us to be contractors. In this capacity, we are responsible for running our own business, paying our own taxes, and seeking our own employment.

How to Get Paid for Gigging

The music industry is different now than it was in the freewheeling world of the seventies and eighties. Cash gigs now rarely exist (outside of tip gigs and busking), so we musicians must become businesspeople. There are various ways that musicians operate as a business entity. By far the easiest and most common one is called a 'sole trader' in Australia, the UK, and New Zealand, and a 'sole proprietorship' in the US and Canada. In this, you earn money through your music, and are responsible for all legal issues, accounting, and taxation. In some jurisdictions, such as the US or Canada, you don't really need to do anything to set up a business. As long as you are operating under your own name, you can be a sole proprietor. In Australia, the UK, and New Zealand however, you need to register as a small business.

As we've seen, contemporary musicians earn most revenue from live performance. The manner of getting paid for a performance depends on the band contract. If a single person owns the band, and everyone else is a subcontractor, the bandleader/owner will invoice the venue and they will pay them. Then everyone else in the band invoices the bandleader and is paid by them.

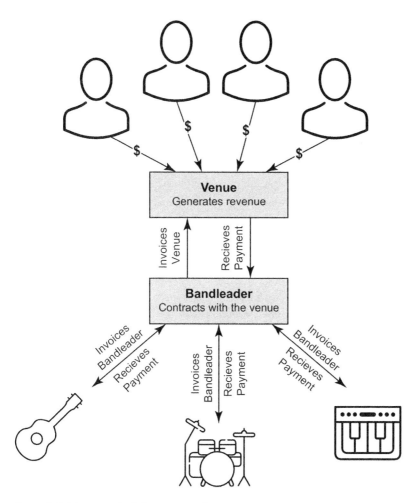

Figure 8.2 Money paths following a performance.

It becomes more complicated if you have a manager or agent involved. Typically, the agent will invoice the venue, and keep their 10%. The manager will then invoice the agent and keep their 10%. Having these people in the mix can slow payment down, but it can also ensure an ultimate payment. However, if a band is set up as a partnership, payment becomes more complicated again. After the agent and manager take their cuts, the payment will be made into the band partnership's account and the various members of the band will split the income depending on their contract.

One thing about being paid. Generally, you will be. It may take a few weeks, but it will happen. Occasionally though you may meet cheats that will book you and then not pay. I've had people move overseas and never pay. I've had people ghost me when I'm chasing them for a gig. Eventually, being cheated happens to everyone. Depending on your jurisdiction, you may have varying legal remedies. Often, if you are a member, your local musicians' union can assist. However, depending on the performance fee, it may cost more than the gig would have paid to recoup the money or be more trouble than it's worth. It is galling, and it is annoying in the extreme to have someone benefit from your hard-won performance skills, but sometimes it's a case of gritting your teeth, trusting to karma, and moving on.

Taxation

As a citizen of your country, you are required to pay tax. Every jurisdiction is different in its approach to taxation, however there are a few common features. There is one tax you will certainly need to consider as you perform: Income tax. There is another, value added tax, that you may need to consider depending on where you live.

If you are doing your job well, you will be earning money as a performer. As we've noted, the easiest business model for you is that of a sole trader, which means you are likely to be considered a contractor to the venue, promoter, agency, or management. Being a sole trader means that you are responsible for paying income tax rather than an employer who pays tax on your behalf. At the end of the financial year, you are likely to owe money to the government for the income you have generated as a musician. It is vital that you put money aside from each performance to cover the inevitable income tax bill at the end of the financial year. Getting hit by a big, unexpected (or semi-expected) tax bill at the end of the year is unpleasant in the extreme.

Some jurisdictions, such as Canada, the UK, Australia, and New Zealand have a value added tax (VAT) sometimes called a Goods and Services Tax (GST). This is a tax that is added to the cost of most services and products. In these jurisdictions you collect a certain amount, 5% in Canada, 10% in Australia, on top of the performance fees you charge. However, you are more than a tax collector for the government: Depending on the jurisdiction, you can usually claim back the GST of equipment you buy for your business. You can apply to collect GST once your earnings go above a certain amount.

Sometimes—rarely—you will earn cash as performing musicians. In this, you might do a gig and receive dollar or pound notes at the end of the performance. While many musicians choose not to claim this money, note that the government regards it as just as much a part of your income as any declared income and failure to declare it is against the law.

Paying tax is a less exciting aspect of being a professional performing musician. However, the goal of your performing career is to maximise your income to keep doing what you love. That makes taxation a necessary part of your career. Learn as much as you can about it, and you might keep some of that lovely gig money.

People You Need

In business, you hire specialists to do things for you. Mechanics repair your van. You take your saxophone to a shop to replace the pads. And in business, there are two people in particular you will need to operate successfully: An accountant and a lawyer. You can try to deal with legal aspects and tax. You can try to repair your car yourself. But it will take longer, and the results will not be as good. In a car, this can mean a breakdown on the way to a gig. In accounting, this can mean extra dollars paid to the tax department. In law, it can mean the difference between keeping your own music, and someone taking it.

First accounting. It may be tempting to try to do your taxes yourself or even go to one of those places in shopping centres that promise to do your taxes for $59 or whatever. However, being a musician is a very specialised job. For that you need an entertainment industry accountant. Like an artist manager, a good accountant will generate income for you. Doing taxes yourself might save you a few hundred bucks, but you will inevitably end up paying more through ignorance of the latest taxation laws. Once you are earning money from your performances, seek recommendations, ask friends, and find an accountant that specialises in entertainment law.

The longer you work in the industry, the greater the chance you will need legal advice. Now, depending on how they're set up, your local musicians' union may provide basic legal advice, however it's a good idea to have your own specialist legal advice when necessary. It's worthwhile seeking a specialist entertainment lawyer where possible.

Insurance

Because you are contractors, not employees, nor patrons of the establishment, you are not covered by the insurance of the venue or promoter. In our increasingly litigious society, as a musician, you need to be insured against a range of accidental damage while playing live. What happens if your gear catches on fire and burns down a venue? What happens if an audience member is injured while dancing? What about if someone steals your expensive equipment? While practices and names do vary from region to region, there are some common insurance types you need to consider.

The first, and most important insurance you can have, is to insure the public at your performances. If a piece of equipment you own gives someone an electrical shock, or someone tumbles off your speaker stack trying to stage dive, you need to be insured for potential litigation. This is called Public Liability Insurance in the US, UK, Australia, and New Zealand, and Property and Liability Insurance in Canada. You are generally covered into the millions of dollars of damage. Many venues will not permit you to play unless you can show you have public liability. If the insurance is in the band's name or business entity, a single insurance cover should cover everyone in the band

Another type of insurance will cover your equipment. There is nothing worse than having your gear stolen or damaged. Some airlines have been known to be less than gentle with equipment. If this happens, you need to repurchase your equipment, and you do not want to have to do that from your own pocket. Many companies around the world will organise musician equipment insurance at reasonable prices. These companies bet on the fact that musicians normally look after their equipment very well, and it is unlikely to be damaged by neglect.

Because you are a contractor, you are not covered by the public liability insurance of the venue or promoter. So what happens if you hurt yourself while performing? Some jurisdictions are beginning to organise insurance that cover the personal injury of performing musicians. It can offer insurance on lost income if you have an accident or get sick.

When choosing your insurance, consider the limitations of your policy, the insurer, and the price. Every insurance policy has limitations you need to consider. If you drop a guitar at a gig, you're likely covered. You're probably not covered against smashing it into an amp. Second, always use specialist music insurers. A normal insurer might try to replace your vintage guitar worth a fortune with a base model straight out of the shop. They will not understand the intricacies of music-specific insurance. Finally, you'll be surprised just how reasonable some insurance policies can be.

Insurance is not a subject that inspires people to go out and write heartfelt songs. It is annoying. It costs money. You hope to never use it, so basically it is easy to regard it as giving your hard-earned money away. But when you need it, boy will you be glad you had it. In some of these cases, it is up to you whether you take them. With Personal Liability, you probably can't (or shouldn't) play without it.

Further Reading

While there are many books on the music business, few of them give more than a cursory outline of live music. In Australia, Shane Simpson's *Music Business* is a great read. Donald Passman's *All You Need to Know About the Music Industry* is a standard text.

Chapter Summary

- Contemporary musicians earn the greatest part of their income from performance.
- There are three sources of income for performing musicians:
  - Performance fees.
  - Performing rights fees.
  - Merchandise.
- There are five main types of performance fee:
  - The set performance fee.
  - The door deal (percentage of gross).

- • Guaranteed fee plus percentage of door after a breaking point.
  - • Net participation fee.
  - • Four walls deal.
- • Another type is the pay-to-play. This is not recommended without some strong reason to undertake it.
- • There are five main contracts you will come across as a live performer:
  - • Live performance contracts which outline the legal and financial arrangements between you and the venue or promoter for a particular gig.
  - • Band contracts that define the financial and legal arrangements between members of the band.
  - • Artist management contracts that define the financial and legal arrangements between a musician or musicians and an artist manager.
  - • Agent contracts that define the financial and legal arrangements between yourself and an agent.
  - • Backline contracts that define the gig requirements for backline engineers.
- • As musicians, we need to be more than just musicians and engage in the music business:
  - • We need to know how to get paid for gigging.
  - • We need to understand the basics of taxation in our particular jurisdiction.
  - • We need to employ specialist accountants and lawyers.
  - • We need to understand the insurance requirements of being a musician.

Notes

1 DiCola, "Money from Music: Survey Evidence on Musicians' Revenue and Lessons About Copyright Incentives."
2 Public performance means a musician or ensemble who does not own the copyright but performs that piece of music live. A live performance occurs when it takes place in public, and the audience is drawn from outside a normal circle of friends and family. Public performance also includes broadcasting via television, radio, telephone line, or other means of transmission.

9 Planning Your Product

Think of any of the bands that have been very successful. Think of KISS and what comes to mind? Outrageous makeup, Gene Simmons' tongue, and great hard rock. What about Michael Bublé? Good looking guy crooning classic jazz hits with a big orchestra. Bjork? Unconventional performer doing unexpected things. It goes on. Shania Twain. Brian Setzer. Taylor Swift. Lady Gaga. These musicians are successful in part because they plan their musical brand and their product as assiduously as Coca Cola or McDonalds do. The world is full of musicians without a strong identity that never go anywhere. You don't want to be one of them.

You can achieve a strong identity through careful planning. Before you rehearse together, before play your first performance, before you head into the recording studio, you need to collectively and individually consider your musical product. Part of this is about the business side of performance. Part of it is about branding the act.

The big performers now have people dedicated to controlling and shaping their brands. They have people to teach them how to be interviewed, people who post for them on social media, who design their websites, and control how the public sees them. You probably don't have that luxury. But if you're going to succeed at any level of the music industry, you need to consider how the public sees you. That's your brand. And that's what we're going to discuss in this chapter.

MY FAVOURITE PERFORMANCES

Certainly, Prince and Stevie Wonder are absolute virtuosos with incredible charisma and stage presence. Whereas Prince is more of a 'showman', and the show is fully choreographed, probably down to each word said between songs. He brings so much theatricality that is unique to him, yet still has room for virtuosic and passionate solos to improvise with. Stevie Wonder has a more casual approach to performing, but, again, his stage presence, his joy, and his energy are all endless. With Leonard Cohen, it is of course an elegant and poetically beautiful performance. I saw him when he was already an old man, but he literally skipped on to the stage. His band was slick and he was impeccable in his performance, but a great singer he is not. But that is not what Leonard Cohen is about. He is about poetry, beautiful songwriting, and the profound message in each of his songs. What I found overwhelmingly beautiful with Cohen was his incredible humility and grace, his gratitude towards the US, the audience. His lightness of being and his sense of humour. He was an absolute delight from the first moment to the end. And it was an honour to be able to see him in my lifetime.

Lara, Vocalist/violinist

Branding

Branding is the business procedure that creates a unique idea, image, and name in consumers' (in this case, your fans') collective mind. It aims to differentiate your presence within the market, attract new consumers, and retain existing ones. The representation of the unique idea, image, and name is your brand, and you need to guard it carefully. It is what distinguishes you from the hundreds of other bands trying to attract fans and their hard-earned dollars. Philip Kotler, a writer and professor of marketing, was right when he said, "Don't advertise a brand; live it".[1]

There are three aspects to a brand:

1. Identity (who you portray yourself to be).
2. Integrity (the portrayal of yourself as someone with honesty and authenticity).
3. Image (who fans understand you to be).

Brand Identity

Your branded identity is the portrayal of who you are as an artist. It tells your audience and fans:

- These are my values.
- This is what I do.
- This is what I stand for.
- This is who I am.

Think of Tina Turner. What values does she encapsulate in her public persona? You might suggest resilience, honesty, dignity, and defiance. What does she do? She sings songs that shout and confront; songs that talk with honesty about relationships. Songs like "What's Love got to Do With It", "Simply the Best", and "We Don't Need Another Hero". What does she stand for? Defiantly breaking through despite the odds. Who is she? She's an energetic and rebellious singer who sings with truth. Now this may or may not be actually true of Tina. I've never met her. It doesn't matter. This is how she is portrayed by her brand.

Brand Integrity

There's a saying. George Burns used it in his routines. "The secret of success is sincerity. Once you can fake that you've got it made". A second aspect to your brand is that of authenticity and integrity. Your portrayal of yourself needs to be (or appear to be) an honest and authentic portrayal of you. Branding academics say brand integrity is the "extent to which consumers perceive a brand to be faithful towards itself, true to its consumers, motivated by caring and responsibility, and able to support consumers in being true to themselves".[2] Unless you are perceived as being honest and authentic, why would anyone come and see you?

Brand integrity is constructed of four aspects:

- Continuity: Are your portrayals of yourself as a musician (or band) faithful to yourself? Are they consistent? Do they inspire confidence that you will be around for a long time, or do they portray you as a fly-by-nighter?
- Credibility: Is your brand true to your audiences? If people come to see you will they get what they are expecting?
- Integrity: Are you perceived as a musician who is true to their morals and values?
- Symbolism: Do you support your audience to be true to themselves? Do you add meaning to people's lives? Are your performances valuable to consumers? Do they care?

Thinking of Tina again, do you perceive her as someone who is faithful to her idea? She doesn't seem to be a fake. She seems genuinely to be this feisty woman that has won through despite the odds. That's something she's consistently portrayed as over a long time. It's something that resonates with her audience. She also portrays this with integrity, as a musician with a strong moral compass who has been through some tough times. Her songs resonate with her audience.

Brand Image

Your brand image is how you are understood by your audiences and fans. Every single time you are interviewed, write a post on your blog or social media, talk with fans, play in public, or connect with anyone, you are establishing your brand image. With every encounter, your fans build an impression of who you are, what you do, and what you stand for. You need to be methodical and plan how you establish your specific brand image. Your brand needs to be unique. Ed Sheeran writes direct, simple songs that talk of common human experiences. He is … interesting looking. He plays guitar adequately. But this could apply to hundreds of musicians in the world. The difference is that Sheeran's branding of himself is strongly personal. He is a commentator on life. He plays the acoustic guitar. This branding has made him an incredibly successful musician. Love him or loathe him, you cannot ignore him. This is largely because of the brand he has built.

Like Sheeran, you want to be thought of as unique and special. You need to build your brand around that. If you don't, there is no reason for anyone to pay more attention to you than any other singer. You'll fade away into the background of the innumerable performers in the music industry with no brand.

Other Brand Attributes

Once you've got these three elements down, you've got a great start to things. However, it's only a start. There are other attributes you need to present to your audience to develop a great brand.

First, your brand needs to be consistent. Whether you're in the media, posting on Instagram, designing a website, or whatever, you should maintain consistency. This consistency is manifest in many ways. From one perspective, it means always presenting the same narrative about who you are and what you do, the same sense of integrity and moral compass, and the same image to your fans. On another level, it means that all the ways you present yourself must have a uniformity. Your website, your albums, and your social media must all use the same colours and imagery. They must tell the same stories. If you achieve that consistency, it will continue to resonate with your fans and build an image about who you are as a performer in their minds.

Your branding must tell a story about you. When you post on social media, or answer interview questions, what story are you telling? What narrative are you establishing? Are you the working-class boy or girl? Are you the straightforward and honest guy or girl from the country? An inner-city hipster all pose and pomade? Every interaction you have adds to that narrative. Make it exciting. Make it consistent. Weave it in and out of your songs.

Your brand needs to be vibrant and engaging. No-one wants to go and see a boring singer or band. You need to brand yourself as an exciting and likeable performer. Use bright colours in your online presence. Be engaging and fun in interviews. This will make you appear approachable and likeable.

PLANNING YOUR PRODUCT

If you're a performer you should know how to play your instrument to a certain degree. But you should also be able to perform in a way that communicates to an audience. That means thinking about who you are, what you want to represent, and how that's going to be represented on stage. Are you going to have lots of bright flashing lights? Are you going to go for new tech lighting? What are your movements? How are you setting up your set list? Are you talking to the audience or not talking to the audience? If you are talking to the audience, think about what you're going to say before you get there; otherwise, you'll come up with banalities that don't mean anything to anyone. I'm not saying it should all be prescripted. That can be a put off. But, you know, you have to put some thought into what you want to achieve. And that's looks, performance, presentation.

Tim, Record executive

Your brand needs to be professional. Whenever you have an opportunity to present yourself to industry and audiences, ensure they consistently know how professional and dedicated you are to your art. You must appear fun but dedicated to your work.

Finally, keep it new. Look at Madonna. She has kept herself relevant now for four decades by reinventing herself every few years. There will come a time when you need to reinvent your branding.

GENERATING A FANBASE

I've mostly made a living playing styles of music that are not part of mainstream music industry in Australia (with little or no support from radio and TV and with little exposure to the masses). Financially rewarding performances have been created over time by creating a following: A 'fanbase'. People who have engaged with the quality of music we create and perform. Short term success includes respecting the business side as much as the musical side. You need to undertake PR campaigns and exposure along with rehearsing and musical preparation. You need to plan repertoire based on what an audience will engage with. I don't have a singular method. I'm pretty versatile. It's enabled me to work in many different areas. I've sometimes worked with mainstream artists and genres where the 'business machine' is run by corporate admin and labels. I've sometimes worked with other projects that have limited and selective markets where I need to target specific parts of the music community to increase the possibility of financial rewards.

Cesar, Bandleader, composer

Your Name

The name of your act is an essential part of your image and brand. Let me give you an example. In the late 2000s Tauheed Epps, whose stage name was Tity Boi, an enormously talented and well-connected hip hop artist, was making attractive attention in the Los Angeles underground scene. However, he couldn't seem to chart with solo tracks. His 2007 hit "Duffle Bag Boy" was mostly remembered for the involvement of Lil Wayne. His name did attract attention, but the wrong kind, being cited as an example of misogyny within hip hop. In 2011, he changed it to "2 Chainz", which he thought of as family friendly. In the same year, his mixtape T.R.U. REALigion climbed to number 58 on the Bilboard R&B/hip hop album charts. He started getting asked to guest on other artists' tracks. In 2013, he was chosen by Adidas as the face of their shoe Adidas Classic, when Rick Ross was dropped for including a flippant lyric about date rape in "U.O.E.N.O." The offensively named Tity Boi had become the acceptable, though still hip, 2 Chainz.

Epps' brand wasn't terribly marketable in 2011. The values embodied within the name Tity Boi were outdated, unacceptable to most people, and—whether intentional or not—unmarketable. You need to avoid unmarketable branding from the start, because you'll do a lot of work on your branding and it is difficult (though not impossible) to throw it out and start again. You need to ask yourself what your brand stands for. What are your core personal values? How do you want others to perceive you?

If you're looking for long-term success, consistency is the secret ingredient. Developing and maintaining a level of trust with those who matter most to you and your business can be effectively reached through showcasing yourself consistently. Whether it's online, in print, or face-to-face, prevailing consistency will allow you to gain trusted footing with your personal brand.

Writing Your Biography

Part of the process of creating your brand is creating your biography. This is a hard ask for musicians because we are so close to our music. Plus, most of us hate writing about ourselves. Still, a music bio is one of the most important tools in your branding toolkit. It becomes the 'about' section of your social media channels, your gigs, your festival applications. Your bio tells potential audiences why they should care about your music. A well-written bio might even get them to listen to what you write. It could even get them to your gigs. It gives the public the story behind the music. It might be used by festivals, by the press, by anyone who wants a quick and easy introduction to you. It's important, so spend some time on it. If you're not sure where to start, here are a few ideas.

Start by looking at the bios of musicians you admire. You'll find them on websites. This will get you into the stride of things. See what they say and how they say it.

You've got to have hay to make haystacks. And you've got to have information to write. As a starting point, answer the following questions about yourself:

- Where are you based now? Were you born there?
- What kind of musician are you? Are you a songwriter? Guitarist?

- How and why did you come to be a musician?
- What genre do you write in?
- Within that genre, what's special about your music? How do you describe the music that you write?
- What music have you recorded and released?
- What are the big gigs that you've done?
- What projects are you undertaking now?

Once you have this starting point, start to link them in writing. Keep it fairly neutral. Write in the third person (she/he rather than I) because this makes it easier to scan and understand. It also makes it easier for venues and media to cut and paste. Maintain a professional distance and clarity in your writing. Avoid superlatives or opinions. But don't worry too much about making it perfect. Don't worry if there's too much. Write a thousand words if you like. Just write. This will make it quick to scan and understand, and will also help you with your website's SEO. It also allows media, bloggers, and venues to simply copy and paste your bio if they need.

Now edit. Cut about half of the information. Then edit down to three paragraphs. Make the first paragraph the main one. (If someone's going to do a quick edit, it might be the only bit they use). Put all the basic information about you and your music here. Then, in the second paragraph, go into some depth about your music. The final one should outline your current projects.

The next step is to purpose your bio. Create three versions:

- One that is less than 30 words. This is for social media or quick introductions.
- A one-paragraph version that is no more than 100 words.
- The full version that is less than 200 words.

Ensure that your work is professional, accurate, and stylish. Don't write yourself up to be more than you are. Find the things that make you interesting and marketable, and concentrate on those.

Finally, make sure your work is professional. Spellcheck (manually as well as computerised). Give it to different people to read and take their criticisms on board.

Further Reading

There are plenty of books on branding and marketing, but few from a music-only perspective. One of the best is Bobby Borg's *Music Marketing for the DIY Musician*. Leslie Meier's *Popular Music as Promotion* takes a more academic approach and is also a good read.

Chapter Summary

- You need to develop a strong brand to differentiate yourself in the music industry.
- Brands are composed of:
    - Identity (who you portray yourself as).
    - Integrity (your honesty and authenticity).
    - Image (who fans understand you to be).
- Brands are:
    - Consistent.
    - Narrative.
    - Engaging.
    - Professional.
    - Relevant and current.
- Your name is part of your brand.
- You need a relevant and well-written biography.

Notes

1 Kotler, *Marketing 3.0: From Products to Customers to the Human Spirit*, 34.
2 Morhart et al. "Brand Authenticity: An Integrative Framework and Measurement Scale," 202.

10 Technology and Live Performance

Technology has always been important to contemporary music. Recordings are disseminated by wax cylinders, shellac and vinyl records, radio, TV, CDs, digital downloads, and streaming audio and video. New forms of instruments and new forms of amplification make instruments louder, permitting bigger concerts. New forms of telling people about musicians, recordings, songs, and performances are constantly being developed. Fresh ways of recording music emerge from the computer labs of music tech boffins. Quite simply, there wouldn't be contemporary music were it not for technology. Technology is as fundamental to contemporary music as apples are to apple pie or arguments are to politics.

That said, live contemporary music is not in its truest sense an art form for mass dissemination. It rides on the back of mass dissemination. Without potential audiences hearing your music on radio, on Spotify, or on YouTube, how are they going to want to come to your gig? Live music exists within the experience. We perform it to a limited number of people at a particular point in time in a particular place. It is precisely because it is performed to comparatively small audiences that consumers regard live music as special. A recording can be played repeatedly and might be heard by millions. A live performance is an experience, capable of multiple repetitions and commodifications, but which happens only once and is available to a restricted group of consumers at that time.

The technologies used in the performance of live contemporary music falls into three categories:

- Performance technology (the technology used in live performance).
- Promotion technology (the technology used to promote live performances).
- Recording technology (the technology used to record actual or facsimile live performances).

Whether it's the technology of instrument making, the technology involved in amplification so you can be heard, or cutting-edge lighting and sound effects, technology is at the core of live music. You can't get away from it, so you might as well embrace it. Let's first talk about the tech used within performance. Don't worry if you're not technical or do not have much of a grasp of audio theory.

I'll try to keep it fairly accessible. There are two main groups of technologies that are used in live performance:

- Technologies to amplify the sounds produced.
- Technologies to enhance the experience.

TECHNOLOGY AND THE SOLO MUSICIAN

I'm a solo musician. I've generally played by myself for my entire professional career. I've played in bands from time to time, but it's never really stuck. I like playing in bands, but it's a catch 22. Playing in bands, but also wanting to play on my own and experiment with the technology.

I love the dynamic of having other musos up on stage with me and being able to, you know, share that joy up on stage, with people with the same commitment level, the same timeframes. But I feel like I can do a lot of things by myself. And it's improving me and my knowledge of music tech. I'm always learning things as well. When I'm playing solo, I play with a range of different hardware and software and, you know, the technology is advancing. I don't know if technology makes it easier for me, but it's opened up so many more doors. With those doors you have to define yourself eventually. There's a thousand blokes that can play guitar and can sing really well. But to be at the cutting edge of that technology and be able to bring something different to the table and something new, I think that's really exciting. And that crosses over well to the audience as well.

Anders, Guitar

Amplifying Technologies

In the Middle Ages and the Renaissance, instruments were fairly quiet. Stringed instruments were strung with catgut, recorders and flutes were quiet, keyboard instruments like the clavichord and harpsichord had limited dynamic range, and so forth. For hundreds of years, considerable inventive prowess was invested in making instruments louder and better. The Boehm system made the transverse flute able to stay in tune when it went louder and softer. The development of valves made brass instruments chromatic. The resonator guitar permitted audiences to hear guitar over a large band. However, these developments still relied on the instrument being heard acoustically. With the development of transducers and valves and then transistors, electrical amplification became possible. This made the quietest instruments loud enough to fill rooms, halls, and then stadiums. Instead of being too quiet, instruments developed the capacity to be too loud. This had many issues from squealing audio feedback to musicians with damaged hearing. But it permitted the development of the modern live music industry.

If you're going to work in live music, you need to have a basic understanding of what an amplifier and mixer are and how they work. In order to discuss this, we're going to need to dive into a little acoustic theory, but I'll try to keep it light. There are plenty of resources on sound and live mixing if you need them.

There are five types of technology that amplifies live performance:

- Input transducers (microphones and pickups).
- Mixing consoles.
- Amplifiers.
- Output transducers (speakers).
- Foldback.

Input Transducers

Microphones and pickups are technically called acoustic input transducers. A transducer is a device that turns one form of energy into another. A light bulb is a transducer that converts electrical energy into light. The screen of your smartphone is a transducer that turns pressure into electrical current. A microphone turns sound pressure waves into electrical energy. The air in which we live is constructed of atoms. When a singer sings, a string vibrates, or a drum is struck, these atoms move back and forth in what we call pressure waves. The microphone detects these pressure waves and turns them into electrical analogue signals. In live situations, we send these signals along a cable to a mixing desk where we amplify them and send them to speakers.

Microphones come in several categories depending on how they pick up sound and the direction from which they pick up sound. The most common type of microphone in a live situation is a dynamic microphone. Other types of microphone, such as the condenser or ribbon, are fragile and a single drop can wreck them beyond repair. They're used in studio situations. Good dynamic microphones, however, are cheap, near-indestructible, have high gain before feedback, and stand up well against long-term on-stage beatings. Moreover, live mics are usually dynamic cardioid mics. This means they pick up most of their sound from the direction in which they're pointing (the performer) and reject sound from behind the microphone (the audience and the equipment). Shure's best-selling SM series of microphones (such as the SM57 or SM58) are renowned, industry-standard live microphones and are used for many instruments. The way sounds are picked up by microphones are described in a polar pattern. The example in Figure 10.1 shows a typical polar pattern for a cardioid microphone. As you can see, patterns are picked up mostly from the front (0°) and entirely rejected from the back (180°). In practice, this varies with the frequency of the sound.

Live performers use mics in varying ways depending on the instrument. Drums often have microphones all over them, either suspended on mic stands or on

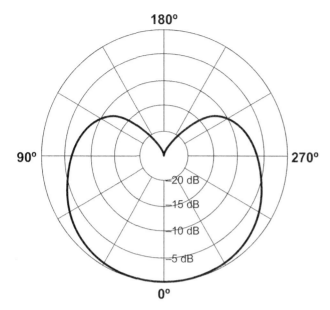

Figure 10.1 A typical polar pattern of a cardioid microphone.

clip-on microphones that attach to the drum frame themselves. A basic setup would have drums clipped to the kick, snare, and a couple of overheads. Mics can be added to individual cymbals and drums, as well as to the bottom of the snare. It is possible (and economical) to buy a package of purpose-built drum microphones that, though they may not be the best quality, will sound good enough to get you by. Sometimes you will see a guitar amp on stage being miked, often by an SM57, to get the particular sounds a guitarist wants or likes rather than (or in addition to) being fed into a DI box. An acoustic piano may be miked in several ways depending on whether it is upright or grand. Other acoustic or semi-acoustic instruments, such as guitars, upright bass, electric bass, or an electroacoustic piano such as a Rhodes, use a pickup that is typically built into or attached to the instrument itself and are designed specifically to pick up the sounds of the instrument. Horns can have specialist microphones that clip on to the bell of the instrument. These days, many vocal microphones are wireless, which means they transmit an audio signal from a radio transmitter built into the microphone to a base station that is plugged into the sound desk. This eliminates the need for miles of carelessly dribbled cables across the stage. Electronic instruments, such as keyboards, keytars, or EWIs, of course, do not use input transducers, but create their sounds electronically.

We should at this stage also discuss audio feedback. Audio feedback is the painfully loud squeal you might have heard at a gig. It is technically called an audio positive loop gain or a Larsen effect. It occurs when your input transducer

(microphone or occasionally your instrument pickup) picks up the output tra-
ducer (speaker). Basically, your microphone is amplifying the actual sounds of
the amplifier and the speaker is amplifying the microphone (this is the loop). As
the sound continues go around the loop, it gets louder and louder and the squeal
occurs. Occasionally, it can be used in a controlled manner (Jimi Hendrix used it
as an effect) however it's usually considered undesirable. More than a few seconds
of it can wreck audio equipment. Audio feedback can be eliminated by keeping your microphone pointed away from the amplifier and by clever equalisation
from your live engineer.

Microphone issues in live performance can be vexatious, particularly for
singers.

- Microphones can pick up from varying directions depending on the make
  and model. The Shure microphones previously mentioned are dynamic
  cardioid mics, which means they take in most of their sound from the
  direction in which they're pointing and reject sound from behind the
  microphone. However, it can also pick up onstage banter movements and
  other sounds.
- Microphones can pick up the softest-spoken phrase. Whatever you say on
  stage, assume that the microphone will pick it up and broadcast it around
  the room. If you don't believe me, Google the conversation between then-
  Australian prime minister Tony Abbott and his minister Peter Dutton about
  global warming in 2015.
- I know we mentioned it above, but it's important. Never point a microphone
  at the speaker. This is inviting feedback.
- Treat your microphone well. Even dynamic microphones are somewhat del-
  icate. Wrecking microphones can get expensive. Don't drop them. Don't
  swing them around on a chord. Don't run over them with a steamroller.
  Don't lend them to your friends. Treat them well and they will give you years
  of service.

Instruments that use a guitar-type lead typically go into what is usually called a
DI unit or DI box (Direct Inject) or occasionally called a balun. Guitar cables
'unbalanced', meaning they have two wires inside them, one to carry the signal
and the other to earth the signal. These are great, reliable, and simple leads; however, they can pick up unwanted interference and noise the further they travel. If
they travel over any distance (say from the stage to the mixing desk at the back
of the venue), there will be noise and crackling and hissing in the sound. For any
distance, it is better to use 'balanced' cables that have three wires, two carrying
the same signal but inverted, both wrapped in an earth that acts as a shield. You
can tell these cables because they are thicker and utilise what we call an XLR
plug (sometimes incorrectly called a microphone plug). The function of a DI box
is to convert the high-impedance unbalanced signal from your instrument to a
low-impedance balanced signal that the mixing desk can handle and that doesn't
have noise.

Amplifiers

Audio amplifiers were developed in 1912 and for the first 60 years of their existence were based around vacuum tube (valve) technology. In the 1970s, they changed to solid-state technology based around the transistor. The amp you plug your instrument into is probably a solid-state amp, though some enthusiasts use valve amps. You will regularly use two kinds of amps. If you are a guitarist, bass player, or keyboard player, you will use an instrumental amp. These are designed to give a good amplified sound with the particular instrument you use. A bass amp differs from a keyboard amp. You can use these in small gigs or onstage for monitoring. In larger gigs, however, it is likely that you will use a front-of-house amplifier run through a mixer and with foldback. These days, amps are often built into speakers (powered speakers) or mixers (powered mixers), but occasionally you can find dedicated amplifiers that run unpowered speakers.

LOUDNESS WARS

The bane of live musicians' existence is a loudness war. A loudness war can happen in this way. Say you have a drummer that tends to play on the loud side. If the room is small, it can get quite boomy on stage. So perhaps the guitarist can't hear themselves over the drums. Surreptitiously, they turn up the volume on their instrument, so the sound on stage is just a little louder. Then the keyboard player can't hear themselves, so their hand wanders over to their volume and gives it a little push. The guitarist frowns, because once again she can't hear herself. So she cranks it a little more. Before you know it, the sound level on stage and in front of house has increased by a lot. The singer is screaming to be heard. They end the gig with a sore throat, and everyone's ears are ringing.

Be very careful of loudness wars. Not only do they have the potential to make a fun gig unpleasant, not only are you less likely to be engaging on stage, but they create an uncomfortable experience for the audience.

Mixing Consoles

Analogue mixing consoles developed in the 1940s from radio mixers. In fact, the first ones were radio mixers, and they were used in studios to record multiple microphones. Live mixing in the 50s and 60s was generally done by checking the levels of the various instrumental and vocal amps on stage and praying nobody turned up the volume through the performance. This made it haphazard. Mixers existed, but they were rudimentary. Developments in the late 1960s, including the evolution of solid-state amplifiers, permitted larger speakers. Studio mixing consoles were quickly being dragged to performances and used to create house mixes and foldbacks.

Modern mixing consoles fall into two categories: Analogue and digital. Analogue mixing consoles are what you might typically think of as a console, with sliders and knobs, and XLR as well as unbalanced inputs. The stage outputs from the band and microphones run to a stagebox, which runs a very thick lead (called a multicore snake) containing all the inputs from the stagebox to the mixing console. Digital consoles can look similar to audio consoles, or they can look like a row of XLR and unbalanced inputs and outputs. Digital consoles are more flexible than analogue ones and can reroute effects quickly, storing certain setups for quick recall. They are often controlled by an iPad or tablet, meaning that the engineer can wander the room while they mix. The other innovation is the digital snake. No matter how good your analogue multicore snake is, it will inevitably attract some noise or issues. It is also very thick. A digital snake is much smaller and turns the analogue signal from the instruments into a digital one at the point of the stagebox.

Regardless of whether a mixing console is analogue or digital, it works in the same way. Inputs from various instruments, mics, and playback devices are attached singly by balanced or unbalanced input. They are assigned to separate channels where each channel is given a level, an equalisation, placed in the stereo mix (panned), and effects such as reverb are applied. They are then sent to a master output where the final level is set. From there, the signal is sent to an amplifier and then on to the speakers.

It is always preferable to get someone else to mix your performance. However, there will be times when you have to do it yourself. Perhaps it is a small gig. Perhaps there is no money for backline. In this case, you should be able to find your way around a mixing desk. It is worthwhile practising doing this.

Output Transducers

There is a real art to designing and building speakers. The mathematics and acoustic theory is complex and involved. You can't just knock together a box in your workshop, chuck in a cheap speaker and expect it to sound great. You need to do the maths, learn the theory, and create lots of awful speakers before you get a good one. At their heart, speakers are output transducers, the reverse to microphones, in that they take one form of energy (electrical) and convert it into another (acoustic). Speakers were first developed for telephones, though it took many years (and the development of audio amplifiers) before we could use them for live performances.

There are two types of speaker: Active speakers and passive speakers. Active speakers have an amplifier built into them. You can take them, plug in a microphone or instrument, and use them as a simple amplifier. They might even have a couple of inputs. Alternatively, you can plug them into the output from a mixing console and use them as a live rig. Passive speakers do not include an amplifier and must use the output from either an external amplifier or (more commonly) the amplifier built into the mixing console. Generally, the larger the speaker, the louder it is. You'll regularly see speakers described as 10", 12", or 15" (sorry metric countries).

You might ask why anyone would ever buy a passive speaker. Active ones might sound like a dream come true. But before you head down to David and Waldo's Awesome Music Shop™ and place thousands of dollars on the counter, consider what you need. Active speakers are a lot heavier than passive ones. If the amplifier breaks, you lose the entire speaker rather than just an amp. Further, you're locked into a setup. If you have passive speakers, you can just buy (or add) larger speakers if you need them. I tend to own active speakers because most of the gigs I do have backline. If I have to run the live rig myself, it's going to be a fairly small gig, and that's not usually going to change. But everyone's situation is different, and you need to look at your own needs before you go blowing lots of money on gear.

There are small self-contained PA systems with built-in mixing consoles. They might look like two speakers, but on the back of them, there is a mixing unit with six or so inputs. They fit together as a suitcase and can be carried or wheeled to gigs. If you buy one of these, remember the nature of speakers is to be on the large and heavy side. All-in-one units are great because every unit can be built to work together and provide great sound, but they might also be underpowered.

Foldback

There are typically two different mixes in live performance. The first is the mix from the audience's perspective called the front-of-house (FoH) mix. The creation of this is within the arcane science of live engineers. However, there is a second important mix that that you rely on as a musician to create the music. We call this the stage mix or foldback.

It is important, as a musician, that you can hear yourself on stage. It is rare, but not completely unheard of, for bands to play unamplified. Some bands playing in small clubs still play as they did in the 1960s, with amps on stage for each amplified instrument and a vocal amp for vocalists. However, this has drawbacks. You will set up the sound so you can have an optimal mix on stage. However, if there is no backline to assist you, you will have limited opportunities to ensure the sound you are hearing on the stage is as it is supposed to be in the venue. For this reason, most situations require a stage mix.

There are typically two methods of monitoring. The more traditional is through the placement of wedges in front of the band. Wedges are triangular speakers that sit on the floor in front of the band and direct sound upward at 45°. During the sound check, the engineer develops a stage sound mix. This may be a single mix for the entire band or, if the outputs are available, for individual musicians. At the start of the 2000s, stage mixes began to be placed under the control of musicians by using headphones and control boxes with several controls for individual instruments. However, they needed to run cabling to each box making it difficult to use if musicians were moving around the stage. More recently, the stage mix has moved into the wireless world. The mix is sent into a control box that individual musicians can control directly via smartphone or tablet apps.

Wireless headphone boxes are connected to the mix and musicians hear the mix through headphones or earbuds. This dispenses entirely with wedges and gives musicians entire control over their mix.

How Big Do You Need Your Live Rig to Be?

The size of your live rig, the wattage of your amplifiers, the size of your speakers, and the number of channels in your mixer all depend on a lot of things. They depend on the size of the room. How full it is. Human bodies absorb sound, something you need to factor into your sound check. If you go to a music shop, you'll see powered speaker with wattages and speaker sizes. Music sales staff are generally amazing and will try their hardest to sell you something appropriate for the gig, but it helps if you know a bit about what you want.

Remember that bit of acoustic theory I promised? Here it is. You might have heard of decibels (abbreviated to dB). In acoustics, decibels measure the sound pressure level (SPL). Our ears hear the SPL as loudness. The higher the dB, the louder we hear a sound. But double the decibels isn't twice as loud. 100dB is many times louder than 50dB. We measure the power of amplifiers in watts, and watts are not a logarithmic value. So, a 50-watt amplifier is only about 3dB louder than a 25 watt. You'll notice the difference, but it won't be as much as you think. To make matters more complicated, the SPL gets weaker the further it travels. Every time you double your distance, the sound reduces by 6dB. Thus, if a speaker is producing 100dB (about the volume of a jackhammer) at 1 m, at 2 m this will be down to 94db, at 4 m, it'll be down to 88dB, At the back of your 32 m room, your sound will be down to about 70dB, or about the same SPL as a vacuum cleaner. This doesn't take into account the size of the room or the people in it either.

Thus, the size of the room will dictate the size your live rig needs to be. The following might give you an idea.

- Small space (e.g., bar, restaurant): 200–250W
- Medium space (e.g., medium size auditorium, church): 250–1500W
- Large space (e.g., large auditorium, church): 1500W–4000W
- Outdoor space (e.g., outdoor festival): 4000W+
- Stadium: 15,000W+

Technologies to Enhance the Experience

The very nature of being at a gig, close to the musicians you admire, listening to their songs, makes the experience special. However, there are technologies that add to your experience and make it … well … even specialler. If you want your gigs to be memorable, you need to utilise these technologies, because many other bands are doing it, and you have to be competitive.

Technologies to enhance the experience come in two main varieties: Lighting enhancements and audio enhancements.

Lighting

Stage lighting is a useful tool for performance. Dimming most of the house, but lighting the stage, brightly forces people to focus their attention where you choose. Different types and colours of lights can add effects and enhance the experience. In short, you need to know how your lighting operates, and how to use it to enhance the experience.

Stage lighting was first used when musicians performed in theatres. When Duke Ellington performed in the Cotton Club, or Benny Goodman performed at Carnegie Hall, they used the stage lighting that was there. When contemporary music gigs moved to small venues, they might have brought some lighting, but they often performed in the ambient lighting of the venue itself. Lighting shows for live performances really got going in the era of psychedelic rock, where audiences would go to LSD-fuelled performances by the Grateful Dead, Jefferson Airplane, and Pink Floyd. Lighting enhanced the experience as much as the drugs did.

There are several types of stage lighting. Traditional stage lighting used high-intensity light bulbs and typically manual control from a traditional lighting desk, looking a little like an audio mixing desk. However, these are now very rare because of their fragility and the huge amount of power they use and heat they generate. Modern lights typically generate power through light-emitting diodes or LEDs. These can change colour and are very efficient, generate little heat, and can be controlled digitally.

Table 10.1 Different types of stage lighting

Lighting Type	Description
PAR Lights	Short for Parabolic Aluminised Reflector lights these are probably the most common stage lights you'll see. Traditionally these used a sealed beam unit and used a gel (a transparent coloured material in front of the bulb) to change colour. They are fairly cheap, require little maintenance, and are fairly durable. Modern ones use LED lights and can change colour from a lighting desk. They shine a particular colour on a region of the stage.
Strip Lights	Strip lights involve several lights set up in a strip. They can be used to create a wash (an unfocussed light that covers a large area). Traditionally they would require a gel to change colour, but modern LED versions can change colour from the lighting desk.
Moving Head Lighting	PAR and strip lights are fixed in place. However, there is a range of lights called "moving head lighting" or "intelligent lighting" that can move a focussed beam around the stage area. Modern LED versions can also change colour. They create a moving and exciting lighting experience.
Spotlights	A spotlight is a powerful focussed beam that creates a defined pool of light with a hard edge. They can be used to highlight a particular area of the stage or the house. The most common form of fixed spotlight is the Fresnel lantern. However, a spotlight can also be mobile when it is called a followspot. Followspots are often operated by a technician who physically points it at the performer, but automatic spotlights are now available.

Gigs can be lit in several ways. Either you bring a simple rig or a few lights. Often the venue will have a lighting rig. Sometimes this is simple, sometimes it is very complex with multiple lights and a complex controller. In larger gigs, your backline will supply lighting. If you're bringing your own lights, your rig will probably be very simple. You might bring some coloured floods you bought from a hardware store, place them on the floor, and plug them in. You might purchase a few cheap lights and a small lighting controller that you can operate between songs. But if you have a lighting rig, it will be a simple one. The next step up with regards to lighting rigs is at a venue. If a live audio engineer also does lights (which they'll charge for), they can also operate lights between operating sound. Rarely, a gig might have a separate lighting operator and live audio engineer. In larger gigs, or in venues that have no lighting, the backline will bring lighting. A modern alternative to a lighting rig in a show regularly performed in the same way with the same lighting is to go with pre-set lighting. A program such as QLab is connected to a DBX lighting rig to adjust your lights.

COLOUR AND MOVEMENT

I'm a very auditory person. But I'm married to an artist. So I'm very conscious of the fact that people go to hear bands for a range of reasons. They go because they want an experience that combines the visual with the aural. They want colour and movement. The jazz singer Kerrie Biddell used to talk about colour and movement. Just because you're playing jazz doesn't mean you deny the audience a bit of colour and movement. For the audience, some good lighting and special effects go a long way towards highlighting what they should be focussing on, as well as giving them some variety. I went to a big band about two weeks ago and what I noticed immediately was: There's 17 people that you can look at. And so you can look at the bass. I'm a bass player, so I look at the bass player for 30 seconds and go, "yeah, that's interesting". And then the trombone player does a little thing and you go, "that's nice". And then you hear the saxophones playing a nice sort of five part voicing thing and you go, "that's cool." So your eyes and your ears are bouncing around. I think that's how the average audience watches a rock band. For a while, their eyes are bouncing around from the singer to the guitarist, and then they notice the drummer's doing some stuff, and then the lighting focusses on the keyboard player for a moment or something else that's going on because there might be some backing singer if it's a big concert. So there's lots of eye candy and ear candy going on, and it makes for a 360° experience. There's sound and lighting and movement and stuff, as well as an emotional journey. They're playing the songs that I love, they're playing some new songs that are fresh to my ears, so it's some new stuff. I think if you're putting together a performance, you've got to take into consideration all of those aspects, not just the music.

Clive, Bass player, songwriter, and educator

Backing Tracks

Not backing tracks, I hear you cry! We're not going to use backing tracks. We're authentic! We don't want to fool the audience. We want to be real! Well, let me tell you something. Every live performance—not only every music performance—is about smoke and mirrors. Cabaret, stage musicals, comedy, jazz, rock. They are all about making things seem greater than they are. Recently, I went with a colleague to a Kylie Minogue show. There were two support acts as well as the main Kylie performance. Every performance used live bands. Every performance also used backing tracks. Ultimately, you have to decide whether to use backing tracks. But you should at least know how they work

Backing tracks are recordings of instruments you don't have in the band. They are designed to make a smaller band sound bigger. They might include strings, horns, second keyboard parts, percussion, or anything you can't include within your ensemble band. Backing tracks have suffered over the years from poor-quality and electronic-sounding implementation, which gives them a bad name. Modern backing tracks, however, can be of extremely high quality and add considerably to an experience. Modern Digital Audio Workstations (DAWs) such as LogicProX, Cubase, and Protools, combined with high-quality samples, can create extremely good backing tracks. Particularly high-quality tracks might use live musicians recorded in an expensive studio.

Backing tracks normally use a standard stereo file. This can be a wav file, an mp3, or any of the popular stereo formats. On one track (say the left track) are the backing tracks, and on the other (in this case the right track) is a click track. Figure 10.2 shows how a set of backing tracks might be created on Logic Pro X.

In this example, the right track of our stereo file is a click track. A click track is an audio cue that is sent to an earpiece worn by the drummer. It is sort of like a metronome: A series of clicks with a different sound for the first beat of the bar. Vocal cues can also be a part of the click. At the start of the track, a drummer may hear: "One, two, ready, go". Slowdowns are typically subdivided to permit the drummer to change tempo with greater accuracy. They may even have an added acoustic click saying, "one and two and three and four and". Rapid changes in tempo are typically preceded by a bar counted in the new tempo. It is up to the drummer to bring in the rest of the band. Playing to a click is an art that takes time for drummers to develop. If you're a drummer, as you practice reading, also practice playing to a click. Both are essential skills for you.

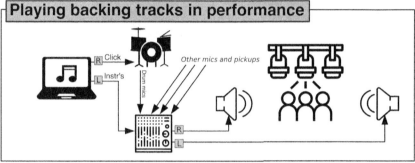

Figure 10.2 Creating and performing with backing tracks with Logic Pro X.

The backing track containing the instruments, in this example on the left track, is sent to an input in the mixing console, just like any other track. This does have the disadvantage that your engineer has to settle for the mix that has been set on the track. More sophisticated playback systems allow you to sync several stereo files together to create more tracks. If you have four tracks, you can have bass on track 1, kick drum on track 2, the rest of the backing tracks on track 3, and the click on track 4. This permits better acoustic sculpting for the particular room. High-end systems such as QLab Audio can play multiple tracks at once, meaning you could have individual sends for each instrument on your backing tracks.

There are several ways of playing backing tracks in performance. The simplest is a smartphone or tablet running software that permits rapid selection of a particular track. (Put it into airline mode if you're going to do this, as you don't want to receive a phone call during your performance!) More sophisticated systems involve the use of a laptop running a program such as QLab. The free version of QLab permits the playback of a single stereo track. The paid audio version is expensive but has many additional features.

Further Reading

There are a lot of books on technology in recording, and some in live sound. While a detailed discussion of the specialist art of live mixing is outside the scope of this book, Bill Gibson's *The Ultimate Live Sound Operator's Handbook* is a great starting place.

Chapter Summary

- The thoughtful implementation of live music technology is central to being a performing musician.
- There are three types of technology associated with the live music industry:
    - Performance technology:
        - Amplifying technology:
            - Input transducers.
            - Mixing consoles.
            - Amplifiers.
            - Output transducers.
            - Foldback.
        - Technology to enhance the experience:
            - Lighting.
            - Backing tracks.
    - Promotion technology:
        - We'll deal with this in the next chapter.
    - Recording technology:
        - No longer the main method of generating revenue.
        - Used as part of a toolkit of the working musician.

11 Getting the Gigs
Promotion, Travel, Contracts, and Talking Business

One day our music executive friend, Tim, was standing on the stage of the old Sydney Entertainment Centre with one of Australia's biggest producers of live shows. The place was buzzing as backline set up for the evening performance. Staff staffed and ushers ushed. This guy turned to Tim, and pointed at the back seats saying, "for all the huge capacity of this venue, after I pay everyone, my profit margin is the last three rows". Now, in a venue like the old EntCent, the back three rows are still a huge number of tickets. Being at the top, those rows have the most seats. However, it's worthwhile remembering that everyone was getting paid. The musicians, the venue, the ushers, the backline—everyone was assured of getting their salary. All except the promoter, who was relying on those back three rows to run his business and feed his family.

Once musicians can play well together, are cohesive and competent on stage, and have a defined product, they have the basics covered, and they need to join the industry. They need to promote themselves. They need to get gigs. They need to talk business. This chapter will explore the process of promotion, of touring, and of the practicalities of getting gigs. It will consider the role of social media in creating a 'buzz', and of being heard above the white noise of every other band.

How to Promote Your Act

So you've got a great solo or ensemble act. Everyone in the band is a great player and a great hang. The band is tight. You've written a few good songs and recorded them. So what's next? How do you get the word out? How do you get people to your gigs? That's the art of promotion, and music promotion is a book unto itself. However, in this section we can cover the basics.

Your Website

A website should be your first promotional technology. While some may regard them as a little outdated, you still need one. You need a place on the web where you can present yourself and your product in a manner you choose. Get some ideas by going to edsheeran.com, taylorswift.com, lukecombs.com, veronicaswift.

com, thebadplus.com, romeosantosonline.com, kendricklamar.com, or any professional musician website.

There are several ways of setting up a website. The first thing you need is a domain name and hosting. These are two different fees. You will pay for your domain name, which can be the generic yourname.com or a local variant such as yourname.co.uk, yourname.co.nz, or whatever. This fee is shared between the registry who look after the domain, and the company registering the domain. The hosting is money you pay to the hosting company to give you an amount of space on their servers. A Google search will reveal a multitude of hosting options in your area. You don't even need to stay in your area. I've successfully hosted sites on providers based in India. Once you've registered for hosting, you will then get a hosting login where you can add content, set up email addresses, and so forth.

If you are not a tech guru, there are a couple of ways you can still set up your own website. You can set up a content management system (CMS) and purchase a theme. Your CMS might be Wordpress, Joomla, or several other systems. Both Wordpress and Joomla are open source software that you can install on your server. You can then buy a Wordpress or Joomla theme, which allows you to put content in relatively easily. Being open source, there are enormous resources out there to assist you with Wordpress and Joomla. The alternative is to use a commercial system, of which the most popular currently appears to be Wix. In this system, you open an account at Wix, pay for your hosting and URL, and create your website from very flexible templates. Wix has a free option, but it comes with Wix branding and advertisements. Currently, the commercial version of Wix costs a minimum of US $13 per month, with an additional $6 per email address.

Your Electronic Press Kit

An Electronic Press Kit (EPK) is your band resume where people can find out about you and your music. It is commonly a PDF document available from download from your website. This is where press and promoters can get quotes about your music and band. It includes the following information:

- Your current contact information.
- A short biography.
- A link to media, including professional pictures, sound links, and videos.
- Quotes from people about your work.
- Any press coverage.
- A list of upcoming gigs.

When you create your EPK, make sure it is a professional document. You should check the spelling and grammar. You should ensure the layout is professional and clear. You should make the text effective. You need not have a designer lay it out, but you should ensure the layout is clear and effective. You can create it using a word processor such as Microsoft Word or the open source LibreOffice Write.

Photos and Videos

Let me tell you something. As ubiquitous as smartphones are and as awesome as they are at taking Instagram pics of your breakfast, they're not good enough for taking publicity photos. Neither is your home camera. Neither (probably) is your friend's DSLR. Your publicity photos need to be taken by a professional photographer in a controlled environment using high-quality equipment. If your college has a visual arts department, they might help. If not, a quick search of the internet will reveal a plethora of professional photographers. If you live in a city, you might even find some who specialise in music photography. Use them. Take photos every year or two. Note, however, that this can be expensive. A friend of mine recently paid over AU $1,000 for three photos. If you're going to be a professional musician, you need professional photos.

Equally, if you're going to use video, make it the best you can afford. I've seen bands—even student bands—pay for professional videographers to record videos. If you're lucky enough to be in a school that has a filmmaking or video course, see if you can work with student filmmakers to do professional video.

Social Media: Engaging With Your Fans

When I first started teaching in the mid-1990s, one of the biggest revolutions was the internet. The mid-1990s internet was slow, ugly, and didn't implement music and video all that well, but it was instantaneous access to information. We all thought it would revolutionise the industry. (It did. Just not in the way we thought it would.) We thought it would allow musicians to put their music online. They would keep in touch with fans directly rather than having to go through the gatekeepers of the record industry. They would promote their own gigs. People would receive promotional emails from them and read them. (Ha!) The trouble was that many people and musicians had access to this. The amount of music produced and thrown up (literally) online ramped up. There was a lot more godawful music available, and this meant a lot of white noise. Without the gatekeepers of the industry—the labels, the producers, the A&R staff—you had to search through a lot of bad music to find good.

One of the biggest innovations of the new version of the internet has been the development of social media. These internet sites where people connect with friends and show what they do. And they're still fairly new. YouTube launched in 2005. Facebook and Twitter both launched in 2006. Instagram and Pinterest launched in 2010. After a slow start, Reddit has become widely popular in the last few years. These are not technologies with decades of history. We're still working out the ethical and moral parameters for their usage, but I'll leave such debates to the philosophy faculty.

Now before we get going, understand that social media is not some kind of musical silver bullet. It will not transform you into a star. It is one tool among many in your toolkit of live music success. However, it is a useful tool. It helps you engage with your fans and encourage them to come to your gigs. The public is already engaged with it. How often do you sit next to someone on the train and watch their thumb flick, flick, flick, as they scroll through a social media site?

Now, everyone loves music. The difficulty is in getting people to notice you over the aforementioned musical white noise. How do you get them to engage with your posts and gigs? Remember, we're talking about three sets of people: Public, audience, and fans.

- How do you get people who have never heard of you (public) to engage with you and come to gigs (audiences)?
- How do you get people who have been to a gig (audiences) to become fans, come regularly, and buy your merchandise?
- How to you keep these fans engaged and returning regularly?

To do this, there are a few things you can do.

Firstly, have professional social media accounts or pages separate from your personal ones. Your personal Facebook account should be just that: Personal and secure. It should be for your friends from far-flung places to post photos of their cats. You need to set up a distinct professional page on Facebook and a professional account on Twitter and Instagram. Dividing your life into your professional and personal life makes sense. You can present yourself professionally on your professional account and personally on your (secure) personal account. Make sure your professional accounts are clean and optimised. You should use the same branding across all of your social media. Use the same images on your professional Facebook, Twitter, and Instagram accounts.

Now, let's talk about images. Remember that professional photo we talked about? This is where it will shine. Social media runs on images. Social media sites prescribe optimal sizes for their images. If you don't use them, they will be cropped, which can mean losing important information. These sizes change occasionally, so check online.

You can use programs like Photoshop, Pixelmator, or the open source GIMP to size these. However, there are plenty of specialist programs such as Adobe Spark Post, Canva, or BeFunky that allow you to create striking images for inclusion on your Twitter feed.

Your profile is your presentation of yourself as a musician. Ensure that it is both up-to-date and constantly updated. Send posts. Change your bio. Use your profile to promote your latest gig, tour, recording, song, merch, or whatever. Facebook has an events feature that allows you to promote your upcoming gigs. Use it.

Post content regularly. Post photos of yourself in action, rehearsing, playing, signing, standing next to fans. (This is where a decent smartphone comes in handy!) Get audiences to tag you. Post videos of yourself playing a new song. Post behind-the-scenes content as it shows you as a real person without the hype and marketing. If you don't post regularly, you won't stay relevant. Document your musical journey as a band. Explain what you're doing and why you're doing it.

Tag everybody. Tag musicians, venues, music brands. You're playing at the coolest place in town. Tag or hashtag it. You love your Korg keyboard? Post a photo of yourself playing it and include @KorgUSA, @KorgUK, or @KorgAU. This is not entirely pandering to a brand, musician, or venue. By including these tags, your posts become more visible. You're using their readership in your own tags. Your fans might tag you in a post. Interact with them. If someone tags you in a post, it will appear on your social media feed. Write back to them. That engagement, that accessibility, is what fans are hoping for. It makes them feel connected to you.

Consider the time at which you post. While you might finish that gig at 1 am, it might not be the best time to post. By the time everyone wakes up, that photo is waaaay down on everyone's social media feed. The best times to post are during the day, during the week. Sunday and between 5 pm and 7 am have the least engagement. There is some variation between different platforms, but this generally works well.

While we're here, you might feel uncomfortable self-promoting. Don't. That's what social media is all about. Particularly for musicians. Tell people about your new gig, tour, album, or merch. While social media algorithms are complex and a chapter unto themselves, if you post regularly about your music, people will see that you are engaged and they will be more likely to follow you than a static page. This is a business strategy and not something you do for pleasure.

One way to get your gigs and band noticed is to use Facebook's paid advertising campaigns. It used to be the case that your notices and gigs would automatically show up on your fans' Facebook feeds. Not anymore. Facebook's revised algorithms mean that you don't necessarily show up on your supporters' feeds. However, you will show up on a wide range of feeds if you pay for the campaign. Sponsored posts appear to a target demographic you define, and they can be surprisingly cost-effective. If you have a gig coming up, a sponsored post can be very useful.

USING FACEBOOK

A couple of years ago, you could definitely use Facebook a lot more to your advantage. Now I find everyone's on the same playing field. Everyone uses it to promote their band. You have to pay if you want people to see your posts these days. It's not like it used to be, where we'd put up a post and it would appear, like we did our first EP. Everyone that was following your page would see that pop up in their newsfeed. If you don't pay for a post now, no one sees it, so I suppose Facebook have got people checking it now and they need to make money for them. They need to pay dividends.

Mik, Guitarist

Social media isn't magic. It is one tool you can use for promotion. But it is a way of engaging with your audience and promoting your band and their performances.

Not only is it worthwhile investing your time and finances in, it is essential. Every other band is doing it. You need to do it as well.

Recordings

This book focusses on the live music industry. We haven't really discussed recordings. Until the late-1990s, the industry was entirely focussed on recording, because that's where the money was. While you could only play to perhaps a few thousand people at the largest concerts, millions could buy your records. Touring was regarded as a way to promote albums. In a way, the tours paid for the studio time. However, when Napster got going, the public quickly got used to free music. Recordings lost their intrinsic value, and they've never recovered. About the best that can happen now is that some people choose to pay for a Spotify or Apple Music subscription, which gives you access to huge catalogues of music for less than the price of a CD. Recordings help pay for the tour rather than the other way around. As I've said, the recording industry is not earning the dollars it used to for musicians. It does for streaming services and—to an extent—for labels. However, that doesn't mean that you should not record. Recordings are terrific promotional tools that can raise awareness of your music and upcoming gigs, and develop your performance, writing, arranging, and production careers.

I'm going to make a controversial statement. Recordings of contemporary music are now merchandise to support your live gigs. Don't get me wrong, they're important. They bring you to the attention of large numbers of people. However, it's rare to make huge amounts of money out of them. One of the best opportunities to generate income from recordings is as merchandise at gigs and (particularly) at festivals.

Recordings are another tool in your music industry toolbelt. They are necessary. Create the best recordings you can. Go into studios. They're a lot cheaper and have better gear than they had in the 1990s. Get the best recording engineers you can afford. Audiences who don't know you will judge you by the recordings they come across on streaming services and social media. However, they are no longer the industry focus they once were.

LIVE MUSIC VERSUS RECORDED MUSIC IN INDIA

Live music is more important than recorded music in India. I encourage artists to record something to put across to clients. I manage this reggae band called [name redacted] and we were talking about cutting albums yesterday. I said, let's just keep the album aside, let's just record one track and use it as a demo for now. Maybe two. Then record an album. I've managed bands where we've recorded an album and we've printed a bunch of them. And at some point at a concert we've seen them on the floor lying somewhere, or you know, a bunch of them lying somewhere on the floor or on the grounds or whatever, like, you know? So it's not really important in the whole game plan of sticking it on as a band. But saying that, there has been a slight difference in terms of how there are a few dedicated and informed music consumers there, you know? There are more now. But they're not more than five percent, ten percent sort of reach. And those people sort of listen to music and recorded music. I'm not too sure if CDs work. But definitely mp3s and online music increase the number of fans. But I don't see recordings as being of much importance. Live music is where the money comes in.

Gary, Artist manager

We're not going to go into the processes of recording your music. I will note that, if possible, try to partner with a good recording engineer and a good studio. They will make your recordings sound more professional. There are also plenty of studio musicians and engineers around the world that can help with your project on websites such as airgigs.com and soundbetter.com.

Getting Your Recordings Heard: Radio

Once you have your recordings, you need to place them. There are two basic options: Radio and streaming services. Radio airplay is still one of the most important ways of getting your music to a local and national audience. Depending on your area (and who you're targeting), you can target national, commercial, and community broadcasters. Internet radio and podcasts are also alternatives.

Radio stations choose songs to play based on many variables. Some of these include:

- Whether the recording is already successful on other stations.
- Whether you are an established artist with a track record of hits.
- Sales and tip sheets from industry publications.
- Listener requests.
- Market tests.
- Record promotors/radio pluggers and label rep influences.
- Reputation in the live arena and via publicity.
- On merit and consultation with station reps.

To maximise your chances of getting on the radio, consider these points:

- Radio stations have a format. Some are jazz stations. Some are country. Some are 'contemporary hit radio'. Ensure that your song and sound is right for the format.

- Community stations are far easier to 'crack' than commercial ones. If you can create a buzz on community radio, you can leverage this to generate interest from bigger stations.
- To maximise your chances of getting your music on radio, develop relationships with radio stations.

If you have the money, you can also hire radio pluggers. Radio pluggers specialise in generating airplay for artists. Major labels usually have them in-house, but independents must contract them directly. However, if you go with a radio plugger, understand that they are expensive and even after an eight-week campaign, you may have no radio plays to show for it.

Getting Your Recordings Heard: Streaming and Playlists

Radio is still important. A lot of us still travel by car. Consumers, however, increasingly use streaming services to find new bands to follow. However, there is a lot of music to wade through on Spotify or Apple Music. This makes it hard to get the attention your recording needs and deserves.

If you are making audio recordings, get them onto Spotify and Apple Music. You do this via a label or an aggregator. You'll know what a record label is, particularly if you have a deal. You may be less sure of an aggregator. It's simple. An aggregator is a company that assists you with global distribution of your music through digital stores (like Apple Music or Google Play) and through streaming services. Basically, you pay the fees, upload your music, and it will eventually appear on the various streaming services. They can charge upfront fees and/or a percentage of the revenue you earn from streaming. Common aggregators include CD Baby, DistroKid, and Believe Digital. However, there are a wide range of aggregators out there, all offering different services and charging different fees. You should search around.

As noted, there is a lot of music on streaming services. Enter the playlist. Playlists are lists of music that are curated either by the streaming service or by a third party. They are classified by genre, so you get hip hop playlists, jazz playlists, indie playlists, and the like. It is possible to pay for inclusion on third-party playlists. Spotify has a sponsored songs feature which allows labels to pay to play songs to free Spotify subscribers. Further labels and the like have paid third-party playlist producers for inclusion on the most influential playlists, a technique that Spotify admits costs around $2,500 per song. Doing so can bring you to the attention of the official and elusive Spotify curators.

One thing though: Don't expect to get rich off streaming. Spotify, for example, pays between 0.6¢ to 0.84¢ per play to the holder of the rights of the music. This will likely at least include your aggregator and possibly your manager, producer, label, and songwriters. 100 plays will net 60¢ to be divided between you all. 10,000 plays will bring in the grand sum of $60. Making money in streaming is about volume. The more plays you can get, the more you will earn. But the volume has to be big.

INCOME STREAMS

Q: Back in the day, you were mostly working with recorded music which was where the money was. We went through a stage of recorded music being less where the money was and live performance being where the money was. What do you see is the relationship between the two as of now?

Tim: The money is with live.

Q: Is it ever going to change?

Tim: No. Well, okay, I mean, possibly. The revenues are going up on recorded music. The tipping points of streaming could be exponentially healthy. It has the chance to flip again. I think artists have got to choose what they want to do and how they want to represent themselves. And for some people that might be writing. You've got three key income streams if you're an artist: Recording, writing, and live performance. And depending on who you are and how you want to skew it, the live environment doesn't suit some people. It just might be too tough on the road, you know? If all Sia did was write songs, she'd still be a very wealthy woman. Artists are going to have to engage people in a competitive world. Engagement skills are that important, even if that is just knowing who you are and how you want to translate that to your tribe.

Tim, Record executive

Getting Gigs

So now you have people wanting to hear you. How do you give them that opportunity? The process of getting gigs varies depending on your level of professionalism and experience as a musician. But there's one constant: It's all around contacts and reputation.

Let's use the experience of Waldo as an example. Waldo is a known bass player in Sydney. He arrived in Sydney from Chile in 1976 with his family. His father was a known guitarist in Chile, who continued to play in Sydney. A lot of Latinos had recently arrived in Australia, so there was a need for musicians at that time. As his father became known in the Latin scene in Sydney, he started giving Waldo gigs. Gradually, people started to know him and like his playing, so these contacts started calling him for other gigs. However, he was interested in more than just Latin music and he started listening to other styles of music: Pop, rock, jazz, funk. Wanting to play in this music too, he purposely set out to make contacts in the rock and funk world. He went to gigs. He spoke to people. Eventually this paid off, and he started playing in different bands. Jazz. Funk. Writing songs. Doing this led to still more contacts. Waldo became known as a bass player who was a good hang, but also technically adept and a talented sight reader. Now, he was still playing Latin music, but people were asking him to play in different bands. Waldo started putting his own projects together. Because he was known in Sydney, he started to contact agents and managers. He made contacts with record company people. With recording studios. That led to a lot of gigs. Venues started calling him to put bands together. An inner-city nightclub called Toucan Tango asked him to put a band together and that kind of led to a three-year gig playing every Thursday, Friday, and Saturday. As Waldo says: "I'm quite good at talking, you know what I mean, talking to people and convincing them that I'm much better than I am". Essentially, Waldo started gigging through just friendship, networking, and reputation.

That's how it worked for Waldo. How would it work for you? The industry has changed since the 1980s. There are more musicians of varying degrees of talent pushing themselves online. But the industry still revolves around contacts and reputation. Contacts come by going to gigs, going to industry events, getting involved in the scene, talking with booking agencies and promoters, meeting other musicians, and so on. Always be looking for opportunities to play, to meet other professional musicians, to meet industry members. Keep records of who you meet. Pay attention when they tell you their names. Have business cards made that clearly state your name, your instrument, your contacts, and your website, and distribute them. Take them to gigs and give them to other musicians. Take them to industry events and hand them out.

Reputation is another matter. Throughout this book, I've encouraged you to treat each gig professionally. I've outlined the way the industry works in my and Waldo's experience, and in the experience of the professional musicians to whom we've spoken. These are a good starting point. However, you're also an individual, and within these guidelines, you need to find your own way of working. But always remember the 60/40 rule. Working as a professional musician is 40% about covering the gig, and 60% not being a jerk.

THE ADVANTAGES OF NOT BEING PIGEONHOLED

We get more gigs than any other person on their label, and it's purely because of our style. We've got a style of music that you can't necessarily bracket into one genre. We've had three number one Australian country hits. A number one popular hit. And then we've got all these different other areas like Blues & Roots; we've won the APRA award for the Blues &

Roots Song of the Year. We've supported Dolly Parton. We've toured with
Birds of Tokyo, James Blunt on a world tour, KD Lang, Pete Murray. None
of them are the same genre. And that's why our booking agency loves us.

Jeremy, Guitarist

Networking Your Way Into Gigs

You might get a few gigs from friends when you first start playing. Perhaps friends
are throwing a party. Perhaps your college requires that you play as part of an
assessment. But these gigs are not sustainable and eventually you must approach
other people about gigs. People who don't disappear from the scene.

Before you approach people about gigs, you need to have a few things ready.
Gigs are not a learn-as-you-earn scenario! Your band needs to be sounding good.
You need to have set lists ready. Your music needs to be written. You don't get a
gig and then form the act. You have the act first and then get the gigs. You also
need to be set professionally. Have a website. Have an EPK. Have photos. Have
good recordings if you can. If you can't point people to your material, they'll have
nothing to judge your act on.

Once you've got a product, you're ready to start developing your network.
Cold calling is not, in my experience, a great way to start gigging. But if you have
nowhere else to start, it's worth trying. Call venues and places that mount acts
similar to yours. Look at gig listings on the internet and in the limited remaining
street press. However, there are other ways to network with the industry. You're
much more likely to get gigs if people know you. Everything in the live music
industry is about personal contacts. If you're at school, you've already got some
great contacts in your fellow students, but don't stop there. When you're handing
out business cards at industry events and gigs, make sure you collect them as well.
Meet people and follow them up. Reach out on social media and email. You can't
afford to be retiring about this, because there are hundreds of other musicians
pushing their own acts. In this way, you'll develop your own industry network
and gather a reputation.

A few pieces of advice on networking:

Be proactive in your networking. Be the one to reach out first and initiate
contact. Talk to people. Go up to them at industry events, stick out your hand,
and introduce yourself. Propose collaborations and follow up. If you constantly
wait for people to reach out to you, you might wait for a while.

Your network is like any group of people: You need to maintain it. Follow up
with people you've not heard from. Use social media if you have to, but reach out.
Get in touch and meet for coffee and brainstorm ideas.

If you don't know someone you should, approach them directly. Social media
is great for this. If you like how a venue works, send them a message. If you admire
an artist manager, reach out to them. Music industry professionals like direct
approaches and hate time-wasters.

Be professional. Always. Be punctual. Be concise in your communications. Say what you'll do, then do what you say. Ensure your brand and promotional materials are effective and well-laid out. People will judge whether they want to work with you based on how you portray yourself as a professional industry person.

Do your research. If you've met someone at an industry event, read up on them before you send them a follow up. Research before you contact someone cold.

Be yourself. Don't portray yourself as someone you're not. If you're a music student with a lot to learn, show yourself as eager, efficient, and professional. If you've more experience, showcase that. Music industry people have a sixth sense for nonsense, no matter how well you dress it up.

Approach networking with a business mindset, but also a personal one. You don't know who you might meet. Industry events are a great opportunity to increase your professional circle. The people going to them, however, will want to work with people they like. Showcase yourself as you are, and you'll be fine.

Touring

Touring is an effective way to increase your fan base and your geographical footprint. If it makes economic sense, it's a good thing to do. Plus, you get to see parts of the world you may have not seen. But it takes commitment and organisation.

Tours can be big or small. The big ones take huge amounts of organisation and logistics. Depending on the level of the tour, one of several people handle the details of touring. The artist manager, the producer, or the bandleader might deal with logistics. Agents may book gigs in the touring areas. The tour may have a tour manager to organise things. Or it may be less involved. The Waifs began touring all over Australia in their teens. Between 1992 and 1996, they lived out of a Kombi. They would decide where they were going next, ring the tourist bureau, get the names of live music venues, and call them. In this way, they got known, and launched a career that is still going. There are few logistics in that.

Touring can be fun. But touring also comes with financial risks. If you don't earn enough from the gigs, you can end up losing money. If the venue doesn't promote enough, and you're on a door deal, gigs can be financial and artistic disasters. However, with planning, budgeting, and care, touring can be rewarding. One thing I like best about being a musician is touring far-flung areas I've never been to before, travelling on the back of my talent, as it were. But if you're going to tour, you need to be organised and effective in your planning.

Planning a tour means organising a budget, travel, accommodation, and events. The question of where to tour is often prescribed. Perhaps you're going to a festival and finding some gigs on the way. Perhaps your agent has booked some gigs in a regional area. Or maybe you're just trying to be like The Waifs, look at what's around you, and go there. Either way, you'll risk less if you plan.

Budgeting a Tour

If you're a name act with an artist manager, your manager will look after tour budgeting for you. However, you may also have to do this on your own. Basically, you need to balance the costs of touring with the income you will receive. Costs include travel, food, salaries, emergencies. Income comprises the money from gigs and merchandise.

Tour Income

Tour income can range from known and fixed incomes to big fat unknowns depending on the contract you establish with venues. If you have a set perfor-mance fee from venues or a festival, it becomes relatively easy to budget. You have this much income. You have these expenses. If you earn more than you spend, it's a successful tour. However, if you are on door deals, you need to calculate. Being a distant gig, you don't know what factors may affect attendance. Perhaps the local football final is on the same night. There may be multiple events, or bigger-name acts in town. The weather may be bad. When you're touring, always work with bad scenarios. Once you know your venue capacity and how much you'll make per ticket, calculate the income at (say) 25% of capacity, 50%, 75%, and 100%. That way you'll know how much wiggle room you have.

It's safest not to include merchandise in your budgeting. If you sell a hundred pink fluffy hippos for your band Pink Hippos, great. You've made more than you thought. Congratulations! But you might also sell none and have the hippo bag in your car on the way home. Merch is the most unpredictable tour income item.

Most tours are a combination of set fees and door deals. Do the sums and work out how to afford the tour.

TOURING IN THE AUSTRALIAN REGIONS

There are significant festivals across Western Australia, but there could be plenty more, given the huge number of musicians in the state. I guess one of the issues in WA is the tyranny of distance. That's something I'm being very proactive about as an executive director of [local music industry organisation]. Opening opportunities for regional and remote artists and not discounting them just because they're a long way away. There is fund-ing available through [local arts organisations] that musicians use to get to the festivals if you're offered a spot. That's slowly shifting the mindset in WA, whereas previously it was like, "yeah, you know, we can only pay $250 for a small spot". Regional artists aren't going to buy into that. Well, actually they will for the opportunity.

There's a great touring circuit from Exmouth down to the Gascoigne that's really opened up the touring circuit. It means people from Perth can tour into that circuit. Or people from the Kimberley can tour down into that circuit and that gets them down to Perth as well.

Bel, Artist manager

Travel and its Costs

There are multiple ways of getting to a gig. The most common is by road, which limits how far you can travel. Often musicians travel in separate cars with their gear in the back, sharing the driving, and sleeping on the road. Sometimes musicians will hire a van and travel together, though this is less common than in the past. Driving on tour has advantages. It is probably cheaper than flying. You can take gear with you without it being damaged. You get the real experience of touring. Alternatively, flying to a tour is difficult because of the luggage restrictions imposed by airlines. That 25 kg of luggage isn't going to go far when you have amps, drums, guitars, and so forth. This is the reason many people use land transport. If you're flying though, see how much it costs to hire gear at the destination.

Travel costs can include petrol/gas, vehicle hire, flights, and shipping. These are known expenses. Knowing a car's range can help you estimate how much petrol you'll need. You'll get quotes from car hire companies if you're hiring a van. If you're flying, ensure that you have the luggage organised before turning up at the airport, because those luggage fees increase the budget significantly. The further you travel, the higher your performance fee should be.

Increasingly, bands are providing a fixed fee to musicians and expecting them to drive themselves to the gig. If the fee is reasonable, this is often a fair way to manage travel costs. If are taking gear, the travel to the gig becomes tax deductible. The further the travel, the higher the fee should be.

Regarding other expenses such as food and drink, you'd be well advised to nominate a per-diem for your band. This is you saying: "This is how much I'll contribute to your food and living expenses during the tour". If they want to eat at the best hotel in town and have a bottle of scotch on the gig, that's their affair. The per-diem can also add up, so be careful but not miserly.

Accommodation

Accommodation is one of the biggest expenses for which you should budget. The more members and the further you travel, the more these costs reduce the incentive for actually playing the show. Some tours include accommodation in the contract, and you won't have to pay to stay. The standard of accommodation is variable, so be warned! If the venue does not include accommodation, always try to increase your performance fee to cover these costs.

When you're touring, expect to share rooms with your fellow bandmembers. I have occasionally toured when I've had a room to myself, but it's rare. On these occasions, be considerate of your roommate. For the duration of the tour, you'll be working and sleeping in close proximity. Be relaxed and be a great band- and roommate.

One last thing: When you finish the gig and pull up to the motel for the night, it's tempting to leave your gear in the car and collapse into the bed or chill with the band. Please. Before you do, get the gear out of the car and put it in your room. The number of times gear has been stolen from hotels is just too high.

Salaries and Emergencies

You obviously need to budget in musician fees. Musicians don't (shouldn't) work for nothing. You need to budget their salaries into the budget. Again, be fair and not miserly, but balance the books.

Finally, things go wrong on the road. I've had trucks break down miles from anywhere. I've had venues refuse payment after a successful gig. (We got the money in the end). I've had musicians end up in gaol. (True!) Always ensure that you have a little money set aside for the weird things that happen on the road. They may turn your hair white (they did for me!), but you'll have some great stories.

Tour Funding

Sometimes, government agencies and industry organisations provide funding for regional touring. This can cover the touring expenses, making an unprofitable tour much more achievable. It is worthwhile searching to see if there is financial help available to help your tour.

Further Reading

There are plenty of books on the market that discuss recording such as Bobby Owsinski's *Music Producer's Handbook*. A great deal has been written on music publicity. I'd direct you to two authors in particular. Ariel Hyatt is a ferocious music publicist with a range of great books on promotion. Derek Sivers is the founder of CD Baby, and also has a range of books on the subject. On the subject of touring, I'd recommend *The Touring Musician's Handbook* by Bobby Owsinski.

Chapter Summary

- You need to plan to promote your act in order to get gigs.
  - You need a professional website.
  - You need an Electronic Press Kit (EPK).

- You need professional photos and (potentially) videos.
- You need to engage with fans and venues over social media.
- Recordings help you promote your act.
- You need to get your music heard wherever you can.
  - Radio.
  - Streaming.
  - Playlists.
- You need to plan in order to get gigs.
  - Your industry network is essential here.
- Touring is a method of introducing your music to new acts.
  - You need to budget your tour carefully, including:
  - Tour income.
  - Travel and associated costs.
  - Accommodation.
  - Salaries and emergencies.
  - There is sometimes financial help from government and industry organisations.

12 The Unwritten Rules of Music Performance

There is a Hunter S. Thompson quote you may have heard. It was actually originally about the film industry, but it's been enthusiastically adopted by the music industry as well. With some justification. Thompson's quote runs: "The music business is a cruel and shallow money trench, a long plastic hallway where thieves and pimps run free, and good men die like dogs. There's also a negative side."

There are some aspects of the music industry that you won't learn in the rarefied environment of the music academy. What follows are the realities of the music industry learned in the trenches of tours and neon-lit venues, of late nights and long days travelling. Some of these are negative, terrible things. Gigs fail. Your friends can stab you in the back. You have to look after your health. Legal issues abound. And yet, this can also happen in any profession. When all is said and done, being a musician can be one of the most rewarding careers. We've both worked in it all our lives, and we wouldn't do anything else.

In this chapter we will concentrate on that cruel and shallow money trench. This is the stuff that you won't learn in the classroom, but that you learn on the bandstand through the process of playing live music. What we say here might seem a bit down-heartening. But really, these are the realities of life as a performing musician. Many performances fail because of preventable mistakes such as poor mixing, being rude to someone, by not working an audience, by not doing preparation, or by not working with a venue. These are the unwritten rules you need to follow to ensure that your performing career is successful. Pay attention, get a pencil, and write these down!

If Being a Musician Is Rough, Should I Even Be a Musician?

This a question all of us face at some stage in our careers. I'll tell you what I've told every student I've ever taught. The only reason to be a musician is because you'd be absolutely miserable doing anything else. However, there are a few extra things you can think about.

Consider Your Priorities

Realistically, going full-time as a performing musician usually requires sacrifices, at least in the early stages. Are you willing to make them? In other words, for the sake of your music career, are you willing to skip some nights out to save cash? Forgo a new pair of shoes? Maybe live with roommates to cut down on living expenses? Many people make a comfortable living at music—and many more people accept a lower standard of living than they might ideally like to have to devote time and cash to get their careers off the ground.

Are you willing to make those kinds of trades, hoping to make it in the music industry? If not, going full-time might not be right for you.

Remember that if you're in a relationship or in a family—say, if you have four other mouths to feed—then this isn't just a decision you're making for yourself. Is everyone else ready to pitch in and toe the line? You will need support, both moral support and maybe even some financial support. This is the time to make sure your priorities are on the same page as your family's priorities. Things could get rocky otherwise.

Are You Already Making Money at Music?

What kind of earning potential do you have as a musician? If you've never had a paying gig, dip your toes in the water a little bit as a part-time musician before you jump into full-time musician mode. Not only will you need a good network of contacts for booking gigs and such that you build up over time, you'll also need a realistic idea of how much money you get paid to play. Which brings us to our next point.

Can You Make Enough as a Musician in Your Town?

Not every town lends itself to supporting full-time musicians. What is the going rate for gigs in your area? Are there enough venues to keep you going? Touring is an option but in the absence of tour support and the ability to demand high guarantees for your show, touring is more likely to cost you money than cushion your bank account. You need to be within easy reach of enough music establishments to keep the ball rolling or you need to consider moving to some place more practical.

You Know It's a Job, Right?

Becoming your own boss and becoming a full-time musician sounds great. But you've got to work at it. You've got to treat it like a job. If you sit on the couch watching television rather than working every day on your music career, suddenly it'll be 560 hours of Judge Judy later, and you'll realise you haven't actually accomplished much. Make no mistake about it—going full-time as a musician is a full-time job like any other. You need to get up every day and go to work.

Do You Have a Financial Cushion?

Even if you have a steady flow of gigs coming in, there's likely to be an earning lag. Sometimes a gig takes a while to pay. Make sure you can manage your finances as you transition. Sure, it's not very fun, but here's what happens if you don't take this concern seriously. You quit the job that is letting you get some music time in, you spend a few months falling into debt, and then you frantically have to take any job you can to make up the shortfall—probably one that leaves you less time for music than you had to begin with. That's a real drag. Be realistic about the timing so you don't end up one step back from where you started.

If Money Is Your Reason for Being a Musician, Go Be a Corporate Banker

Honestly. I mean that. Go do something … anything else. Hold a stop/go sign. Work in an office. Code. Become a lawyer. You'll have a much easier life. You can make money in the music industry, or any of the creative industries, but it's going to be much harder. And there'll be less of it, unless you are very lucky.

However, most musicians don't do it for the money. Most don't do it for the applause or the fame. We do it because it is our imperative. The soul crushing 9-to-5 is fine for some people. However, it's not for we working creatives. Some of us engage with music only by maximising our income streams into performing, teaching, writing, and recording. Others have a day job or a side gig.

Your Audience Is Your Income

This might sound obvious but apparently it's not, because we've seen this in action. Never, ever, ever alienate your audience. We've seen big acts who play with their back to the audience, who get angry when they don't get the accolades they feel they deserve. If your audience feels disrespected, they will not return. They will leave halfway through the gig, and they will not come back. On the other hand, if you engage with your audience, if you look at them, talk to them, prepare for them, they will love you forever. We've both seen so many musicians who just sit down and don't engage. They're the ones that create eminently forgettable musical performances, not the memorable and successful ones.

Always Be Respectful of Everyone Associated With Your Performance

Normally everyone at the performance wants you to succeed. The venue, the waiters, the security: Their success is your success. If you are respectful of them, they will be of immeasurable help to you. Be courteous and respectful. Say hi to the waiters and the box office staff. Say thanks when they bring your meal. If you're the opening band, get your gear off stage quickly. A little courtesy and thoughtfulness will make everyone a little happier and make the event more pleasant.

Now we're not saying that you won't encounter dismissive venue owners, harried waiters, and overly officious security. Obviously you will. But you have no idea why they're like that. Perhaps their dog just died. You don't know. And your responding in kind is not going to make things any better. Smile, take your instrument, and go set up.

Be Prepared to Work. And I Mean Really Work!

If you're serious about your music, you'll need to work. The top 25% of musicians, the people that earn 97% of their income from their music, work on average between 41 and 44 hours per week on their music.[1] They spread those hours between gigging, performance, composition, and recording, but you take the point. The hours are long. This is not an industry for those who want an easy life. There's this image left hanging over from the seventies that being a musician is a glamorous lifestyle full of travel and booze and sex. Well, let us tell you: It isn't the seventies any more, and music is now, more than at any time, a business. Gigging, preparation, and touring are not glamorous. It's hard work. Be prepared for that.

You Will, at Some Stage, Play Godawful Gigs

If you're serious about your music, if you practice hard, prepare hard, and attempt to create memorable gigs, you should lessen the number of gigs that fail. However, sometimes gigs fail for reasons that are out of your control. You'll be playing to an empty house because there's been no promotion. Or you'll be playing to a crowd who are more interested in watching a sporting event. Or a gig will fail for a hundred other reasons. We've all played those gigs. And they suck at your soul and make you reconsider being a musician.

So, what do you do if you're in this situation? If you're in a band, the experience is a little less fraught. You can support each other with humour. You can grin sheepishly and get through the gig somehow. Such gigs enter into your band's folklore. Do you remember that gig we played in such-and-such a place? God that was awful. You'll get through it. However, it can be more daunting if you're a soloist. In that case, you need to grit your teeth and get through it somehow. Try not to watch the clock and, if you're not playing for anyone else, play for yourself. Make the performance as good as you can. For you. This is the strength of character time. In both cases, you need to talk with the venue or promoter afterwards to see how you can improve the gig. Even if you're not playing there again. Someone will be.

HORRIBLE GIGS

Recently, I did a gig with a band that is usually fantastic. Fun to play with, fun to watch. The singers are engaging and talk to the audience. The band is really in the pocket. They have followers all around the state.

We were booked to do two gigs in a regional area a couple of hours out of Sydney. From the start we were suspicious of the first gig. This is in a town of about 22,000 people, and the venue had booked us from 10.30pm until 1.30am. Apparently that's the time that the football finished on the television. I could count on one hand the number of gigs I've had that went until 1.30am. The stage ... if you could call it a stage ... was about six inches high and had waist-high barriers advertising beer. Plus, the venue had supplied the sound guy, so it was all a bit unknown. But, like the professionals we are, we set up, sound checked, and went and had dinner. We came back to a nearly empty room. The foldback had been changed so I couldn't hear the keyboard in the wedge over the deafening guitar. We stumbled through the first set, ignored by the audience who were pretty drunk. We went to the dressing room and looked at each other in disbelief. It was horrible. In the second set, some guys who were tripping on something came in, and started dancing. Fortunately they turned out to be pretty harmless and lightened the show.

When a gig is bad, it's diabolical. It's soul destroying. Particularly when you work hard at what you do. It makes you want to go and take an office job. It's rare for me, but I literally could not wait for that gig to be over. Fortunately, the second gig (which was in a country town of about 2,500) went off. Everyone in town must have come to the gig. It went way too quick.

David, Pianist, author of this book

Things Will Go Wrong

One of the joys of live music is its very fraughtness. Sometimes the backing/click track will play the wrong song. Sometimes the keyboard cable will fail halfway through the performance, and the poor sound guy will take five minutes to work out what's gone wrong. Sometimes a light will explode half way through (and no, that doesn't count as pyrotechnics). These have all happened to us. When they do, if it's bad enough, if the band trainwrecks, if the sound goes, stop and start again if you can. Audiences are incredibly forgiving of technical issues in live music. However, if it's something minor, or if you can't stop, keep going. If it's a small enough error, it's likely that no one will notice.

If You Get Lost, Shut Up and Listen!

Sometimes, and this is particularly the case if you're a reader and inexperienced, you might lose your place on the music. You'll miss a repeat and gradually (or suddenly) you become aware that what you're playing is not what everyone else is playing. In this case: Stop and listen! You'll eventually get on the right track.

THE THREE STOOGES

Sometime in the mid-1970s, living in Los Angeles, I was hired to play in a big band backing a male "Sinatra" style singer in San Francisco. The pay was okay, and they were putting us all up for two nights. Rehearsal one day, gig the next. There was a Vegas-style production number featuring a dance troupe from Oakland, and the chart was at least five or six pages long. The promoters were a bit clueless as to how a show should be put on, the rehearsal was unorganised, and went badly. The trumpet players were not exactly first call guys. Some in the band referred to them as The Three Stooges.

Cut to showtime. During the production number, the trumpet section got lost, and although there was no way they were going to come back in correctly, they kept trying, playing a few bars, hoping they were in the right place, trying again and again for the rest of the piece. The way they were flailing, playing, pointing, yelling bar numbers at each other, flipping pages forward and backward, there were probably as many eyes on them as there were on the dancers.

The only bright spot was one particular line from the show's newspaper review the next day. The reviewer was not kind at all, and the line below, in reference to that production number, has stayed with me since then:

"The band, most of whom were clearly intoxicated, struck up several tunes at the same time".

Brien, Trombonist

Other Artists Will Act Dishonestly

Recently, there were two acts that played a similar repertoire, one based in Sydney and one based in Brisbane. The Sydney act had booked a gig in Brisbane, which had offended the sensibilities of the Brisbane band. The Brisbane band organised for all their friends and family to call the Brisbane venue and tell them they weren't coming to see the Sydney band because they were so terrible and the venue shouldn't hire them. So the venue cancelled the performance with the Sydney band. In another example, two musicians were headlining a show. Musician A had got the gig through her contacts. After the show, Musician B talked to the venue manager and tried to get her to book his show, and kept calling, without referencing Musician A.

In university circles, there's a thing called Sayre's law. It states that academic politics is the most vicious and bitter form of politics because the stakes are so low. We could say the same for the music industry at a certain level. You can try to work with integrity. You can try to work with others with integrity. However, not everyone has the same outlook, and you will get burned sometimes. It might be by an agent, or by your fellow musicians, or by people in your own band.

The thing to do is to continue to act with integrity. You are the only person who has to live inside your head. Be angry. Work to minimise the damage. But don't lose yourself in the bargain.

In both cases there was a happy (depending on your point of view) ending. In the first one, the promoter for the Sydney band rang the venue up, explained the situation, and the venue reinstated the act with a cancellation clause if they did not sell 250 seats. The band filled the room that night and everyone was happy. Except the Brisbane band. In the second, Musician B played the venue once to 20 people, and Musician A hired a new person on the bill. Happy endings don't happen all the time. Not every dishonest musician has their comeuppance. But boy does it feel good when they do!

Most Revenue in Venues Comes From Alcohol Sales

As much as it makes musicians uncomfortable, the vast majority of revenue in most venues comes from the bar. Basically venues employ you so that people will come to the venue and drink. You are a drawcard. Now, the fact that you are a drawcard can be depressing. The fact that you are being used to push a mild and addictive poison may make it even more so. Alas, this is something that you just have to make your peace with if you're going to play as a live musician.

Many (Not All) Venue Managers Don't Really Know What They're Doing

Venue management is often a young person's job. The people who decide whether or not to book you might be straight out of university with a hospitality degree. Often, they're way too young to have much experience in the music industry. They may even have an inflated view of their own self-importance. Trying to get through to them with promotion about your band can be very testing, and the only advice is to keep trying.

But sometimes you'll come across venue managers who are great. They might be experienced, super smart, or both. These venue managers are worth their weight in gold.

LOOKING AFTER THE BUSINESS

So my thing is if you're a good entertainer then I want to make sure that you're working. And if you're a venue I want to make sure that you keep entertainment in your venue by giving you good entertainment, so it's a two-way street. I'll make sure that if something happens and I need to replace someone, that person will be able to perform at the same standard. I constantly keep in contact with the audiences and talk to them about what they want, and I try and provide it. Because essentially this industry is only going to stay alive as long as we keep looking after it.

Back in the 1990s, agents were making so much money from venues and from taking commission from acts that they were pillaging and ruining venues. They were managing acts and putting the acts that they managed into venues. That way they'd get paid by the venue and also get a commission from the act. They were technically double-dipping and making a fortune. They'd sign venues up to contracts where they couldn't go and book anyone outside of that agency for two years or whatever it was. And suddenly, as a result, venues just no longer had entertainment. They just closed their auditoriums. A lot of venue managers developed the mindset that entertainment didn't work. But it was only because agents were getting greedy. I've spoken to managers of venues and been horrified by the money that was lost, when agents should really only have been taking 10%. It saddens me because a lot of acts talk about how our clubs don't book entertainment anymore, that they're only worried about gambling machines. But it was our industry that stuffed it up. It really was. And it's from sheer greed. From people that didn't know anything about entertainment taking advantage of venues. I still see that sometimes. An agent can't do enough for you to try and get the act in, but as soon as the tickets aren't selling, they don't care. They're getting their money. This instead of going, "Hey, this is really bad, how about we look at a way we can work this", you know? No, they don't care, they'll just hang you out to dry.

Anthea, Promoter and singer

Look After Your Health

I know this is going to come over all fuddy-duddy and professorial, but you need to look after your health. Let me say that again, and I'll bold it this time. **You need to look after your health!!!!!!** Music is a high-pressure industry. I've had marvellous, talented, gorgeous friends and musicians die in various preventable ways. And it's heartbreaking. If you stay in this industry, you'll see it too. Do not let yourself become a statistic.

Musicians sometimes die from alcohol-related conditions or injuries. I've known musicians, good friends, who have died in their sleep choking on vomit after a big night out, musicians who have died from liver disease. I've known alcoholics who need a six-pack of beer to wake up to in the morning, who shake on the bandstand if they don't have a few shots before the gig. As musicians, we are constantly surrounded by alcohol—because we work when everyone else plays. Approach alcohol cautiously. Amy Winehouse died at 27 because of alcohol poisoning. We all like a beer, but working in the music industry with its easy access to booze and audiences that want to buy you drinks, well, it's easy for that alcohol to become an addiction. And musicians already have addictive personalities.

In the movie Love Actually, Bill Nighy's rock and roll character turns to the camera at one stage and says: "Hey kids. Don't buy drugs. Become a pop star and they give them to you for free!" Okay, funny gag. But it belies a deeper problem in the music industry. The music industry has long been associated with drug taking. At some stage, you will be offered illicit drugs. Lots of musicians have taken them over the years and lots of musicians have died. Charlie Parker died at 34, a victim of heroin addiction. Janis Joplin died of a heroin overdose at 27. Ray Charles was arrested three times for heroin possession and nearly went to gaol. In the 1980s, James Brown is reported to have done PCP, heroin, and marijuana. The wonderful, beautiful, and talented pianist Bill Evans was addicted to heroin until he died. And these are some of the best musicians in the history of contemporary music who have either died or almost ruined their careers. Think long and hard before you accept illegal drugs at or after live gigs. A drug addiction is no laughing matter.

There is a tendency among musicians to permit themselves to get flabby. (Or—if they are lucky—to rely on good genes to keep themselves looking good.) The music industry is not forgiving of bodies. It is high-stress. You are working odd and often long hours. On the road, it is hard to find healthy food to eat. Despite the occasional unfit musician, you really can't work in this industry and be overweight. There is no use artistically sneering at the physical education students running on the track at your university. Go and get some endorphins happening. Join a gym. Work out. Do yoga. It doesn't matter. You have only one body, and you need to look after it.

Mental health issues are also rife in the industry. Getting up on stage as often as you can, opening yourself up to an audience, touching them emotionally, and putting yourself out there is mentally draining. Sight reading is mentally draining. Receiving criticism, no matter how well intended, is mentally draining. You need to have coping strategies. This book does not provide psychological techniques for coping with mental health. The process is different for everyone. But you do need to find coping strategies. Whatever works for you. Mindfulness exercises, meditation, yoga, exercise. Talk to a psychologist or a counsellor. But do something to maintain your mental equilibrium.

MENTAL HEALTH AND MUSIC

There's definitely a correlation between people in the creative arts and mental health issues. Whether people with a propensity towards mental health issues drift towards the creative arts or whether the creative arts actually precipitates mental health issues, I don't know. But so many of my musician friends have been through episodes of anxiety and depression. Some of it is just situational depression. Bad things happen and they get depressed. But a lot of my friends have had enough of that happen in their lives, added to the insecurity of being a musician; well, that's the stuff that has led them to have chronic anxiety or depression.

It's easy to get caught up in your instrument and your career when you're in your 20s and have apparently boundless energy. By all means work hard. Push yourself. Work yourself to capacity if you want to be successful, because you're probably going to need it. But bear in mind that it comes at a cost. It comes at a physical cost, and it will probably come at a mental cost. At some point or other you will need to take care of that.

I've seen a lot of musicians quit the industry. Trombone players who end up being roof tilers, singers who end up being scaffolders. They just end up working outdoors away from the musical instruments, away from the music industry. I would suggest that in hindsight, now that I'm 60 and a lot of my friends are the same age, the ones that have survived the music industry have found a way to de-stress, and somehow a lot of them do things like meditate.

After a lot of resistance, I've finally taken up meditation in the last six months after some particularly difficult times. And I've finally kind of accepted that doing meditation wasn't something that you do when you're weak, meditation is something that you actually do to support your capacity to endure the rollercoaster ride that is being a professional musician.

I think it's interesting that many of the musicians I grew up with went for 10–20 years of doing no physical exercise whatsoever. And a large number of them now work out in the gym, or swim, or do something. I happen to play field hockey. I would recommend that every musician finds something that they like doing that gives them some physical exercise to get their muscles working. Also to get their lymph system working, because there's no pump to your lymph system. You've got a heart that pumps your blood, but movement is what pumps your lymph system, which moves the impurities out of your blood. I'd recommend you exercise even if it's just walking half an hour, an hour a day, do something, get out of the piano room and go walking, get some fresh air. I would definitely recommend that.

Clive, Bass player, songwriter, and educator

Drunk or Stoned Musicians Fail

This is a hard truth. If you are serious about your music, avoid consuming substances that affect your performance before you play. You are a professional within an industry. Yes, that industry occurs in an environment populated by consumers that are drinking and having a good time. But the time to join them, to make use of the band rider, is after the gig, not before. You are there to create an environment where people have a good time. Having a few drinks will not help either your playing or the audience's enjoyment. It is no longer 1972, and the rock and roll lifestyle has given way to an industrial approach to performance. Alcohol, believe it or not, does not make you sound better. Listen to singers in a karaoke bar if you need evidence. If you want to drink or take substances outside of the venue, that's your call. Don't do it at the gig.

Doing What You Love Isn't Always What It's Cracked Up to Be

You know the saying that is displayed on every cheesy, kitten-infested inspirational poster in the world? "Do what you love, and you'll never work a day in your life". Well, let me tell you from personal experience, that's a crock. Don't get me wrong. I love working in the music industry. But there are days when it's hard work. Touring is exhausting. On a per hour basis, what we do doesn't pay that well. Perhaps the quote should be: "Do what you love and you'll completely overwork, spend hours and hours on every project which will become an endless and impossible search for perfection. But you'll have fun doing it". Hmmm ... maybe it's a bit long, and there'd be less space for kitten pictures.

Live Music Is a High-Risk Business

We talked about the risks of music and the type of performance fee you negotiate. Music is always a high-risk business. Someone is placing themselves and their cash and time on the line. Sometimes it's you. Sometimes it's someone else. It's possible to lose that money. Be ready for that.

Always Have a Fallback

You should always have a fallback when you're working in the music industry. Being at university is a great time to plan this. Choose your electives so you can work in a different field as well. Learn to code, or learn hospitality, or bookkeeping. Come out of university as the best musician you can be, with as much industry knowledge as you can possibly possess to make your career a success. But always keep that secondary knowledge up to date. There might come a day when you need it. Besides, coding, hospitality, or bookkeeping will just make your performance career better.

Music Performance Anxiety

When you've played in public, you may become nervous prior to or during your performance. That's normal. When you perform, you're undertaking something difficult in front of people who, whether known or unknown to you, are important to your future. However, when those fears become exacerbated to the point of affecting your performance ability and career, it is known as music performance anxiety (MPA). MPA can irreparably damage your personal life and professional career, so treatment and prevention are very important. Psychologists consider music performance anxiety to be a subtype of social anxiety disorder. It is typified by the presence of specific fears related to performing music, and it can be related to both solo and group presentations, as well as to any instrument, including singing. MPA can impact not only your performances but your career and quality of life. It is a condition you need to take seriously.

If you suffer from MPA, it's important to realise you're not alone. Music performance anxiety has affected some of the finest performers, including concert pianist Vladimir Horowitz, guitarist Eddie Van Halen, Beach Boy Brian Wilson, singers Adele and Carly Simon, and Ozzy Osbourne among others. After forgetting the lyrics to one of her songs, Barbra Streisand refused to perform in public for three decades, so great were her fears. Cher used to have such bad performance anxiety she couldn't look at the audience, singing instead to Sonny Bono. Performance anxiety has caused discomfort to generations of music students, their teachers, and their parents. Probably one of the best (or worst) stories about performance anxiety in music concerned the 19th century pianist Adolf Henselt. The mere thought of giving a concert made poor Adolf physically ill. When playing with an orchestra he would hide in the wings until the opening *tutti* was over, and then rush out and literally pounce on the piano. Once, he forgot to put aside his cigar—this was in 19th century Russia after all—and played the concerto cigar in mouth, smoking away, much to the amusement of the Czar. Henselt only gave a few concerts throughout his career for obvious reasons. For the last 33 years of his life he gave only 3. His MPA had won out. Or the story of German opera tenor Jonas Kaufmann, who had suffered from MPA early in his career. One day, in the middle of performing Wagner's opera *Parsival*, he suddenly found he could not sing on stage. He was literally paralysed with stage fright, as the orchestra gave him his cue several times. Eventually he learned to manage his MPA and is now back to the opera stage. Despite their MPA, these musicians learned to manage their fears. Otherwise you'd never have heard of them.

Recent advances in the theorising and measurement of MPA have increased our understanding of the condition, but we still don't really understand how it develops and how it affects each performer. A certain amount of anxiety helps performers by developing the arousal necessary to ensure excellence in performance. Being nervous and excited is part of the process of performing. But when it gets too great, it becomes problematic.

A lot of our insights into music performance anxiety come from a related sphere: That of elite sports performance. If you're an athlete, you can also suffer from performance anxiety, which can affect your body. As musicians, we use our bodies every day to play. We exert fine motor control over our fingers, our breathing, our tongues. It's demanding. Musicians (and elite athletes) have tried many approaches to performance anxiety. They have been told to relax. (Trust me, that helps a lot! In Oppositeland!) They have been told to undertake hypnotherapy. They've taken beta blockers. Nothing they do seems to work consistently across all sufferers of MPA.

MPA is far, far too big an area to address in this book. However, know that many musicians have suffered from MPA and many have successfully managed it. If you suffer from MPA, see a performance psychologist. Also, get hold of a copy of Don Greene's *Performance Success*. It's a great read.

Finally: Live Music Is the Best, Most Joyous Business You Can Be In

When you're on stage with a band that's really in the pocket. When every single member of the band is better than you. When the singer turns to you and indicates it's your solo and actually listens. When you can play no note wrong. When the audience is paying attention, applauding, and loving what you do. When these things happen, there is an intense joy in playing live. Everyone in the band—even the old curmudgeonly saxophonist—is grinning from ear to ear. And people not in the band cannot fathom it. Part of the reason an audience comes to hear you play is that you can do something they can't even begin to understand. And it's a little like magic to them. They come to experience that joy you are generating on stage, and to take a little bit home with them.

For many of you, being a live musician is a chance worth taking. Much of what separates the people who do music full-time from the people who don't is that the full-timers gave it a shot. Give yourself the best odds with careful planning and then, when you're ready, cross your fingers and give it a shot too.

As musicians, we are lucky to be able to play live. Don't ever let the annoying parts of the industry get you down. Yes, you need to develop a website, to pay attention to every little detail of a gig, to deal with tricky, even crazy personalities, and look after promotion. But we are doing what we love.

Don't take it for granted.

Note

1 DiCola, "Money from Music: Survey Evidence on Musicians' Revenue and Lessons About Copyright Incentives."

Conclusion

As you finish this book, you might think all we care about is making money. That we're some sort of top-hatted musician/academic capitalists focussed solely on raking in the bucks. That's far from true. Besides being professors, we're both practicing musicians with established careers. But we've been doing this long enough to realise that the music and the business are two sides of the same coin. Music is an art. Musicians are artists. We've both been lucky enough to make music with some amazing and inspiring performers. But art alone doesn't put food on the table. It doesn't pay the rent. It doesn't give you the luxury to actually be an artist, because you have to concentrate on the 9-to-5 day job.

You've got to have the art. Of course you do. But as artists we have to live in the real world. In addition to the art, you need the business acumen to game the system and earn a living. Fundamentally, you need to know all the things in this book.

WHEN AUDIENCES START TO NOTICE YOU

When audiences start to notice you, be ready to learn quickly as much as you can about absolutely every aspect of the industry and what you need to do to make a gig successful, e.g., social media, websites, writing your own bios, putting together emails and flyers, keeping track of mailing lists and increasing your mailing lists, booking shows, doing a successful sound check, being on time and not being an asshole, being professional, knowing how to network, and taking things slowly. Building a career takes time. Do what you need to do outside of music at first to get by, and keep pursuing the music, just keep doing it if you love it. If you want to make money just from music, it helps to be a great writer so you can pursue publishing deals, otherwise technically brilliant players can fill their books with sessions for other bands and projects to help with the bills. Line yourself up by playing in a few bands to keep the gigs coming in so that you are working as much as possible. As time goes on, learn to say no to badly paying gigs so that you can focus on expanding the better paying ones. Always be thinking of the next step of your career and plan ahead. As a performer, if your audiences simply aren't growing, think again about what you are doing, change it, do something different. Remember, you can't rely on friends and family to be your only audience!

Lara, Vocalist/violinist

An old friend used to say that there were three gates you needed to go through to be a successful musician. The first gate was: Am I good enough? This is a question only you can answer. Do you have the talent and the dedication to be a musician? Are you a good enough technician, interpreter, and performer? Is your music theory strong enough? You'll know the answer to that. The second gate was: Am I tough enough? There are hard yards in being a musician, and you've got to stick at it for a long time. The last question was: Do I want it enough? Do you want this more than anything else? Can you imagine yourself being a corporate lawyer? Or a bus driver? Or a doctor? If that's you, then you have your answer. But if you still want to be a musician, you know what you have to do.

The days of relying on recordings to generate millions are gone. They are long gone. They're probably not coming back. Some musicians might tell you that's depressing. I think it's an opportunity. As a musician playing in a contemporary genre—hip hop, jazz, rock, pop, indie, country, Latin, whatever—the lion's share of your musical income will come from live performance. It is worthwhile taking gigging seriously and doing everything in your power to maximise this particular income stream.

It's never been easy being a musician. It's even less easy now. The industry is more competitive and more difficult than ever. However, we're not musicians because we want the easy life. We are musicians because we would be miserable doing anything else. The 9-to-5 regime just isn't for us. Even if we work a day job, even if we spend our afternoons teaching our instrument to sometimes unwilling students, we do it to support our music. If you're serious about being a musician, your live career deserves your focus. Work on both your art and your business. Realise that it's not an easy road but do it anyway. Maximise your income streams. Practice. Rehearse. Write. Get a handle on the technology. Love what you do. Create memorable live performances.

And when you're playing on stage with that cooking band, and everything is working well, no one's on an ego trip, and the audience is eating out of your hand, remember that feeling. That's why we are performing musicians.

FINAL ADVICE

Musicians need a strong work ethic!! Practice, practice, and then more practice. Maintain an open mind to learn from as many different musicians and genres as possible. Learn to read music. Learn about less mainstream genres of music. A versatile musician has more work possibilities in a place like Sydney, Nashville, Toronto, or Glasgow. Play and jam as much as you can. Whenever possible, play with musicians that are better than you. Be the worst musician in the band rather than the best. Ask for advice. Follow good examples from teachers, mentors and colleagues. Be patient. Steady improvement. Work hard!! Then practice more!!

Cesar, Bandleader, composer

Glossary

Canon   A canon is a collectively established group of pieces that are considered 'worthy' and regularly performed. While it applies mostly to classical and jazz genres, rock, country, and folk also have songs that are played more than others, and musicians that are considered to be more 'worthy'.

Chops   Your chops are a contemporary music term for your technical skills.

Chord Chart   A chord chart is a notation that shows only the chords. It is used by rock musicians and sometimes by jazz musicians.

Copy   Copy is text about your ensemble or performance. It is used on websites and other promotional tools.

Cut the Gig   To be able to play well, or at least competently, in performance.

Cutoff   The visual signal to finish a piece. Often done when the band is holding a single note.

Dep   A deputy musician who is sent when the main musician can't make the gig. (This process is called "depping".) (See *Sub*).

Downbeat   The time a show is scheduled to start.

EPK   EPK stands for Electronic Press Kit. It is a sort of electronic resume that is used to generate interest in your music.

Hang   The 'hang' is socialising between bandmates between shows and sets.

House Band   A group of musicians who regularly play at an establishment.

Jam Session   An informal musical event. Musicians play songs from the canon, improvise, and play together.

Lead Sheet   A lead sheet is a notation that shows the melody and the chords only. It is used by jazz musicians and sometimes by rock musicians.

Noodling   Noodling is playing music (either from your part or general practice) between running through songs. It is a bad practice that interrupts the flow of rehearsals and makes it difficult for musicians (and the bandleader/conductor) to talk. It is also distracting. Avoid it.

Payola Scandal   The payola scandal was a government investigation of the process of paying radio DJs for playing certain records. It rocked the music industry in 1959 and several prominent DJs lost their jobs.

Scat   Scat is a form of vocal jazz improvisation that uses nonsense syllables.

Sightlines   The visual lines of sight between musicians on a stage.

Sub   A substitute musician who is sent when the main musician can't make the gig. (This process is be called "subbing".) (See *Dep*).

Subs   Subwoofers.

Surtitles/Supertitles   A caption projected on a screen above the stage in an opera, translating the text being sung.

Train Wreck   A train wreck is an industry term for when someone in a band makes an error affecting everyone else in the band so that the band is forced to stop partway through a song.

Bibliography

Baker, David. *Jazz Improvisation: A Comprehensive Method for All Musicians.* Van Nuys, CA: Alfred Publishing, 1997.

Beevers, Christopher G., and Björn Meyer. "Lack of Positive Experiences and Positive Expectancies Mediate the Relationship between BAS Responsiveness and Depression." *Cognition and Emotion* 16, no. 4 (2002): 549–64.

Berliner, Paul. *Thinking in Jazz: The Infinite Art of Improvisation.* Chicago, IL: University of Chicago Press, 2010.

Blume, Jason. *This Business of Songwriting.* New York, Billboard Books , 2006.

Borg, Bobby. *Music Marketing for the DIY Musician: Creating and Executing a Plan of Attack on a Low Budget.* Milwaukee, WI: Hal Leonard, 2014.

Braun, Anna M. "Effects of Differentiated-Tempo Aural Models on Middle School Orchestra Students' Attitudes and Motivation toward Practicing." Walden University, 2007.

Brown, Steven Caldwell, and Don Knox. "Why Go to Pop Concerts? The Motivations behind Live Music Attendance." *Musicae Scientiae* 21, no. 3 (2017): 233–49.

Bruser, Madeline. *The Art of Practicing : A Guide to Making Music from the Heart.* New York: Bell Tower, 1997.

Cecconi-Roberts, Lecia Anne. "Effects of Practice Strategies on Improvement of Performance of Intermediate Woodwind Instrumentalists.". PhD Dissertation. University of Missouri, Columbia, 2002.

Coker, Jerry. *Improvising Jazz.* Englewood Cliffs, NJ: Prentice-Hall, 1964.

Colson, John F. *Conducting and Rehearsing the Instrumental Music Ensemble: Scenarios, Priorities, Strategies, Essentials, and Repertoire.* Lanham: Scarecrow Press, 2012.

Covach, John Rudolph, and Andrew Flory. *What's That Sound?: An Introduction to Rock and Its History.* 5th ed. New York: W. W. Norton & Company, 2018.

DiCola, Peter. "Money from Music: Survey Evidence on Musicians' Revenue and Lessons About Copyright Incentives." *Arizona Law Review* 301 (2013): 301–370.

Donald, Larry Scott. "The Organization of Rehearsal Tempos and Efficiency of Motor Skill Acquisition in Piano Performance." DMA Thesis. The University of Texas at Austin, 1999.

Duke, Robert A., Amy L. Simmons, and Carla Davis Cash. "It's Not How Much; It's How: Characteristics of Practice Behavior and Retention of Performance Skills." *Journal of Research in Music Education* 56, no. 4 (2009): 210–321.

Earl, Peter E. "Simon's Travel Theorem and the Demand for Live Music." *Journal of Economic Psychology* 22, no. 3 (2001): 335–58.

Ericsson, K. Anders, Michael J. Prietula, and Edward T. Cokely. "The Making of an Expert." *Harvard Business Review* 85, no. 7/8 (2007): 1–8.

Garofalo, Reebee. *Rockin' Out: Popular Music in the USA*. 5th ed. Upper Saddle River, NJ: Pearson/Prentice Hall, 2011.

Gibson, Bill. *The Ultimate Live Sound Operator's Handbook*. Milwaukee, WI: Hal Leonard, 2011.

Gladwell, Malcolm. *Outliers: The Story of Success*. New York, Little, Brown and Co, 2008.

Green, Alfred. *Rhythm Is My Beat: Jazz Guitar Great Freddie Green and the Count Basie Sound*. Lanham: Rowman & Littlefield, 2015.

H. H. "Mr Cab Calloway's Cotton Club Band." *The Observer* (March 11, 1934): 25.

Hallam, Susan. "What Predicts Level of Expertise Attained, Quality of Performance, and Future Musical Aspirations in Young Instrumental Players?" *Psychology of Music* 41, no. 3 (2013): 267–91.

Harlow, Bob. *The Road to Results: Effective Practices for Building Arts Audiences*. New York: Bob Harlow Research and Consulting, 2014.

Harrison, Clive. *The Songwriting Labyrinth: Practical Tools to Decode the Mysterious Craft*. Sydney: Rumpelstiltskin Press, 2015.

Huizinga, Johan. *Homo Ludens: The Study of Play-Element in Culture*. Boston, Beacon Press, 1950.

Hyatt, Ariel. *Music Success in 9 Weeks: A Step-by-Step Guide to Supercharge Your Social Media & PR, Build Your Fan Base, and Earn More Money*. 3rd ed. Brooklyn, NY: Ariel Publicity, Artist Relations, and Booking, 2012.

Kotler, Philip. *Marketing 3.0: From Products to Customers to the Human Spirit. Marketing 3.0: From Products to Customers to the Human Spirit*. Hoboken, NJ: John Wiley and Sons, 2010.

Kronenburg, Robert. *Live Architecture: Popular Music Venues, Stages, and Arenas*. London: Routledge, 2012.

Lehrman, Matt. "What Is Audience Engagement? (Part 1)." *ArtsJournal* (2015). http://www.artsjournal.com/audience/2015/11/what-is-audience-engagement-part-1.

Malone, Bill C., and Tracey E. W. Laird. *Country Music USA*. Austin, TX: University of Texas Press, 2018.

McPherson, Gary E. "Five Aspects of Musical Performance and Their Correlates." *Bulletin of the Council for Research in Music Education* 127 (1996): 115–21.

McQuail, Denis. *Audience Analysis*. Thousand Oaks, CA: SAGE, 1997.

Meier, Leslie. *Popular Music as Promotion: Music and Branding in the Digital Age*. Hoboken, NJ: John Wiley & Sons, 2016.

Moore, Ali. *Rocker Jeff Beck Returns to Australia*. Australia: Australian Broadcasting Commission, 2009.

Morhart, Felicitas, Lucia Malär, Amélie Guèvremont, Florent Girardin, and Bianca Grohmann. "Brand Authenticity: An Integrative Framework and Measurement Scale." *Journal of Consumer Psychology* 25, no. 2 (2013): 200–18.

Napier-Bell, Simon. *Ta-Ra-Ra-Boom-de-Ay: The Dodgy Business of Popular Music*. London: Unbound, 2015.

Owsinski, Bobby. *The Music Producer's Handbook*. 2nd ed. Milwaukee, WI: Hal Leonard, 2016.

Owsinski, Bobby. *The Touring Musician's Handbook*. Montclair, NJ: Hal Leonard, 2011.

Passman, Donald S. *All You Need to Know about the Music Business*. 10th ed. New York, Simon & Schuster , 2019.

Patterson, Ian, and Shane Pegg. "Nothing to Do: The Relationship between 'Leisure Boredom' and Alcohol and Drug Addiction: Is There a Link to Youth Suicide in Rural Australia?" *Youth Studies Australia* 18, no. 2 (1999): 24–8.

Pattison, Pat. *Writing Better Lyrics*. Cincinnati, OH: F+W Media, 2011.

Pine, Joseph, and James Gilmore. *The Experience Economy*. Boston, MA: Harvard Business Review Press, 2011.

Pulman, Mark. "Popular Music Pedagogy: Band Rehearsals at British Universities." *International Journal of Music Education* 32, no. 3 (2014): 296–310.

Richards., Matt, and Mark Langthorne. *Somebody to Love: The Life, Death and Legacy of Freddie Mercury*. Richmond, CA: Weldon Owen, 2016.

Sackett, Aaron M., Tom Meyvis, Leif D. Nelson, Benjamin A. Converse, and Anna L. Sackett. "You're Having Fun When Time Flies: The Hedonic Consequences of Subjective Time Progression." *Psychological Science* 21, no. 1 (2010): 111–17.

Santana, Paula, Rita Santos, and Helena Nogueira. "The Link between Local Environment and Obesity: A Multilevel Analysis in the Lisbon Metropolitan Area, Portugal." *Social Science and Medicine* 68, no. 4 (2009): 601–9.

Simpson, Shane. *Music Business: A Musician's Guide to the Australian Music Industry by Top Australian Lawyers and Deal Makers*. Sydney: Omnibus Press, 2012.

Sivers, Derek. *Anything You Want: 40 Lessons for a New Kind of Entrepreneur*. New York: Penguin, 2015.

Söderman, Johan, and Göran Folkestad. "How Hip-Hop Musicians Learn: Strategies in Informal Creative Music Making." *Music Education Research* 6, no. 3 (2005): 313–26.

Tirro, Frank. *Jazz: A History*. 2nd ed. New York: W.W. Norton & Company, 1993.

Walmsley, Ben. "Why People Go to the Theatre: A Qualitative Study of Audience Motivation." *Journal of Customer Behaviour* 10, no. 4 (2011): 335–51.

Wegner, Lisa, and Alan J. Flisher. "Leisure Boredom and Adolescent Risk Behaviour: A Systematic Literature Review." *Journal of Child and Adolescent Mental Health* 21, no. 1 (2009): 1–28.

Whaley, Garwood. *The Music Director's Cookbook: Creative Recipes for a Successful Program*. Galesville, MD: Meredith Music Publications, 2005.

Witt, Stephen. *How Music Got Free: The End of an Industry, the Turn of the Century, and the Patient Zero of Piracy*. New York, Viking, 2015.

Index

Printed in Great Britain
by Amazon

86110072R00119